PRAISE FOR NEVER ENOUGH

"Like going to business school and therapy all in one book."

—**James Clear**, *New York Times* Bestselling Author, *Atomic Habits*

"A massively important topic written by a guy with firsthand experience. Everyone should read this."

—**Morgan Housel**, *New York Times* Bestselling Author, *The Psychology of Money*

"An incredibly candid and personal story of a great young investor and his learnings from his successes and failures to date. I read it in one sitting and loved it. A must-read."

—**Bill Ackman**, CEO, Pershing Square Capital Management

"*Never Enough* is a gripping reminder about what's worth wanting and being careful what you wish for."

—**Shane Parrish**, *New York Times* Bestselling Author, *Critical Thinking*, and Founder, Farnam Street

"A thrilling and unique story. Humble dude goes from $0 to billionaire with a surprise ending. His choices along the way fill you with envy or disgust, and make you question what you'd do if this happened to you."

—**Derek Sivers**, Author, *Anything You Want*, and Founder, CD Baby

"*Never Enough* might be the best book I've ever read about making loads of money—the conundrum of wanting more and more, even knowing it won't make you happier, and seeing it produce so much pointless and ridiculous behavior. Andrew Wilkinson has stepped off this hedonic treadmill to give us a gripping first-person account of his singular experience as an entrepreneur and investor. He is breathtakingly honest about the one subject that rich people find it hardest to be honest about."

—**Jacob Weisberg**, Author and Cofounder, Pushkin Industries

"A raw, unfiltered look at the dark side of entrepreneurship, *Never Enough* strips away the glitz to reveal the grit. Essential reading for anyone seeking the unvarnished truth about the entrepreneurial journey."

—**Sophia Amoruso**, *New York Times* Bestselling Author, *Girlboss*, Investor, and Entrepreneur

"Andrew is what happens when a billionaire meets Zen Buddhism. If you want money but also happiness (don't we all?) read everything he writes. But if I was you, I'd start with *Never Enough*."

—**Codie Sanchez**, Founder, Contrarian Thinking

"What makes *Never Enough* so compelling is the extreme candor with which Andrew describes his remarkable hardship-laced entrepreneurial journey. Warts and all, he tells it exactly as it unfolded. The take-home value is off the charts!"

—**Mohnish Pabrai**, Businessman, Investor, and Philanthropist

"Andrew Wilkinson tells an incredible true-life story: high-tech digital nomad crosses paths with the Norman Rockwell world of Warren Buffett, Charlie Munger, and Berkshire Hathaway. A must-read for dyed-in-the-wool value investors and high-tech digital nomads alike."

—**Guy Spier**, Investor and Author, *The Education of a Value Investors*

"The best, most life-changing business books are written by people who've quietly spent decades building massive companies and then, after years of others begging, finally give in and tell their stories. That's Andrew and this book."

—**Sam Parr**, Cohost, *My First Million* podcast

"Andrew Wilkinson is—without a doubt—one of the great young founders of our time. This book provides excellent insight into his life and work."

—**David Senra**, Host, *Founders* podcast

NEVER ENOUGH

NEVER ENOUGH

FROM BARISTA
TO BILLIONAIRE

ANDREW WILKINSON

Matt Holt Books
An Imprint of BenBella Books, Inc.
Dallas, TX

This book is based on the notes and recollections of the author, deposition transcripts, transcript of recordings, business records, and emails. Some names of individuals and other identifying details have been changed or omitted to protect their privacy. In passages containing dialogue, quotation marks are used when the author is reasonably sure that the speaker's words are close to verbatim and/or that the speaker's intended meaning was accurately reflected.

Never Enough copyright © 2024 by Andrew Wilkinson

Matt Holt is an imprint of BenBella Books, Inc.
10440 N. Central Expressway
Suite 800
Dallas, TX 75231
benbellabooks.com
Send feedback to feedback@benbellabooks.com.

BenBella and *Matt Holt* are federally registered trademarks.

Printed in the United States of America
10 9 8 7 6 5 4 3 2 1

Library of Congress Control Number: 2023051445
ISBN 9781637744765 (hardcover)
ISBN 9781637744772 (electronic)

Editing by Katie Dickman
Copyediting by Michael Fedison
Proofreading by Ashley Casteel and Cape Cod Compositors, Inc.
Cover design by Rodrigo Corral Studio
Printed by Lake Book Manufacturing

Special discounts for bulk sales are available.
Please contact bulkorders@benbellabooks.com.

To my boys. I hope this helps you make sense of me.

It's good to learn from your mistakes. It's better to learn from other people's mistakes.

—**Charlie Munger**
1924–2023

CONTENTS

Joseph Heller and I were at a party given by a billionaire on Shelter Island.

I said, "Joe, how does it make you feel to know that our host only yesterday may have made more money than your novel *Catch-22* has earned in its entire history?"

And Joe said, "I've got something he can never have."

And I said, "What on earth could that be, Joe?"

And Joe said, "The knowledge that I've got enough."

—**Kurt Vonnegut**

Chapter 1

WHAT'S YOUR NUMBER?

It was 5 A M. I sat bolt upright in bed, and I smiled ear to ear.

That's because today was the most important day of my life. It was a day I had been waiting for for more than a decade. A pinch-me kind of day. A day where nothing could go wrong.

I quickly showered, dressed, and tiptoed out of my house, so as not to wake my two young sons. The only sound amid the darkness of the morning was the idling of the SUV waiting for me at the end of my driveway, and the *click-click-click* of my suitcase along the cobblestone walk.

I was giddy with excitement as the driver took exit 26 to the airport, and probably would have remained that way if I hadn't peered down at my phone to check my email. There, buried between a hundred messages from CEOs and bankers and lawyers I employed, was a single, simple Google Alert with my name on it: "Andrew Wilkinson." When I clicked on the alert, popping it open in my phone's browser, in the title of an article, next to my name, was a word I had never seen attributed to me before.

It was a word that made me feel nauseous and euphoric all at once.

A word that could only be attributed to around three thousand people on the planet. A term that could get you knighted by the queen or a date with a celebrity—or maybe inspire a violent protest outside of your home. It was a word that was used as a compliment or a vicious diss, depending on the room. Discussion of it consumed the nightly news, the halls of Congress, trolls on Twitter, and dripped vitriol or admiration from almost everyone who uttered it.

The word that sat next to my name was *billionaire*.

It made me feel exposed. Like I was standing amid a crowd and someone had thrown a bucket of crimson paint over me and now everyone was staring, wondering who I was and what I'd done to deserve this.

Just a few years earlier, when I was in my early twenties, I'd had the same unsettling feeling when someone had labeled me with another, less intense, designation—that one being *millionaire*—but it seems I'd surpassed that number, some 750-odd times over, and according to a journalist's sloppy accounting, that *m* was now a *b*.

"Andrew Wilkinson, Billionaire."

Now it was rattling around in my head like a loose marble as I hopped out of the SUV and aboard the jet waiting for me, a Bombardier Challenger 605, with plush beige leather seats and ornate wooden accents. A little living room in the sky.

"How's it going?" my business partner, Chris, asked as I slumped into the seat across from him. "Excited? Stressed? Petrified?"

"I'm good," I said, forcing a smile.

"You all right?" he asked, noticing something was up.

"A little wigged out that someone has just called me a billionaire on the internet."

"Oh, come on," he said with a grin. "You've been called worse things." We both laughed as the plane began to taxi along the runway.

In reality, I wasn't a billionaire, yet. But I was close. I could feel the word's hot breath on my neck. It wasn't a matter of if, at this point, just a matter of when. The label—that word—was making up ground, and of course I wanted it to catch me. I wanted to win the Olympic Gold of business, whatever that meant.

As we took off, I looked out at the coast of Vancouver Island below. At the specks of people milling about. A couple of kayakers on little boats the color of condiments floated across the glacial sound; a bicyclist swept along the water's edge between the Amabilis fir trees and the black cottonwoods. From above, we all look like little dots, trundling across the earth, trying to do our own unique thing. Write a play; start a business; have a family. As our altitude continued upward—now two thousand, three thousand, four thousand feet—I wondered what these people on the edge of the island were thinking about at that moment. I imagined some of them worrying about a promotion at work, reaching the next rung of their own ladder; another one stressing about getting a new, bigger, better house; another doing the books of their café, hopeful they could grow their profits this year. I knew that, somewhere down there, some of those worries belonged to people who worked for me: a programmer at one of our software companies; a journalist at the online news outlet I owned; a chef at one of our restaurants.

And I wondered if any of them were truly happy.

In truth, I knew I wasn't, even with all the money I had.

I'd noticed a trend among many of the people I had met over the past few years, where, in business circles, someone would ask the question: "What's your number?" What's the number you'd need to see in your bank account to feel as though you had "enough"? It was a gaudy question, for sure, but it was a question that I found fascinating. That's because everyone—and I mean *everyone*—irrespective of where they sat on the pecking order of success, answered the question in almost the exact same way: they would be happy if only they were able to "double" what they already had. The person with $500,000 in the bank would feel secure once they had $1 million. Someone with $1 million in savings just needed two. The person with two just needed four, and so on, all the way up to the people worth ten times that, who just needed an extra zero on the end of their net worth.

As much as I hated to admit it, this was surely true for me. For as long as I could remember, I had dreamed of being called a billionaire. There wasn't a good reason I wanted this title. I wanted to get rich for animal reasons. Because I remembered how it felt to be broke. The feeling of my gut clenching when I tried to buy a coffee with my credit card, muttering under my breath, praying I didn't hear the shrill beep of shame—DECLINED!—which happened more times than I cared to remember.

I was terrified of not having enough. Of this sensation that burned into my stomach like an ulcer, making me grit my teeth. For a long time, I couldn't stop the feeling. I was too young to even know how. It was an undercurrent of anxiety pulsing through me.

The first time I felt this feeling abate wasn't because of therapy or a Klonopin, but rather a summer vacation with my family to Savary Island, a remote sliver of land off the coast of Vancouver. The island doesn't have cars or even electricity, and when you arrive by boat, visitors have to lug their bags along steep and windy pathways to reach their hotel or cabin. I distinctly remember watching a family of five struggle with their suitcases along a dirt path, puffing and panting as they went, a kid plowing into his father who'd stopped to put down a bag and catch his breath. Which is when I had an idea. I rounded up my younger brothers and our cousins and told them I would pay each of them five pieces of candy per bag they carried. Then, I hung out on the dock as new boats came in, and I offered weary travelers my sales pitch.

"Why not enjoy a leisurely stroll while we carry your bags? We'll take them from dock to door for ten bucks."

Like sea-level Sherpas, we'd load up and hike across the island, visions of penny candy propelling us forward. We'd drop the payload and immediately head to the general store, gorging ourselves on fuzzy peaches and licorice, with a few dollars profit left over for me. Holding that money in my hand, even though it was just a few dollars, was a salve to me.

My journey into the business world had begun.

When I got a little older, I started babysitting. Flipping burgers. Selling computers. Finding every conceivable way to stack up dollars.

By the time I was in middle school, I would drop my backpack at the door, run to the VCR, and for the three hundredth time slide in a copy of *Pirates of Silicon Valley*—a horrendously cheesy made-for-TV movie about Steve Jobs where I studied every move Jobs, Gates, and Wozniak made. I slept next to a dog-eared copy of *The Journey Is the Reward*, an eighties biography of Jobs, and when my class made a time capsule and I was asked to write a letter to my future self, I confidently predicted that, by 2035, I would be running Apple Computer (and married to Lindsay Finch, my fourth-grade crush) and included extensive directions on how to operate the company.

It was the beginning of a lifelong obsession with making money. By the time I was in my early twenties and running my own company, I scratched business ideas on scraps of paper sprinkled around my office and in the margins of books. I shouted voice reminders into my steering wheel, to be garbled by Siri for later. I kept a meticulous database of ideas. Tasks. Next actions. Things to invest in. Deals to do. People to do business with. Books to read. Businesses to start. Then, I whipped myself like a packhorse. Harnessing my anxiety and using it to tick off my endless list of to-dos. After doing this for long enough, a method emerged from the madness and it started working. The people at the bank started calling me "Mr. Wilkinson" and offering me stately looking credit cards that landed on the table with a satisfying metal *thunk*.

Then the money came. And came and came and came.

But in my mind—regardless of my bank balance—I was still a dust bowl farmer, trying to stave off starvation and stock up for the winter. Sowing backup crops and stuffing the cellar with savorless root vegetables to feed my family. I needed more businesses, more employees, more stocks, more cash flow. More, more, more. And yet a sense of abundance, of enough, always managed to elude me. I'd often caught glimpses of it in the rearview mirror of my life, reflecting on past concerns, wondering, *Why was I so stressed about money?*, even as I fretted over my current financial situation. I just couldn't see the bigger picture in the anxious present moment.

In this moment, gaining altitude, what I needed to unclench the pit in my gut was to hit that number with nine zeros at the end of it. A number so unfathomably large that I couldn't possibly feel this way anymore.

What I didn't yet know was that this trip—the business deal Chris and I were about to potentially do—was going to make that number official. And let me finally relax.

As my hometown of Victoria disappeared below the clouds, at thirty-five years old, as this number drew closer and closer, it struck me how much my life had changed since I'd been raised in this sleepy Canadian town with my parents and two younger brothers. Despite being the oldest, I was the shortest at six foot three. All three of us had smooth dark brown hair and the same frantic, bouncing walk—always in a rush to get where we were going, driven by a bubble of anxiety. A mild curve in my spine—scoliosis since birth—caused my head to subtly tilt to the left, giving the impression that I was enthralled by whatever someone was telling me, head always cocked just so, even if I was bored out of my mind.

My childhood began in the larger city of Vancouver, about fifty miles from where we would eventually settle, in Victoria. Our affluent childhood street had been so quiet you didn't need to lock the front door. Just steps from a huge park on Vancouver's west side, the oak-lined road was filled with chirping birds and free-range children playing street hockey, building forts, and biking in roving packs. But unlike my neighbors, who had flat-screen TVs and rec rooms that would put a Toys "R" Us to shame, *money* had always been a trigger word in our house. Our bank account rarely grew past five digits and sometimes dwindled to three.

This was my secret. My mission, accordingly, became to fit in with these well-heeled aliens. I longed to have the Jonathan Taylor Thomas haircut, Etnies skate shoes, always untied, and low-slung Tommy Hilfiger jeans.

Instead, I'd scour the bargain bins at Winners, sorting through last year's brands and cobbling together my costume, a simulacrum of wealth. If you squinted, I looked the part, but it was a thin veneer. I felt like a pauper compared to my exorbitantly wealthy friends' families, however ridiculous the comparison.

It grated on me.

I wanted to snatch the silver spoon out of their mouths, melt it down, and use the money to transform our lives: a photo of my family grinning with the Disney castle in the distance. Sun-baked skin. Pooka shell necklaces. Swimming with dolphins in Maui. Unfathomable wonders.

But let's be real, this isn't a Charles Dickens tale. I grew up middle class. We weren't living on food stamps and our rent always got paid. I had a loving family, and there was always food on the dinner table. There was just never a feeling of abundance. Of safety. My parents stretched a dollar a long way. The subsequent result was a quiet, simmering anxiety stoked by a daily four-word refrain: "We can't afford that," about anything my friends did. It had a visceral psychological impact on me. The desire for more was constant, some Freudian lizard brain-like impulse stuck on a loop. That, and the muffled Charlie Brown voices of my parents arguing about bills.

Thankfully, that was all in the past, or at least that's what I thought. I told myself it was a million lifetimes ago from where I sat now, safe in my cocoon, a private jet heading to Los Angeles to do the most important business deal of my life.

On the plane I looked across at Chris, who was hidden behind a copy of the *Wall Street Journal*, a glass of Diet Coke bubbling away in the cupholder at his side.

"What do you think he's going to be like?" I asked.

"Well, he says the secret to a happy life is low expectations, so let's assume he's going to be a humongous jerk," he quipped with a chuckle.

The "he" we were talking about was Charlie Munger, a man who had been one of my business idols for over a decade, and the reason for this exciting and also petrifying trip.

I knew everything about Munger: how he had grown up just five blocks from his far more famous business partner, Warren Buffett, in Omaha, Nebraska; how, when they were young, he had worked at a local grocery store Buffett's grandfather ran (somehow, the two men never met); and how, years later, in 1959, when they had met at a dinner party, they had become fast friends and eventually business partners at Berkshire Hathaway. Fast-forward to today, and Berkshire is in the top ten of the Fortune 500 list of the biggest businesses in America, a lofty place it has occupied for the last twelve years. Munger is worth several billion; Buffett, who is the CEO, ten times his partner. They are considered two of the greatest business minds of the past century.

When Chris and I started our company, Tiny, we had said that if we could pick just one person that we'd want to meet it would be Charlie Munger. We had even commissioned bronze busts of Munger and Buffett, then placed them on the fireplace mantel at our office. Some of the people who visited us and didn't know who these men were asked, "Are those your grandpas?" But many instantly recognized our heroes and were equally enamored, inquiring if we could make a bust for them, too. (Given that I saw everything as a potential business idea, I noticed so many people wanted busts of Munger and Buffett that we spun this into a side business that still makes tens of thousands of dollars a year.)

I could tell you the companies Munger and Buffett had acquired in any order: by revenue, industry, or alphabetically: Acme Brick Company, Benjamin Moore, BNSF Railway, Dairy Queen, Duracell, Fruit of the Loom, GEICO . . . I could keep going, but you get the point. If there was a version of *Jeopardy!* just about Munger and Buffett's holdings, I'd be the contest's Ken Jennings.

"Berkshire Hathaway owns 5.6 percent of this company."

"What is Apple?!"

"Berkshire Hathaway owns 26 perc—"

"What is Kraft Heinz?!"

I'd read every book about these titans, mainlining their investing wisdom like an addict obsessed with the next fix. ("The big money is not in the buying or selling, but in the waiting.") I could carol their quotes like a theater kid can recite their favorite scene in *Hamilton*, intonations and all. ("It's far better to buy a wonderful company at a fair price than a fair company at a wonderful price.") I could even recount the play-by-play of their returns on investment like a sports buff reliving the final inning of a World Series game. (Berkshire Hathaway's stock increased by a mind-boggling 1,800,000 percent between 1964 and 2014.)

But I didn't want to be a spectator, merely able to recite the company's history. I wanted to play the game. I wanted someone else to recite my own company's history one day.

For as long as I can remember, I had wanted to be *someone*. Someone who had enough.

A Jobs. A Disney. A Buffett. A Munger.

While I wasn't even close to these leviathans, I had been successful by any sane measure. Our company, which we had built from the ground up, owned more than thirty different businesses, had over a thousand employees, and generated hundreds of millions in revenue. Our little empire consisted of a seemingly random assortment of businesses of all sizes, each scratching a different itch, something we'd gotten interested in along the way during our nearly twenty years in business.

When a mutual friend introduced us to Munger, he had told us that he had a technology business he might need our help with. We had jumped at the chance and immediately made plans for a visit. This was, after all, the moment my entire life had been leading up to, and I was going to seize it.

When we landed in Los Angeles, a large blacked-out SUV was waiting for us on the tarmac. We climbed inside, and the driver took us to our hotel to freshen up. We had flown in our "uniform," jeans and T-shirts, but decided to change into a "ninety-year-old-appropriate" outfit, as we joked, which we guessed was khakis, Oxford shirts, and some sort of comfortable thick-padded footwear, perhaps with Velcro.

On the drive over to Munger's house for dinner, Chris and I discussed our plan. Chris had been my business partner for over a decade, and he was so adept at understanding my thinking that we were now able to start and finish each other's sentences, I assumed just like Munger and Buffett. I'd met Chris, of all places, at the local TD Bank, where I was a customer, after my first business, MetaLab, which designed apps for Silicon Valley startups, had taken off.

Back then, in 2009, I'd stopped by my local bank branch on Douglas Street to get a new business credit card, and the teller had told me that a financial advisor, a "Mr. Sparling," would like to say hello. When I was introduced to Mr. Sparling, I was struck by how young he was. He looked more like the son of Mr. Sparling than the advisor himself. He had a boyish face devoid of facial hair and was wearing an ill-fitting suit that hung off his small frame. He was infectiously friendly, almost obnoxiously so, with a down-home charm, and, after a brief conversation and noticing his office was covered with plaques that proclaimed him one of the bank's top employees, I blurted out, just going with my gut, "Would you ever leave the bank? I need to hire a CFO."

A decade or so later, and here we were, running a billion-dollar company and about to have dinner with one of our mutual business idols, Charlie Munger.

"Whatever idea he has, we just have to play it cool," I said as we turned onto Munger's street.

"Yup," Chris said. "Hear him out and then evaluate." We wanted to be respectful, but not fawning.

I'd seen billionaires' homes before, having gone to meetings with investors or suitors of businesses I had bought and sold in the past, and their (multiple) homes are often gargantuan, covered with art and sculptures that you would normally see in a museum; manned with a battalion of harried staffers and driveways as long as a city block; almost always filled with rows of shiny quarter- and half-a-million-dollar cars. Some have helipads. Munger lived more like a wealthy dentist, or a small-time media mogul whose movies had gone straight to cable, not someone who was worth more than the GDP of Monaco.

The house was tucked away on a quiet side street in Hancock Park, one of Los Angeles's most exclusive neighborhoods. Though the homes on this street were worth millions, you wouldn't think this of his particular home, a modest single-story bungalow, barely taking up three thousand square feet within its exterior walls. It was whitewashed stucco with a terra-cotta tile roof typical of the neighborhood. A simple path of stepping stones led from the sidewalk to the double front door, which was painted a cheerful yellow and featured an old-fashioned brass door knocker. The front yard was small, with just enough room for a few rosebushes and a single palm tree swaying gently in the breeze. An old-fashioned white picket fence surrounded the perimeter. Clearly, Munger had opted to keep things simple.

I could hear my heart pounding in my chest as Chris and I stepped out of the car at dusk, walked along the brick pathway, and approached the front door. I pressed the bell, and we waited.

I felt like I was on a first date with my celebrity crush, perspiring profusely, rehearsing my introduction in my head, and overwhelmed by the tingling anticipation of what the night might bring. I took a deep breath of the warm summer air and tried to take in the moment. The floral honey smell of the purple jacaranda tree in the yard. The far-away sounds of Los Angeles. I looked around, now noticing the blinking red lights of the security cameras pointed at our faces and, a moment later, like a grand reveal on the stage at a theater, the door opened and a man in his mid-forties greeted us with a warm smile.

"Welcome," he said. "I'm Oscar, Mr. Munger's assistant. Please come in." As we stepped into the entry, Oscar directed us toward the study where he told us Munger was waiting.

As we were guided down the hall, I looked around to take in every morsel I could. The walls were filled with books—new and old—decadent wallpaper in the dining room and a calm color palette of beige curtains and comfortable chairs. His artworks were not Picassos or Rembrandts (which Munger could easily afford) but small pretty oils and prints. There were thoughtful mementos everywhere: a couple of porcelain ducks in the living room, oriental bowls on bookshelves, a sterling silver tea set in the dining room, various gifts and photos from a long and storied career. It resembled what I imagine someone's wealthy grandparents' house would look like. The only sign that a billionaire lived here was that array of security cameras perched on the front wall, like birds, aimed at the front of the property.

When we entered the study, filled from floor to ceiling with old books, Munger was sitting in a La-Z-Boy chair, his legs crossed, a huge pile of books stacked on the table beside him, with two giant halogen lights beaming down on him like he was a sculpture in an art gallery. He had, I later learned, lost one of his eyes during a botched cataract surgery years earlier, and the lights helped him read.

He was sitting across from Andrew Marks, the mutual friend who had set up the dinner, and who introduced us.

"Charlie," Marks politely interrupted, "these are my friends Andrew and Chris. They have a mini–Berkshire Hathaway focused on tech companies up in Canada."

"Hello," Munger said as he peered up at us. I was struck by how much he looked like the bust on the mantel in my office, shocked, even, at the likeness, with that almost perfectly round face, a thin sliver of silver hair, and thick wire-framed glasses.

"Great to meet you, Charlie," I said, excitedly. "We're huge fans."

Chris, full of equal enthusiasm, overlapped what I had just said. "Huge fans. Great to meet you, Charlie." (It was as if we were the co-creators of one giant palindrome of a sentence.)

Munger was ninety-seven, but it quickly became clear that he was as lucid as ever.

We chatted briefly in the study, and then we were shown to the dining room, with tapestry-like wallpaper made up of green and pink flowers. As we found our seats, I was relieved to see Chris and I had dressed appropriately, as Munger was wearing gray suit pants, a green checkered shirt, and his own style of what I assumed were thick-padded Dexter shoes—a company I knew Berkshire Hathaway had acquired for $433 million in 1993.

Here, Munger held court and was almost exactly how I'd imagined he would be. Brilliant. Funny. Sharp.

He was full of salient one-liners that could have been thought up by a team of writers somewhere but that he was clearly just plucking out of his own brain. "Being in a business with bad economics is like being the shuttlecock in someone else's badminton game," he said as he took a bite of his steak. "When you understand how hard a problem is, it's half solved," he proffered as string beans dangled from his fork. In another aphorism, between bites of his mixed green salad, he exclaimed to me and Chris: "You only have to be right once to become very rich."

These weren't just one-liners that meant nothing to him; they meant everything. They were formulas and strings and values to live by that could reap an ever-compounding 1,800,000 percent return on your investment. He was a walking, talking encyclopedia of not just how to get rich, but of how the system worked, and how it could yield high-quality goods and services for everyone, no matter where you sit on the financial ladder. And while he was insanely rich, he preferred to live like he was not.

Decades earlier, he explained, when he had made his first million dollars, he didn't spend a penny, but instead reinvested every dime while he continued to live off his average annual salary. Things hadn't changed too much. He told us that, up until the last few years, he had flown to each Costco board meeting economy on Alaska Airlines, despite the fact that Berkshire owned not just one, but a fleet of *thousands* of private jets via their ownership of NetJets. When I commented on his green shirt in passing, saying how I liked it, he lit up with excitement, then, gesturing to his shirt, remarked, "I've been getting these flannel shirts from L.L. Bean for years. But the last time I checked, they were at $59.95 each! I decided to compare prices at Costco and found a nice flannel shirt for $49.99. My nephew then showed me AliExpress, we compared prices, and found that you can get two packs of flannel shirts for only $34.99!" (We later learned that the massive gold watch he was wearing was actually not gold at all, but a $30 "special" he had proudly found online.)

Over the years, I've met people who pretended not to care about their wealth, who wore thousand-dollar plain white T-shirts or drove a twenty-year-old Honda Fit to their secret private jet, but it seemed that he truly didn't care about any of the luxuries. He simply loved learning, then applying his knowledge by betting heavily when the odds were in his favor. More about the intellectual pursuit than the private jet.

One of the things I'd also observed over the years about business ty-coons, especially those in Silicon Valley, is that while they were all clearly brilliant in their own way, many of them often acted as though they had the answer to everything. Elon Musk, who is a genius when it comes to electric cars and rockets, has espoused on social media his expertise on everything from global monetary policy (something he clearly knows very little about) to epidemiology and the machinations of viruses (something he knows even less about). Steve Jobs, who a generation of entrepreneurs grew up idolizing, myself included, understood consumer electronics and marketing better than anyone on the planet, but he was so resolute in his own genius that he thought he knew more about his own cancer than his team of oncologists, and tried to treat his pancreatic cancer on his own fruit diet. Which, of course, failed.

When it came to Munger, though, what I found so strikingly different about him was that while he was clearly an oracle when it came to investing and capitalism and his areas of interest, including science and psychology, he wasn't resolute or opinionated on other topics. He was even humble about not being a know-it-all on investing, noting that there were some businesses he didn't feel comfortable speculating upon. One of his favorite refrains when discussing a complex topic was simply to say, "It's hard," with a shrug—the debating equivalent of folding your hand—before moving on to the next topic.

He didn't need to have the answers to everything; he stuck to what he called his "circle of competence," the areas in which he was an expert. In fact, he told us that he preferred to avoid stupidity instead of trying to be intelligent. In the age of social media and Wikipedia, a lot of people act like they know the answer to nearly everything. But when politics came up with Munger, he refrained from offering any firm viewpoint, only positing that politics writ large is simply too difficult to understand without devoting your life to it. "It's a mistake to be deeply ideological about almost anything," he said. "It's better to have doubt."

Of course, that didn't mean he wasn't broad. Especially when it came to business. Halfway through our dinner, a guy about my age burst into the house through a back door. He spoke a mile a minute, like he'd just chugged five Red Bulls.

"Charlie! We need to get that offer in," he yelled, while nodding a frantic hello to the rest of us.

He ran Charlie through the math on what seemed to be some sort of real estate deal. Munger sat calmly listening as he listed off metrics I could barely follow:

"Location."

"Doors."

"Rent."

"Good," said Munger, after a moment. "Go ahead."

The young man picked up his phone and began shouting terms into it as he strode out. And as quickly as he appeared, he was gone. The whole interaction took maybe sixty seconds.

Seeing the confused looks on our faces, Munger explained that this young man was one of his business partners, Avi Mayer, and he had just approved a multimillion-dollar deal to buy a building and that they owned apartment buildings together. Avi's story was a remarkable one. It turned out that in the early 2000s, Avi, a neighborhood teenager, had shown up at Munger's door with a Hebrew Bible, hoping to convert Munger to Judaism. While he had proved unsuccessful at converting Munger, the two had hit it off and Munger began to mentor him. Over time, they began purchasing buildings together. Now, a few years later, they owned thousands of apartment units worth over a billion dollars. Not too shabby for a side project started in his nineties with a neighborhood kid.

After that, we moved to the living room, where we were served strawberry shortcake for dessert and where the talk transitioned to us.

"So," Munger said as he looked at me and Chris, "tell me about your business. Andrew Marks says you're very smart."

By chance, Chris had ended up sitting across from Munger, and so he was the one that took the lead, and while he was always confident in a business deal, given the audience, he somehow felt the need to stand up to explain our business strategy and the kinds of companies we liked to acquire. Munger barely flinched as Chris ran through our revenue and growth numbers, all of which were phenomenal by anyone's standards. It was almost as if Chris were talking to a stone statue.

As Chris concluded, sitting down again, Munger simply said one word: "Good."

Then, it was clearly my turn.

I stayed seated as I told Munger how I had always been entrepreneurial, and how in high school I was making thousands of dollars a week running an Apple news website out of my bedroom. How I dropped out of journalism school after three months and, while making $6.50 an hour as a barista, started MetaLab, which designed apps, and which, within the first few years, was making millions of dollars in revenue. "Then, Chris and I discovered you and Warren, and your investing philosophies," I said, "which changed the course of our careers."

Here, Chris took over once more, like we were a less funny Penn and Teller showing how a magic trick worked onstage. "Before long, we were buying up technology businesses. Not the kind favored by venture capitalists, the kind of companies some people would perceive as boring," he said. "We like to joke that we own the dry cleaners and auto dealerships of the internet. Simple, profitable businesses that do something the world needs, purchased at a fair price. The founder either stays on, or we work together to find a new CEO, and then we just leave the company alone and hold forever, similar to what you do at Berkshire."

I noticed as we were talking that Munger was still a stone statue. I couldn't tell if he was unimpressed, or bored, or what.

Nothing seemed to faze him. He sat, arms crossed, head tilted downward, eyes staring away from us, almost as if we had just done a style of interpretive dance that he was still taking in and unsure how he felt about it. He was almost totally impassive in his demeanor. Then, I said something that seemed to catch his attention.

"We really like being quiet and private up in Canada," I said, as Munger listened. "We don't do many interviews." Munger didn't blink an eye. "And we have no intent on ever going public."

This caught his attention.

"You guys seem smart, but being public has its benefits," he said, leaning in.

"Why?" Chris asked. "Doesn't it create a slew of problems?"

"No, no, no," Munger said. "It creates a slew of opportunities."

He started to rattle through a long list of reasons why being a public company can be ideal. He explained that "the man who taught Warren how to invest" at Columbia University was Benjamin Graham, who described the stock market as "Mr. Market," a character whose mood swings depended on the news, the weather, and just about anything else that would put him in a good or bad mood. "Sometimes Mr. Market is fearful and undervalues your company. Other times, he's euphoric, sending your stock to the moon, far beyond any sane valuation," Munger explained. "This creates opportunities for investors. It gives you the ability to buy back your shares at a great price, or to use them to buy other companies. Being public is wonderful, if you do it right. The key is to avoid thinking about it too much, being honest and diligent, and slowly building a reputation for doing the right thing."

This was all fascinating, even if I knew most of it from my years of reading about Berkshire Hathaway, but then Munger said something that made me almost fall out of my chair.

"Well, I have a problem you may find interesting. The majority of the Munger family's wealth is in Berkshire Hathaway, but in the seventies my friend and I acquired a legal publishing business. Like most newspapers of the time, it made ungodly sums of cash, but since the early 2000s, it has been in decline. That company still exists, and it's a public company called the Daily Journal Corporation, and I'm chairman. With the traditional publishing business in decline, we bought a legal software business, and that's the future of the business. We also took some windfall profits from the publishing business during the financial crisis, and I bought some stocks that have since grown considerably. But I have a big problem."

He waited for a beat, as if we were actors on a stage, reading from a script, and it was our line of dialogue.

"What's the problem?" Chris and I asked at the same time, leaning forward.

"I'm too damned old! I'm ninety-seven, and the CEO is eighty-three!"

We all laughed.

Then, something happened that we hadn't expected. First, he went very quiet—he was thinking, calculating, doing some sort of algebraic equation, and then he looked at us and said, "You know, there's another way for you to go public."

"What's that?" I asked.

"Well, somebody needs to take over for us at Daily Journal. We could just merge our companies and you two could take the reins. You have all these wonderful technology businesses, and we have hundreds of millions of dollars that need investing and a software business that could use your expertise," Munger said.

At that moment, it was as if someone had pressed a giant PAUSE button in my mind. Did Charlie Munger just say "merge" and "our" and "companies"? I had known flying down here that he wanted to talk to us about us helping him with his software business. I figured this was like Charlie asking his web whiz nephew for computer help. Never in my wildest dreams did I imagine that he would suggest merging our companies together.

I was shocked.

If you would have gone back in time a decade earlier and told me that ten years from now, in this very moment, I'd be sitting in Charlie Munger's dining room, across from him in his $34.99 plaid shirt, and that, between bites of cake, he would ask me if I wanted to merge my company with his as peers, I'd have suggested you might need to check yourself into an institution. Forget going back a decade. Even just an hour earlier, as I took a deep breath on Munger's front stoop, if you'd have told me this is where our dinner would end up, I would have told you to cut back on the ayahuasca ceremonies.

But here we were.

I scrambled to formulate an appropriate reply. "This sounds very interesting," I said to Munger, smoothing my dessert napkin with shaking hands and trying to act as calm and collected as possible, when all I really wanted to do was jump on the table and scream euphoric expletives. Chris, who was clearly in the same shocked mindset as I was, went briefly catatonic, like someone had just punched him in the face and he wasn't sure how to respond.

Munger looked between us like we were two bronze statues sitting on his mantel. "So?" he asked, pulling us both back into reality.

"How, um, how do you imagine it would be structured?" Chris asked.

Munger went on to outline how such a deal could work. For example, Chris and I might become majority owners of the new company, and Munger and the other Daily Journal shareholders would own the rest of the combined company. We'd be the public face of it; he'd stay on the board and coach us through it. We'd run all of the day-to-day operations, and we'd be able to enjoy the benefits of being a public company without the headaches of actually going public. He concluded by telling us to think it over.

As we left Munger's house, we were giddy. Not only had we just dined with one of our business heroes, not only had he let us sip from the pool of his ninety-seven years of prophetic wisdom, but he also wanted to explore the idea of us, two random guys from Victoria, Canada, to take over the business he'd helped build. To pass the baton to us.

There, on Munger's driveway, Chris and I jumped into the air and high-fived, like we were Maverick and Goose in the first *Top Gun*.

"Holy shit," I said to Chris as we got in the car. "We're going into business with Charlie Fucking Munger."

At least, that's what we thought was going to happen.

Chapter 2

THE WILKINSON CURSE

Two decades before I was negotiating billion-dollar deals with Charlie Munger, my dad purchased a $1,500 computer that would change my life forever. It would also lead to my parents' divorce, my mom and brothers barely speaking to me, and a lifelong crippling anxiety about money.

It was the mid-1990s at the time and we lived in a small house in Shaughnessy, one of the wealthiest neighborhoods in Vancouver. The rent was affordable given the neighborhood, but still a stretch for my parents, who often told us that, with our income, we should be living out in the suburbs. They had always prioritized living in good neighborhoods with the best schools, which added to their financial strain.

Most cities feel like they were built on top of a Walmart parking lot. They're grids of hot asphalt stretched out for miles, packed with gray concrete filing cabinets filled with office workers that shoot into the clouds. Vancouver is different. It sits in the heart of the Pacific Northwest on top of what was once a lush rainforest. The contrast is obvious: even its most soulless downtown office building looks out on a waterfront skyline of the Salish Sea, with snowy mountain peaks in the near distance. Twenty minutes in any direction and you're in the middle of breathtaking nature.

As a sulky teenager, I didn't understand the distinction. We often rented our spare bedroom to foreign exchange students as a way to supplement our income, and—having never been on a plane or seen another major city—I remember wondering why on earth they would come to such a dull place. Years later, when I traveled for work and saw what the rest of the world was like, it made a lot more sense: I had grown up in one of the world's most beautiful cities without realizing it.

In the early nineties, we rented a small house on Devonshire Crescent. A three-story 1920s home with green stucco siding, an unfinished basement, and a kitchen that would have felt at home in a '70s issue of *Home + Living*. Despite its dated appearance, my mother kept the place immaculate and strategically spent nominal sums to reupholster antique furniture, which helped give the appearance of a nicely (rather than newly) furnished home. She ran the place like a well-oiled machine. Beds were to be made (smoothed at the end). Dishes to be washed (always rinsed twice to eliminate the risk of residue). Tables to be set (knife blades facing inward), with each member of the family sitting in their assigned spots. Dad would come home from work through the back door looking like a drowned rat in his trench coat, his briefcase soaked, hair askew from his rainy bus ride home. In those days, I didn't really know what my dad did for work, but I knew it made him unhappy. To me, a "job" was a thing you brought home in a briefcase, looking sad.

At dinner, Mom would sit at the head of the table, with me to her right and Dad to her left, my two brothers pushing their spaghetti around on their plates.

As we got older, Dad used these dinners to teach us about the world. He'd make a statement and our job was to take the other side and debate him, or vice versa. Sometimes it was silly things, like whether TV was rotting our generation's brains; other times it was more serious questions of morality or politics. I loved arguing with him. To me, it was just a playful debate, with no hurt feelings in the end, but I unfortunately took this habit into the wider world and learned the hard way that debating people's closely held beliefs was not a good way to win friends.

Technologically, it felt like our household was twenty years behind. We were forbidden from playing video games, and TV was limited to a squat thirty-inch Sony from the late '80s that required jamming a finger into the spot where the power button should be and rooting around until it thunked on. Unlike my friends, we didn't have cable. It cost too much, and besides, my parents wanted us to read books. To drive this home, they opted for a rabbit ear antenna that allowed us to get a handful of grainy channels, making hunkering down with a good book seem more appealing than a television that sounded like an AM radio. This empty space inadvertently fueled my interest in computers. Desperate to play video games like my friends, I spent endless hours trying to figure out how to download games onto our ancient home computer.

I'd do my best to nod along as my friends discussed the details of Friday's episode of *Buffy the Vampire Slayer* or *Boy Meets World*, but in reality, I had never seen either of them. While my parents were miserly when it came to TV, toys, vacations, and video games, the books were bottomless. Our library cards were well worn, and my bedside table was covered with dog-eared stacks of whoever's books I was obsessed with that year. J. K. Rowling. Philip Pullman. Michael Crichton. F. Scott Fitzgerald. These books became my escape, a portal into another world where none of my problems existed, summoned by flapping open a paperback.

We were expected to do some basic chores. Nothing crazy, but I *hated* chores and I'd do almost anything to avoid them. My brothers and I would rotate dishwashing duties, having to clear the table and wash the dishes one night each week. Even as a child, I noticed how much time and work it took for one person to clear the table, scrape the plates, load the dishwasher, and hand-wash the remaining pots and pans. "What if we all just cleared our own plates then stack them next to the sink?" I proposed during one night of dish duty. "It would be thirty seconds of work for everyone, but it would make this go way faster." My parents just laughed and refused, thinking I was trying to weasel out of my responsibilities. It infuriated me. It made no sense. It would make it go twice as fast. A little assembly line. A massive efficiency gain. Looking back, I realize that the same qualities that made me a lazy brat as a kid ended up being the ones that made me a successful entrepreneur. As Bill Gates put it: "I choose a lazy person to do a hard job. Because a lazy person will find an easy way to do it." For as long as I can remember, I wanted to do things the easy way. To have control. To grab the wheel and make things work better. To this day, if anyone tells me what to do—no matter how reasonable—I will dig my heels in and resist, flashing back to being a kid.

That said, I have a begrudging respect for the way my parents ran things. They produced relatively productive members of society, even if over the years it resulted in some mandatory therapy and many anal-retentive arguments with romantic partners regarding household organization.

In elementary school, my whole world was within a half-mile radius. A little snow globe accessible in minutes on my lime green single-speed Schwinn. There was Devonshire Park, where I'd spend hours climbing trees, whipping my neon pink Aerobie Frisbee with my brothers, and later, smoking my first joint. Just across Granville Street was Shaughnessy Elementary, a public school that might as well have been private. The school was surrounded on all sides by multimillion-dollar homes and filled with the children of the new rich, who wanted their kids to remain grounded and attend public school. Many of my classmates were the silver spoon offspring of the city's first-generation wealth: corporate lawyers, investment bankers, and real estate developers.

While the location of our home worked wonders for our education, ensuring that my brothers and I got the best schooling the Canadian government had to offer for a fraction of the price, it had disastrous effects on my desire for physical things. It also drastically increased my father's longing to provide them. That was because my friends—and their fathers and mothers, accordingly—lived entirely differently than we did.

Their homes were monumental, with labyrinths of rooms, cutting-edge technologies like flat-screen televisions, and endless supplies of junk food. My friends took vacations plucked from the pages of travel magazines. They skied in Whistler, flew first class to the cobblestone streets of Europe, and sprawled on beach chairs in Hawaii on winter breaks. We Wilkinsons, on the other hand, were lucky if we took the ferry to a nearby Gulf Island to stay at a family friend's cabin that my father had finagled for the weekend. My friends' parents drove the Porsches and Range Rovers that sat sparkling in their driveways, like they'd just left the dealership, while we drove a gun-metal gray Volvo 245 DL station wagon from the mid-1980s (manual transmission, no air-conditioning, no power steering, no airbags) that my father would hand-wash when he could no longer see out of the rearview mirror.

The difference between them and us was made blatantly clear to me when, after school, I first hopped on my bike and zigzagged past the oak trees that lined our block, to get to a new friend's house. Between bouts of Ping-Pong, dips in their heated pool, and multiplayer melees on their PlayStation (which, of course, we didn't own), my friend asked me if I was hungry, then ushered me into a pantry that looked like a small supermarket, shelves packed with Dunkaroos, Chips Ahoy!, and Cosmic Brownies. "Take whatever you want," he said as he tore open a giant bag of 3D Doritos without a care in the world, as a cleaning lady tailed us, tidying the trail of empty packets and crumbs we left behind.

To me, this felt like the ultimate excess, the equivalent of a bacchanal in Sodom and Gomorrah. Afterward, I felt guilty for not saying "thank you" to the cleaning lady for tidying up after us.

Mom was quiet and serious, with a warm laugh that would burst out of her, often when my father made a joke. She had long, straight black hair that she parted down the middle. She held herself, and by extension her family, to a high standard. She sent handwritten thank-you cards in perfect loopy handwriting scratched out in a gel pen. She did things the *right* way and became an expert at anything she applied herself to. If she gardened, she read every book on the topic and could hold court with even the most seasoned botanist. She cooked as well as any sous chef. She knitted ornate creations that made her a big name at the local wool store. She was a hyper-diligent perfectionist who felt there was a right way to do everything and expected the same of those around her, especially us. She always looked a few years younger than she was, the result of her obsessive daily application of sunscreen. ("I got asked for ID when I was thirty," she liked to tell me, the world's gentle pat on the head for her skincare diligence.) She was fanatical about grammar and speaking well. "Me and Nick were playing soccer earlier" got me a "Nick and *I*" interjection in a singsong voice. She had an incredible memory and an ability to build deep connections with other people and make them feel seen. They'd always light up when she'd ask how X or Y's third cousin once removed was doing after their surgery, or how they were feeling about a work problem.

This same thing applied to her three sons: she took a keen interest in our lives, social and emotional, and I'd tell her all about the girls I had crushes on, who was giving me trouble in school, and every detail of my latest existential angst.

Both of my parents had disruptive, chaotic childhoods, each for different reasons. My mom was committed to providing a better foundation for us. She was a stay-at-home mom who ran our household with the precision of the air traffic controller overseeing a chaotic landing strip, but her real expertise shone with money and how *not* to spend it. She was a prudent saver who counted pennies and strategically managed our nominal family finances, hoping to make the most of the dwindling income that my father brought in, as his struggling architecture firm rode the ups and downs of the real estate market. She felt that everything in our home needed to be just so, thoughtfully appointed and well cared for, but more importantly, acquired for a bargain, without giving away the truth about our financial situation, a family of five living on one highly unpredictable income. We didn't eat junk food, we didn't buy new gadgets, we didn't go on trips, and we took extra care not to break, stain, tear, or dismember anything in our house, for fear we couldn't replace it.

I felt that I was an imposter among the rich kids in my neighborhood, but I did my best to look the part. In time, I put the pieces together. I bought the right brands on discount. I biked to school so nobody would see our old car. I figured out how people were related. How their families made their money. Whose dads were suing one another. I learned to talk the talk.

This pervasive sense of being other, living next to these more affluent families, made money the white-hot burning center of everything that was wrong with *our* particular family. Tolstoy once wrote, "Happy families are all alike; every unhappy family is unhappy in its own way." This was our way.

Bills. Credit cards. Debt.

And young Andrew, with his green single-speed Schwinn, didn't like it one bit. It felt to me, even back then, like we were doing it all wrong. It felt harder than it needed to be, like riding my bike up a huge hill in its first and only gear (which I had attempted and failed). I had this nagging feeling that the other dads knew something mine didn't. One thing was clear: if I didn't figure it out, I was going to be poor when I grew up. And being financially limited meant family tension. Yelling. Dollar-store Christmas presents. Driving a car that was made before the Berlin Wall fell.

There seemed to be no plan, other than that we had to keep our heads down and power through, trying the same thing over and over, and getting the same results. At dinner one night, I asked my dad about his retirement savings. He quipped with a playful smirk that he didn't have a pension, so *I* was his retirement plan. A joke that filled me with a dread, as thoughts of what lay ahead swirled in my mind.

In contrast to my own father, I'd watch as my friend Nick's dad, Andre, a real estate developer, would pull up in his sparkling BMW 7 Series, plop his keys down in the hallway of his mansion, alongside a money clip plump with $100 bills, and make dinner (often schnitzel—he was Hungarian) for me and Nick. I was flabbergasted. Why was this guy, who was obviously far wealthier than my own father, not working late? My dad got home exhausted at seven o'clock only to work until midnight from home. He never made dinner or came home early. He always looked stressed. Andre, on the other hand, looked like he was on vacation at Club Med. What did he know that Dad didn't?

Fascinated, I'd pepper him with questions over the dinner table.

"How do you get the money to build a building?"

"What happens after you sell all the apartments?"

"What do you do with the profits?"

"How much does each building make?"

Over time, I pieced together his story. He had moved to Canada from Hungary with $140 in his pocket. After becoming a flight attendant for a small airline and saving up some money, he started renovating and flipping houses. Over a decade, he graduated from houses to condos and built housing for thousands of people. He now owned a wide variety of real estate that paid him passively, including strip malls, a hotel, and a large portfolio of residential real estate. He was one of the most successful real estate developers in Vancouver, with millions of dollars of passive income flowing to him annually, like clockwork. His biggest problem seemed to be boredom. We'd often catch him playing online poker in his home office.

"So, you don't actually have to do much work day-to-day? The money just flows to you because you're the owner?"

"Exactly. My buildings work for me. I build them, but once they're running, they're like a machine: I just check in now and then."

My eyes bulged. At that moment, I vowed to crack the code. No more riding uphill in one impossible gear. No more fights about money. I'd make everyone in my family happy with vacations and toys and schnitzel—sweet, delicious schnitzel.

For my parents, on the other hand, their financial pressures seeded every single argument they had. Either there wasn't enough coming in, or there was too much going out. It became routine for me to sit at the top of the stairs to listen to the muffled voices below, trying to decipher their latest argument.

My father had broad shoulders and a hulking frame, an artifact from years of playing rugby and rowing in high school. Over the years, he had softened a bit around the middle, and his weight oscillated up and down like a stock ticker as he experimented with various diets. He was tall and looked a bit like Bruce Willis (when the actor still had hair) with his sharp and handsome jawline.

Despite his busy work schedule, he always made time for my brothers and me on weekends. We'd spend hours building Legos, crafting pillow forts, and painting model airplanes. An eternal optimist, he often made light of his troubles, jokingly blaming them on Murphy's Law: "Anything that can go wrong, will go wrong." But he also shouldered an insane amount of financial stress, which, depending on how things were at work, fueled an unpredictable temper. He had gotten into architecture, where, despite winning awards and rising to the top of his profession, the financial rewards had been sparse.

I remember lying in my bed as he was tucking me in one night, asking him questions about our family. He told me about "The Wilkinson Curse," how our family had consistently won the proverbial lottery and then blown it out of stubbornness or just plain bad luck. He had a narrative he stuck to: things were hard—there was no way around that; just power through.

He was a walking contradiction. His face was constantly painted with a tense "everything is fine" smile, which was fueled by two emotions: eternal optimism and deep, guttural panic. These simmered in a dichotomous stew that made him an odd combination of happy-go-lucky sweetness and bubbling stress, which could boil over at any time.

His temper tantrums felt straight out of *America's Funniest Home Videos*. Never directed at a person, they almost always involved inanimate objects that had upset him: the unstable IKEA bookshelf he'd spent hours assembling only to realize it was missing a critical screw, the box cutter that had fallen off course and sliced his finger while opening a package, the floppy disc full of work files that kept rejecting his passwords. In these moments, life got to him, and he'd explode like an angry orangutan.

"GOD DAMNIT FUCKING THING!!!!!" he'd scream, sometimes melting down onto the cusp of tears. The scary part wasn't the anger; it was seeing how overwhelmed the dam was and how easily the floodgates could break open. Even as a kid, I read these explosions in Morse code: "I can't cope," over and over again.

I think he knew there were ways to do things to lessen his stress, but it seemed like he had a psychic block. Life was hard, and there was no way around it. Like the baker who would hire staff *if only he had time*. Up all night, covered in flour, desperately trying to make the day's bread for a lineup of customers while simultaneously manning the cash register.

His bookshelf was lined with books like *Rich Dad, Poor Dad*; *The 7 Habits of Highly Effective People*; and *Good to Great*. He looked up to successful businesspeople, and told me about how Jimmy Pattison, the wealthiest man in Vancouver, had built his empire brick by brick starting with a single car dealership, before diversifying into radio stations, publishing, billboards, fisheries, and more, bringing in over $6 billion a year. When I was eight or nine, we saw Pattison eating at a restaurant and Dad nervously ushered me over to shake his hand. It felt soft and pillowy, like it hadn't done any manual labor. I was intrigued.

Dad was constantly encouraging me to start little businesses. When I started a lemonade stand and told him, proudly, about how I'd raked in $40, he asked me, "What's next?"

I'd looked at him, perplexed.

"Okay, think about it, let's say you make $10 an hour selling lemonade. That means you could pay another kid $5 an hour, have them run the stand, and then use your profits to go start another one. And another. And another."

His constant questions sparked a habit that would benefit me massively in business. After any win, I'd hear Dad's voice echoing in my head: "What's next?"

Instead of allowing myself to relax and enjoy what I had—to celebrate an achievement or take a vacation after a long sprint at work—I'd instead wonder how to do it again, but bigger and better and more efficiently. This workaholic but enjoyable habit made me highly adaptive in business but created an inability to relax or run in place. It created a fortune but pushed me into emotional overdraft.

He taught me about compound interest. The idea that tiny sums of money can turn into unimaginable amounts over time if consistently invested.

"Einstein called it 'the Eighth Wonder of the World,'" he told me. "If you saved and invested just $5 a day, every day for the rest of your life starting now, you'd be a millionaire by the time you're fifty."

I loved this stuff, but it all sounded a little fantastical. After all, if this was true, why wasn't *he* a millionaire?

What I found so odd was that he knew all this. He had read the books. But for some reason he just couldn't put it into practice. It was like watching a drowning man flail next to a life preserver a few feet to his right.

In this and other ways he was the antithesis of my mother. Vinegar to her baking soda. And this was how I spent my childhood: sandwiched between two very different people with very different approaches to life. The chaotic optimist contrasted with the serious, meticulous planner. Both would have huge impacts on me, and I'd unknowingly take on both the best and worst qualities of each, which later proved to be both my superpower and kryptonite.

If it had been up to Dad, we'd be living a life well beyond our means and putting trips to Cabo on a credit card; my mother, on the other hand, would rather burn the furniture for firewood in order to stay warm. The two of them could not have been further apart in their feelings and attitudes around money, and neither of them seemed content with their current situation.

When it came to these misalignments, it seemed to me that my mother always won the arguments, at least in the moment. Our desire for a new, fancy television, or my father's yearning for a classic car, or my obsession with owning my own computer, being among those constant debates. I'd hear their voices, usually disagreeing about some new expenditure—echoing up the staircase, where I'd sit listening, refereeing in my head. Eventually, he'd give up and apologize, but my father's resentment would then fester until it finally erupted in the worst possible scenario: he would sneak out and purchase something big without discussing it with her. Something we very clearly couldn't afford.

And on one warm Saturday in 2002, he left the house on one of these shopping sprees to purchase something that would change my life forever.

_____

My obsession with computers started when I was seven. My father would bring me along to work on the weekends and plant me in front of a Mac Plus, a gray rectangular cube of eighties industrial design perfection that showed a little smiley icon when it booted up with a ding so beautiful it was as if Beethoven himself had composed it. What someone else might interpret as neglect, abandoning a seven-year-old in front of a screen so you can catch up on work for several hours, felt to me like pure bliss. I spent whole afternoons goofing around and learning what this or that button did, or how to change this or that icon. I fell headfirst into the world of fonts and colors, animations and video games. I printed silly signs. I made invitations for my birthday parties. I made fake business cards: I was the CEO of AndrewCorp. I was hooked and I couldn't get enough. It offered me my own little world where I could be a grown-up. Complete control. A place where nobody could tell me what to do.

As time went on, my obsession became an addiction. I begged my parents to let me ride the bus to the local Apple dealership after school (there were no Apple Stores yet, just retailers). I spent hours lusting after the shiny Bondi blue iMacs and pored over *Macworld* magazine the way another kid might gaze upon a contraband copy of *Playboy*. Steve Jobs had just returned to Apple at the time, and had released an iconic ad campaign, a collection of black-and-white images of innovators and artists like Bob Dylan and Martin Luther King Jr. with the tagline "Think Different." He made computers—typically the realm of awkward nerds—seem rebellious and cool. To me, Jobs was a demigod, and I wanted to join his cult.

The problem was, I couldn't afford that shiny blue iMac.

By the time I was eleven years old, with pimples forming on my face like the terraform of a distant planet, I started going to Simply Computing, a rundown Mac store in a nondescript building on Broadway, where I started acting as if I were a salesman at the store, much to the amusement of the real salesmen. I'd walk around greeting customers, even though I had no business being there whatsoever. My goal was simple: I was on a mission to convert old ladies, who knew nothing about computers, to buy a Mac instead of a PC. And as time went on, and I honed my skills, I became pretty good at it.

"Well, you know, Macs don't get viruses," I explained to one elderly lady, who was thankfully around my same height and so old she didn't question my own age.

"The user interface is just so much simpler than Windows," I uttered to another. "Here, let me show you the Finder; are you familiar with what a GUI is?" (Of course, they were not familiar with what a GUI was.)

While most boys my age dreamed of being captain of the rugby team or going out on a date, my singular obsession was computers. My obsession was so severe that my unfortunate nickname in school was "Palm Pilot" because I walked around taking notes on a little black-and-white PalmPilot personal organizer, an early precursor to the iPhone. As you can imagine, the girls at school found this irresistible.

At the computer store, the *actual* salespeople at the shop, the ones who got a paycheck and didn't show up voluntarily, thought I was peculiar, but harmless—and probably appreciated the fact that I was doing their job for them. Some even seemed grateful (or at least pretended to be) when I ushered a new elderly customer to the checkout counter as I pushed my glasses up above my nose and explained that "Doris here would like to get an iMac." Turning to Doris, I'd explain politely: "This is Frank—he's a cashier and he'll take care of you from here, ma'am."

One day, during one of my sales pitches about megahertz speeds and hard drives, an old lady named Marcy Smorden asked if I might show her how to navigate the Mac's folder system. After an explanation of the desktop, she was so impressed with my knowledge that she not only purchased a computer, but she also offered me my first real job.

"Can I hire you to teach me how to use my new computer?" Marcy asked.

"Of course," I said. "How would that work?"

"I'd pay you $20 an hour, you come to my house, and teach me how to check my email and use my printer."

I couldn't believe someone was going to pay me, with real money, to use a computer! The store soon started to refer me to more old ladies to teach. It was the perfect symbiosis—they sold a computer, and I helped the patron learn how to use it. Two weeks before my twelfth birthday, I started my first company. It was called "New Tricks," with the brilliant marketing tagline: "Teaching Old Dogs New Tricks." I made a red and blue logo that belonged on an old man's clothing line, and even had business cards printed out that said "Andrew Wilkinson, CEO."

In hindsight, I realize that these elderly women were likely just paying me to keep them company and had little to no interest in learning what the difference was between Mac OS 8.1 and Mac OS 8.5. But putting aside my terrible marketing prowess at the time, that first company, with its half-a-dozen elderly customers, taught me one of the most important lessons of my life so far: that a business, even one run by a twelve-year-old, was at its core about solving problems for other people.

Until then, I thought that a job, or a business, was something that was dictated to you. There were set paths: as a teenager, you could work at McDonald's, or babysit, or do a paper route. I slowly came to realize that almost any need, problem, or desire can be turned into a business of its own. In this case, septuagenarians struggling to check their America On-line email accounts. ("Welcome! You've got mail!")

I started seeing opportunities like this everywhere.

As it turned out, my dad loved computers, too. And while some fathers and sons talked about basketball teams and who just got drafted by whom, my father often joined me in reading *Macworld* magazine and making trips to the various computer stores around town. My mother, on the other hand, wasn't sure how to feel about technology. It was hard to discern whether these glowing cubes were enhancing her children or making things worse, as we spent hours each afternoon glued to them playing games and editing silly little videos that we'd film with our stuffed animals, a consolation prize for our lack of cable TV.

Computers are like dogs, as they age much faster than humans, and we'd always have a five- or ten-year-old computer, akin to having a cabinet-sized 1950s radio set in the age of the Sony Walkman. I was relentless in pointing out this fact and took every opportunity to plead with my parents to buy us a new computer. It was at the top of my Christmas list for almost a decade, until it happened. I was thirteen. I had been particularly irritating of late, driving home how important a new iMac would be to handle the deluge of high school homework and pointing out the many educational software packages it came with.

"You guys don't get it—it will help me get better grades!" I said to eye rolls from my mother.

Dad felt bad, though—I could tell. He had seen my passion and wanted to give me a computer of my own.

Then, one day, he just did it.

He went rogue and showed up at the house with a gleaming new box that he opened in front of me, exclaiming, "It's a brand-new Mac!"

My mother stood off to the side looking incensed. It's not that she didn't want to give me what I wanted; it's that she didn't want my father to just go off and make such a big purchase without discussing it first. But in his mind, he knew a discussion would end with a firm "no."

Later that night, I didn't listen to the arguing from the top of the stairs. I just basked in the warm glow of my computer screen. I wasn't quite sure how to feel when I heard that familiar sour orchestra roaring through the floorboards and it became clear to me that my father had broken Mom's cardinal rule of the Wilkinson family finances: he had purchased the computer *on credit*. My mother was apoplectic. I couldn't make out full sentences, only a machine-gun fire of words: "MORTGAGE," "OVERDRAFT," "CREDIT CARD," "DEBT." Like turning the volume knob on an old radio, this time I chose to zone it out and focus on the task at hand: setting up my new Mac.

———

Four years after I got that first computer, a lot had changed. We moved to a new house in Victoria, Canada, and people started knocking on the door asking for me.

"Seven more today?" the UPS driver would say.

"Nice!"

"Have a good day, Andrew!"

"Same to you, Jim!"

"Same to you, Dave!"

"Same to you . . ."

There were few things that brought me more joy than hearing those postal trucks from UPS and FedEx pull up in front of our house. The truck doors would slam, followed by footfalls up our rickety, half-built front steps, with makeshift two-by-four handrails that ran up either side of the stairs, a remnant of a long-forgotten weekend home improvement project that my father had lingered over for the past few years.

A knock, and then: "Andrew!" my mother or father or one of my brothers would yell, without even going to see who was there.

I'd run down the stairs, past family photos that had been hung in happier times between my parents, and there at the front door would sit a new pile of packages, each one plastered in red and orange stickers that screamed out "FRAGILE" and "LITHIUM-ION BATTERIES INSIDE" as if to warn something terrible could happen if I didn't adhere to these warnings.

I had just turned fifteen, and my body was as lanky and skinny as the mountain hemlock trees that lined our block. And while I'd sprouted to six feet, my arms were in on some sort of practical joke that I had no part in, dangling down longer than they should, like those on a disfigured Mr. Stretch toy. I'd scoop up the packages with these stretch toy arms and set off back to my room. Until the door clapped again.

I used to joke that these delivery drivers were "my own personal Santa." Of course, it wasn't Christmas, and they weren't Santa. At least not in the traditional sense. I had given up on relying on others to get what I wanted. After years of pleading with my parents to support my computer obsession and being shut down, I had taken matters into my own hands.

In my day-to-day life I was as awkward as a teenager could be. I had a voice that jutted into random octaves at crucial times, another practical joke my body seemed to be playing on me, along with more acne that had now grown more crimson in color. But on the internet, I was running a digital empire that delivered everything I'd ever wanted right to my front door. And I didn't have to pay for any of it.

Three years earlier, in 2001, my parents had sat me and my brothers down in the living room and told us something terrible was happening. Of course, they didn't have to tell us it was terrible; that part was painted on their faces.

"We can't afford to live in Vancouver anymore, so we're moving to Victoria," Dad said, with a tense smile. The last three words hit me like staccato bullets. Moving. To. Victoria.

I felt like I was underwater. My father's voice turned into a faded jumble and my heart started pounding. I was in my sophomore year of high school. I'd just found my people. I had an amazing group of friends. There were girls I had crushes on, who wrote notes to *me*. I was starting to get invited to parties. Things were *good*. Now, like a transplanted organ, I was being rejected. Forced to live in Victoria, the painfully boring, small, menial place where my grandparents lived. A city a fifth the size of Vancouver, where the most exciting activities were high tea at the Empress Hotel and a tour of the Butchart Gardens.

While I empathized with the financial situation, I couldn't help but blame my parents. Why hadn't they saved? Why didn't my dad take his own advice? I was furious. My whole life was being upended because of the same thing that caused every problem: money.

That summer we moved was the worst to ever happen to our family. While my parents tried to make the best of it, obviously they were depressed. And if that wasn't enough, life dealt them multiple crippling blows to ensure it. Within weeks of moving, my dad's brother Geoff suddenly dropped dead at the age of forty-four, which was especially hard given that his older brother had also died suddenly just five years earlier, leaving my father as the last remaining son. Shortly after that, my maternal grandmother was diagnosed with stage four ovarian cancer. Our new home in Victoria was like the world's saddest silent meditation retreat. We'd all shuffle past one another, each making our way to a TV, book, or computer for distraction, our mourning a trifecta: our old lives in Vancouver, our uncle, and our grandmother.

My snow globe had been smashed into a million tiny pieces.

I began to spend morning to night on my computer. Feeling bad about the move, my parents got us blazing-fast cable internet and I spent every waking moment steeped in internet culture. One day, I was in a chat room dedicated to discussing Apple news, and I got into a conversation with three fellow fifteen-year-old nerds: Chris, Clark, and Colin. We were four bored kids trying to entertain ourselves through summer break and we were scattered across North America: Maui, Calgary, Tucson, and Victoria. Chris told us that he was in the process of rebooting a website called Macteens, an unfortunately named tech news site that until recently had been run by a few fellow teenage Apple fanatics who had shut it down when they went to college.

We decided to run the blog together, with me and Colin focusing on the content and Chris and Clark on design and development. We got to work and before long, we relaunched the site and started writing stories about all forms of Apple-related minutiae. Rumors. News. Reviews.

While I was browsing other Apple sites, trying to figure out what we should write about, I kept seeing similar websites that reviewed tech products. I asked around and I realized that these companies were sent "review units." Free computers, speakers, headphones, hard drives—you name it— by the companies that made them, in hopes that they would be reviewed and written up, getting the companies press. My eyes lit up. It seemed too good to be true, but this could be the holy grail: free, unlimited tech gear.

Like an email spammer, I started sending hundreds of emails. I contacted every tech company I could find asking to review their products, and that's when the UPS guys started knocking. At first, once a week. Then every day. Then every few hours. Before long, my room was a cornucopia of every tech product imaginable. I felt like I'd hit the jackpot.

The website turned out to be a hit. We started breaking real investigative news stories ahead of everyone else. I'd rush downstairs at five in the morning to hit *publish* and watch as hundreds of thousands of visitors came to the site. Some of our stories even got picked up by mainstream media outlets like CNBC and the *Boston Globe*.

By day, I was an awkward sixteen-year-old in tenth grade who was barely passing math. Nobody knew about my secret alter ego running a clandestine media empire. Somebody who mattered and moved the needle, a master in my own weird, nerdy world.

The next summer, I sent a one-line email that would change my life.

I had saved up enough money to travel to Mecca for Apple nerds—the Macworld conference in New York—where Steve Jobs usually launched Apple's new products. I sent an email to my contacts on the Apple PR team:

"I'm going to be at Macworld next week and was hoping to interview Steve. Possible?"

I knew this was bold. I was a nobody. Interviews were typically doled out to *Newsweek* and the *Wall Street Journal*, not tiny websites run by kids.

A few minutes later, I got a reply:

"Steve's schedule is too hectic, but I can get you in for a group tour of the new Apple Store in Soho?"

I was shocked. I'd expected to get fully shut down or not even get a reply, and now I was getting a behind-the-scenes tour of their first ever Apple Store, which nobody had seen the inside of yet. While I was upset that I wouldn't get to meet Steve Jobs, I realized something important. I had asked for something amazing and gotten something great in exchange. If I'd asked for a tour of the Apple Store, I probably would have gotten a "nice try, kid," but by shooting for the moon and asking for something that was hard to give, I was met with a compromise that was better than I could have hoped for. It's a strategy I went on to use throughout my career: there's no harm in asking.

Given I was still a teenager, my dad accompanied me to New York (with me paying for his plane ticket) and, on the appointed day and time, we showed up at the sparkling new Apple Store, still not open to the public. It was an architectural marvel, a completely reimagined US postal building with an impressive floating glass staircase on the corner of Prince and Greene Streets in the heart of SoHo. I was excited, but calm, chatting with some big-time journalists waiting for what we assumed would be some PR flack to let us in.

Then, a black SUV pulled up and a man got out.

The man was wearing a black mock turtleneck, black jeans, a pair of gray New Balance shoes, and circular rimless glasses. As the signals traversed my nervous system, my heart started thumping and my hands started quivering.

"Hi, nice to meet you. I'm Steve," the man said, looking me right in the eye and shaking my rigid hand before shuffling past to shake hands with each of the journalists.

This couldn't be happening. Trying to calm myself, in my head I kept repeating, "He's just a person."

This was my dream. I had to get it together. I took a deep breath, pushed through the crowd and, as I did with the parents of my friends, started peppering him with questions.

"What was the inspiration for the design of the new iMac?"

"Which model do you use personally?"

"How did you make this crazy glass staircase?"

Like most grown-ups, Steve seemed amused by this gawky teenager, fifteen going on thirty-five, trying to keep his voice from cracking and playing adult. He humored me as I dominated the questions from the group of journalists.

My father watched me as I stood talking to Jobs, surrounded by reporters from the *New York Times* and *Time* magazine and the *Wall Street Journal*, and camera crews from CBS and CNN and CNBC, reporters who had spent a lifetime reaching the pinnacle where they could interview Jobs himself. Here was this oddly shaped kid discussing the design choices of the latest iMac with the master of all ceremonies.

When we came home, I went back to my regularly scheduled programming of being a high school kid who was afraid to talk to girls and who juggled mounds of homework between posting gadget reviews on my site.

And while those delivery drivers continued to bring me Apple-related gad-getry—new laptops and mouse pads and ergonomic keyboards to try—and our website was bringing in hundreds of dollars a month in revenue from advertising, which we placed on the site next to our reviews, there were still things that were out of my reach. Things that I not only yearned for, but that my father and brothers did, too.

Before long, like a voice that couldn't be silenced in my father's head, he just started shopping again. One evening, after another of those cataclysmic blowout fights between my parents, I heard the car creep into the drive-way, the door slam, the footsteps on the gravel outside. Then, the front door swung open, followed by my father yelling, "Andrew! Tim! William! I need a hand getting something out of the car!"

My mother watched as we lugged a huge TV box from the trunk, up the still-half-built front steps, with the makeshift two-by-four handrails, and into the living room. As we unpacked this new beautiful 65" flat-screen spectacle of technology, in awe of its symmetry and its astoundingly small size, Mom walked into the living room and stood at the doorway just star-ing at my father, fuming. And it didn't stop there. Months later, he pulled into the driveway with his dream car, a mid-'90s Saab 9000, which to my father was a symphony of Swedish engineering. To my mother, it was yet another expense we simply couldn't afford.

But that night, my brothers sat in front of the new television, basking in the loudness of their favorite cartoons, while I went into my own room and closed the door, aware of what was coming. I booted up my computer and began working on my website, which became a salve for my anxiety about the argument below. And for a moment, it was.

But this time was different. I had to know what was said, and had to understand why we as a family always came back to this. So, I walked out of my room and just sat on the stairs.

I looked at the family photos that lined the stairwell, and as I felt the mood in our home turn sour, I decided then and there that I would make enough money that finances would never be a problem for me or my brothers or my mother and father—and especially for *my* future family. But how? I didn't know this at the time, but I sure as hell wasn't going to strike it rich in the world of journalism.

Chapter 3

HAIR FOLLICLE FINANCING

When I looked in the mirror and saw the string of bright red hickeys on my neck, the dozens of drinks hit me like a freight train of nausea. Without a moment to think, I vomited into the toilet, throwing up the remnants of a night I couldn't even recall.

I splashed some cold water on my face and peered through the bathroom window at the bright daylight outside. Was it morning? Lunchtime? Afternoon already? The sunlight made my stomach lurch. My head hurt even more as I tried to deduce what had happened. I looked in the mirror, which is when I remembered sliding my credit card across the counter in a hotel lobby at some point in the evening.

I shuffled back into the room, which was pitch black except for a sliver of light sneaking in between the curtains. My head was pounding, and the light felt like daggers jabbing my eyeballs. Before I began the epic quest to find a painkiller, I first had to figure out where I was, how I got there, and who the girl sleeping in my bed was.

I glanced at the notepad on the bedside table and saw the watermark of the St. Regis Hotel in San Francisco. "Okay," I thought, "I'm still in San Francisco—that's good." Then, looking around the cavernous room, I realized I must be in the penthouse suite. I knew this room. I'd dreamed of staying in it. It cost $20,000 a night. But who paid for it? Me? 23-year-old me? As I stumbled around the room, navigating with vertigo, fleeting scenes from the night before began floating back to me. A full glass of free-poured whiskey at the bar. Thinking this was probably a bad idea but downing the glass anyway. There were more drinks, bottles and bottles of brown and clear and sparkling concoctions and me clinking glasses with ... was that someone in a Facebook T-shirt? But who?

I grabbed my phone from the bedside table, where I saw messages from a Facebook VP, trying to recruit me; a startup founder's angry assistant emailing about a lunch meeting I was now thirty minutes late for; and texts from my team back in Victoria asking me a string of questions about our various projects.

As I scrolled through the endless messages, I walked into the living room to see bodies passed out all over the floor, young men and women sleeping in various contorted positions, like mannequins left in the room with abandon. I noticed a couple of people wearing Facebook T-shirts—a spotted memory from the night before. One of them was surrounded by a collection of tiny liquor bottles, lined up like toy soldiers. As I made my way into another room, I saw a couple of my own employees in repose, using towels as blankets.

I tiptoed around everyone, desperate to escape the very suite I'd always dreamed of staying in but that now looked like a frat house with a high thread count.

A couple of years ago, this scene would have been my fantasy. I wanted money, girlfriends, and friends to party with. I wanted the penthouse suite, even the hickeys.

Yet, this certainly hadn't been my plan. None of this had.

Almost a decade earlier, after the sudden success of my tech news website, Macteens, I had decided that writing was my calling in life. That I would set out into the world and become an intrepid reporter. I'd cover Apple, interviewing Steve Jobs and waxing poetic about his company's latest product announcements and rumors, and reviewing all the latest gadgets. Yes, I imagined, I'd likely have to start as a tech reporter for the Victoria paper, the *Times Colonist*, but then I could move to the *Globe and Mail* in Toronto, and soon after, join the upper echelons of journalism: the *New York Times* or *Wall Street Journal*.

Back when I had just graduated high school, in 2004, I had told my three partners at Macteens that I was going to college and gave up my quarter of the business. Then, I stuffed all my worldly possessions into two large cardboard boxes and boarded a plane to Toronto for my first semester at Ryerson University, Canada's top journalism school.

In what would end up being a series of delusionary dreams that turned into stark realities, within the first months of school I realized I'd made a terrible mistake. While my professors talked about the coming age of journalism like we were in the 1950s and we were approaching a golden era and could all expect jobs at *Life* magazine or the *New York Times* or *The Times* of London, I looked around and saw I was about to join an industry dying of terminal business cancer.

It felt like I was a guy training to develop film and print photos onto 4x6 photo paper, right when digital photography had just hit. Even then, I was consuming news on blogs like *Engadget* and *Gawker*, not in print newspapers. Even if I was struck by journalistic lightning and was one of the few people on the planet who became a successful journalist, there was a 0.0001 percent chance I'd ever be a reporter at *The Times*. Forget riches, I'd be lucky to graduate with a paying job.

So, I did the only rational thing. I dropped out.

My parents were distraught. It wasn't just that I quit college, it was that I had absolutely no plan of what to do instead. When I had left home, they waved me off, assuming they had successfully launched me into adult independence, but here I was, back in their spare bedroom playing video games. Any chance they got, they would remind me that they couldn't support me, peppering me with the realities of life. "The electric bill was $140 this month," my dad would say as he sat drinking his morning coffee. "Can you believe how much toilet paper is now?" my mother reminded me. "Thirty-four dollars!" my father said one day as he looked at me from across the couch. "Thirty-four dollars to fill the Volvo; that's more than I usually spend." These lectures were often supported with visual presentations: itemized receipts informing me about the considerable cost of my presence in their home.

Soon after I moved back in, they ceased being my parents. Unlike many of my friends, whose families provided them with free rent in cozy basement suites and had even been known to buy beer for their parties, my new landlords were ruthless. They began charging me $500 a month rent, due on the first of the month. An above-market rent at the time and a not-so-subtle reminder to grow up and move out—quickly! It wasn't that they were being mean, it was more that they had thought their oldest son would be the least of their problems, and only a few months after leaving, I had landed on their doorstep with a splat.

It didn't take long for my savings to dwindle, and I was broke. One morning, I woke up in the spare bedroom of my childhood home, realizing that my landlord-parents weren't messing around. If I didn't get a job, they were going to evict me.

I'd always liked coffee, so I figured I'd try my hand at being a barista. I printed out my resume and dropped it at a dozen coffee shops around Victoria. The next day, one of them called me and asked me to come in for an interview.

The café was called 2% Jazz and, ironically, it was located right next to the offices of the *Times Colonist*, my hometown paper that, until I dropped out, I had imagined I'd one day work for. At the time, the only coffee you could find in Victoria was horrible diner drip—jet black with a lingering battery acid aftertaste. But this place was different. It focused on second wave espresso drinks made with care. I'd never seen latte art before, but they served lattes with hearts and beautiful rosettas. They roasted their own beans and played great music. They made coffee seem cool.

I walked in, dressed in my most appropriate hipster attire—ridiculous baggy jeans and the most ironic vintage T-shirt I owned. Sam Jones, the owner, sat me down and told me he was going to make me a shot of espresso. He told me the story of the South American farm his beans came from and showed me the grinder he had used for years. He explained the inner workings of the espresso machine and then, after pulling a perfect shot, he watched me drink it and asked me what I tasted. I rattled off some random adjectives, describing "notes" and "flavors" and "fruits" that I wasn't sure I could even identify, but that I thought sounded good. Whatever I said, it worked, and he hired me on the spot. He must have been desperate.

I absolutely loved the job. Sam kept a constant soundtrack of amazing music in the background—mostly DJ Shadow thumped into my ears as I burred coffee and dripped espresso. In the background there was always an orchestra of murmuring energy from lots of caffeinated patrons clacking away on keyboards and sharing ideas. I enjoyed practicing my latte art as I chatted with regulars, many of whom reconfirmed my decision to drop out when they'd tell me about the latest struggles at the next-door newspaper, which seemed to be doing endless layoffs.

These conversations, and seeing all the busy patrons on their laptops, made me realize that I needed to figure out my life and find a more sustainable job: I couldn't be a barista forever. Part of that was due to the lack of money—I was making $6 an hour as a trainee barista—but also the indignities of being the lowest person on the totem pole of a small coffee shop.

After a few months, the excitement began to wear off. I started to hate the sound of my alarm. I hated riding the bus to work at 5 AM. I was bored out of my mind when I had to mop the floors and count the till. And given my meager pay, I barely had any cash left over once I paid rent to my parents.

So, I started doing some soul searching. I enrolled at the local community college but skipped all my classes after the first week. I tried to get a job at *Engadget*, a popular tech blog I read constantly, but they weren't interested in a random teenage dropout. I was aimless, tired, and frustratingly poor. Both my literal and professional bank accounts were empty. I had nothing but ambition, this vague sense that I should do more with my life than mop up spilled coffee to the beats of DJ Shadow.

The change started with a book called *The Google Story*. I'd been reading about technology companies, not because I had a gift for coding or some impressive startup idea. The world of technology just felt shiny and new, a fresh start for a young adult who had dropped out of two schools in less than a year. I had stumbled upon the book and decided to give it a go, wondering how the biggest search engine in the world had become just that, and while flipping from page to page, I realized that while the dot-com bubble was a lot of half-baked hype, with almost every internet company raising too much money at absurd prices and then imploding, the new breed of internet companies were radically different: they actually made money.

As I turned the last page of the book, and put it down in front of me, I had an epiphany that there was a gold rush that was about to happen with tech, and I wanted to be a part of it. I decided that the only solution to this was to move to Silicon Valley. Of course, I also knew that this would require acquiring an actual skill. So, I started reading more books about tech.

For a while, nothing changed. I read. I mopped. I made coffee. I was stuck.

That was until I met Jeff and Chris, two guys who came into the coffee shop every day. Chris had a big blond Afro and mellow stoner vibe, while Jeff had dapper hair slicked with pomade and wore a collection of pressed polo shirts. They were an odd couple, to say the least. They would both come into the café and sit for hours at the espresso bar with their laptops, nursing their cappuccinos and the free Wi-Fi. I started stealing glances at their screens and asking questions about what they did. It turned out they ran a small design agency called The Number building websites for local businesses. In between customer orders, I kept asking questions about how their business worked.

"So, how'd you guys learn HTML and CSS?" I'd ask while pulling a shot.

"What do you charge someone for a website like that?" I'd query as I mopped the floor behind them. "How do you find your customers?"

They were more than happy to share the secret of their success, and as they broke it all down, I couldn't believe my ears. They told me they were able to do three to four projects at a time, and that they charged five to ten thousand dollars per website. By my almost-failed-junior-year math, that was twenty to forty thousand dollars per month in revenue. A veritable fortune compared to my $1,500 a month barista paycheck.

As I talked to them, and secretly took notes, scribbling down acronyms on the back of receipts, I realized that I had it all wrong: I was the guy *making* the espresso, but I wanted to be the guy *drinking* it.

These two could whip together a website in a week while sipping espresso and laughing. I was mopping floors at 5 AM while they slept like angels, taking leisurely mornings that started at ten with an espresso made by yours truly. While I was working *hard*, they were working *smart*.

They were smart, there was no question, but what they were doing wasn't rocket science by any means. At Macteens, I'd learned how to use Photoshop to design websites and built them with basic HTML. I was just a bit rusty, but I was sure I could pick it all back up.

One afternoon, I clocked out of work and went to a nearby bookstore to buy some books on web design. My bible became a book called *Bulletproof Web Design* by Dan Cederholm. I devoured every word and line of code in the book, which led me to take a few online courses, and I basically just fell down the best rabbit hole. Before long, I was trying to reverse engineer every one of Dan's websites, figuring out how he did drop shadows, copying the fonts he used, and learning how he made the buttons on his sites look perfectly glossy, a style, I learned from another book, called "skeuo-morphism"—popularized by Apple. I was fascinated by the simplicity of his designs and admired his dedication to the tiny details that made his work stand out.

Night after night, I upgraded my skills from kludgy Dreamweaver HTML to slick modern web design and development. I realized that with a few manic nights and a couple of good books, I could basically learn any-thing. I had found college brutally boring, offering too little of the infor-mation I actually wanted to learn. Now, reading these books and learning on the fly, I realized I was an "autodidact," a pretentious way of saying I preferred teaching myself to being taught. It was all in a book.

Designing websites came naturally to me. Growing up helping my dad at his architectural firm and playing with computers, I had an intuitive sense of layout. I knew where the eyes went first, and how to guide them from one section to the next. I'd spend hours reverse engineering famous websites and nudging pixels ever so slightly to make everything look *just so*. What surprised me most was that it didn't feel like work. I was having fun. I would sit down at my computer at lunchtime, and before I knew it, it would be dark outside. Sometimes I'd pull all-nighters and go for breakfast at a diner near my parents' place before setting off to work at the coffee shop at sunrise.

I was obsessed.

But a hobby doesn't pay the bills, and I decided that although I was still a complete novice, it was time for me to look for some actual design work, which led me to a job board called Authentic Jobs for contract web design. I applied for every single project I could find listed—I must have put in requests for more than a hundred of them. Then, for reasons I still can't ex-plain, someone gave me a chance. His name was Kavin Stewart, and he was a product manager at a company called Offermatica. He offered me $2,500 to design two pages.

I felt like I had struck gold. I got to work designing and laying out the pages, and somehow, I pulled off the job without anyone realizing I was completely incompetent. To Kavin, this was just another project. To me, this was the most incredible opportunity of all time. I had somehow found a job that fit me perfectly. It combined the sales skills and ability to talk to anyone that I'd picked up as an unpaid computer salesman and barista; the tech skills I'd learned from trying to install video games on my parents' crappy old computer; and the interest in design and business that I'd picked up from Dad. More importantly, it appealed deeply to the little boy in me. Nobody—and I mean *nobody*—could tell me what to do. I was an entrepreneur. The owner of the company. The boss.

When I received my first payment, the amount of money that got wired to my account was about 30 percent higher than the invoice I sent. I asked the teller to double-check and told her that the client must have made a mistake. When she came back from speaking with her manager, she told me it was the exchange rate. One dollar in the US was worth a dollar thirty in Canada, something I was completely unaware of. A $2,500 project had become a $3,250 project.

As I walked out of the bank counting my money, I said this was it: I was pushing my chips all in on web design. With my newfound wealth, I immediately quit the coffee shop and moved out of my parents' house, which was not the most responsible decision, since I had a new apartment lease and no consistent income. But it was meant to be irresponsible. I knew the pressure of a lease would light a bonfire under my ass—I had to make it work.

In those early days, I was in a constant panic about money.

Chronically stressed about how I'd pay for dinner, let alone rent, I began frantically searching for more freelance job boards trying to find my next client. Thankfully, my newfound skills were in high demand. While the bubble from Internet 1.0 had exploded in 1999 and trillions of dollars had vanished from the tech market, now, in 2006, it seemed that more and more startups were opening for business. I'm not going to pretend I was an oracle who knew about the coming era of web tech people would soon be calling

"Web 2.0," which would usher in an era of social media, but what I did know was that all of these new startups needed one thing, and that was a website.

First thing first, I needed my own site to showcase my design prowess. There was one problem: I only had one project under my belt. Who would hire a guy from Victoria to do a website with one single project on his site? That's when I had my second big epiphany, one that changed everything for me.

Perception is reality.

People were willing to pay me to design websites for them that made them look legitimate. Why shouldn't I do the same for myself? If I pretended to be an established design agency instead of some random nineteen-year-old living in an unfurnished apartment, I could probably get more business and charge higher rates. What I needed to do was legitimize myself.

Step one of that process was finding a name. Something catchy and sophisticated. In HTML, there's a tag called Meta, which defines the information for that page. I thought Meta sounded nice—it hadn't yet been appropriated by Facebook—which led me to the name MetaLab. I designed a slick-looking website, full of design flourishes I'd just taught myself (thanks to Dan Cederholm), and I created a page featuring my "team" of professional designers and developers alongside a now cringe-inducing tagline: "We help people make cool stuff." Of course, I didn't actually have a team, so I asked a few of my programmer friends if I could use their pictures on the site. I told them if I actually won a job, I'd hire them for the project. Once enough people said yes, I started sending out cold emails, soliciting work for my huge design agency, MetaLab.

In retrospect, I had no business starting a business. I think this shed light on an important truth of the internet, that anyone—anyone—with a little sweat and hustle, a sprinkle of bullshit on top, and a heaping of luck could start a company. It's the old fake-it-until-you-make-it strategy, which obviously doesn't work in most other industries. You can't fake a bakery. I couldn't have faked a car repair shop, or law practice, or really any business that requires extensive training or investment. But I realized that the internet offered a kid like me a critical loophole, letting me bootstrap my fake company until it was actually sort of real. Of course, behind that strategy was an impressive amount of arrogance. I'd built exactly one professional website, but I believed that if someone hired me, I could build another one.

Given the demand for designers, it didn't take long before I had more customers. One of my first clients wanted to redesign their marketing website, to "create something modern and polished." When they offered me $5,000 for the project, I acted cool, but in my head I was ready to scream with sheer astonishment.

A few days later, I sent over my initial designs. The company loved them, and immediately asked me to code a JavaScript prototype. In my head, I started to panic, because I didn't really know how to code anything more than a basic website. I certainly didn't know how to build something of this level, with all the fancy design elements I'd included.

"No problem!" I told my new customer as sweat beads formed on my forehead.

In a panic, I reached out to a developer friend. I sent him the design of the site and asked him how much he would charge to write the code.

"Maybe a thousand bucks?" he told me.

Expecting to get negotiated down, I told my new client that it would cost $2,000 for the coding of the prototype. The client sent a one-line email response: "Perfect." My jaw dropped. It wasn't intentional, but I had just made a 50 percent profit margin after I paid my friend.

I'd read so many books on businesses and design, but it wasn't until I made money as a middleman that it all started to make sense to me. In that moment, I immediately stopped seeing the world as a barista, or even the customer, but as the boss.

This was how every business worked—creating the demand, building the systems and processes, hiring other people to do the work, then charging enough for whatever it is that you're selling that you turn a profit.

Counterintuitively, you didn't actually do most of the work yourself, and yet you earned the profits for putting it all together.

It didn't take long before I had more work than I could handle and I knew I needed a real employee, a team that was more than just a few pictures of my friends on my own site.

My first hire was Luke. His qualifications? He was my girlfriend's best friend's boyfriend, had a great sense of humor, and he knew how to code. I offered him $30 an hour, which was double his current pay at the local university IT help desk. After learning my lesson with the JavaScript project, I decided to charge customers $60 an hour for my programmer's time. In doing so, I had the realization that if you sell your own time hourly—say, as a contractor or employee—you can only ever sell eight to twelve hours in a day. You're capped. But if you sell other people's time, or better yet, a service with a markup on your cost, you can grow your income infinitely without doing the actual day-to-day work.

I realized that, at the café, my boss, Sam, had been doing the same thing with me. He was probably making hundreds or even thousands of dollars a day in profit off of me and my coworkers' labor, sometimes without showing up to the shop for days at a time. But I had to give him credit: he had taken on a lot of risk to get there. He'd started with a street-side coffee cart, working long hours himself, before signing a lease for the café. He'd come up with the concept, hustled to get some press and generate word of mouth in the neighborhood; he'd hired, trained, and bet on his employees. Ultimately, the buck (and a huge amount of stress) stopped with him. When it worked, you could reap the benefits of the reward. I still hadn't learned the lesson of what happened when it didn't work.

For now, I was doing the same. And while I secretly wondered why Luke and the other employees I worked with didn't go do this themselves, I soon realized that it was often due to their desire for certainty. While I'd wanted to shove aside every boss I'd worked for and grab the wheel, I realized that most people abhorred risk. They wanted safety and security. A steady salary and rails—things I had none of. I was perpetually a month away from going broke and constantly pouring my profits into hiring new people, signing scary-looking contracts full of terms I didn't understand with companies that could sue me into the Stone Age should they so choose, and guaranteeing credit lines personally.

Risk, in this case, equaled reward.

Over time, my reward grew. I started going to fancy restaurants and told women I met that I was an "entrepreneur." (I know.) I started paying for big nights out with all my friends, and for the first time, throwing down my credit card without even looking at the bill. I did, however, feel like I was out of my depth. I was pushing the boundaries of my own competence. I had no clue what I was doing when it came to business. I didn't understand accounting and I certainly didn't have an MBA or any formal training. The only business principle I had figured out was that my bank account should be bigger on the thirtieth of the month than on the first, which it usually was. And yet I had the foresight, and the constant nagging sense, that this could all come crashing down.

I believed the only way to stop that from happening was to keep pressing the accelerator.

Rather than rely on job boards to find new customers, I started networking. I flew to every conference I could find online. TED, Summit Series, and Y Combinator's Startup School in Palo Alto. I'd walk around a litany of soulless convention centers and hotel conference rooms, pounding coffee, passing out business cards, and "pressing the flesh" as it was called. I started to cold-email CEOs of startups that had just raised ungodly sums from venture capital. I had a simple insight: most CEOs checked their own emails, and it was easy to guess their email addresses. What did I have to lose? Whenever I saw a company announce a big raise on *TechCrunch*, I'd figure out the CEO's email and contact them. With the confidence that only a one-line email can convey, I'd send mysterious messages like, "Hey, big fan of your business. Would love to work together." Believe it or not, these random cold emails—most of which took me less than a minute to send out—ended up winning some of MetaLab's biggest clients and helped me build friendships with some of the most successful people in business.

One day, while on a flight to yet another conference, I was flipping through *Inc.* magazine when I read about a company called Basecamp. It was run by two guys in Chicago, Jason Fried and David Heinemeier Hansson, and they had used the profits from their web design agency to build their own project management software. Along the way they built a cultlike following by sharing the contrarian path they'd taken on their blog. Unlike seemingly every other tech company that raised venture capital and took huge moon-shot risks, Jason and David focused on a more sustainable approach: simply running a profitable business. To the rest of the business world, this would seem like the most basic tenet of running a company, but believe it or not, this was a novel (and outlandish) concept that offended most of Silicon Valley.

Their approach was one that appealed to the little boy deep inside of me who was sick of his parents telling him what to do: they had 100 percent control to set their own destiny, answered to no one, and had become multi-millionaires doing it. While running a web design agency was a million times better than being a barista, it was also exhausting. Every agency in the world is chronically two to three months away from going out of business, and MetaLab was no different. These guys, on the other hand, had taken their profits and used them to start a software company, which had a massive advantage over an agency: their customers could sign up and use the software without ever talking to a human. It was completely automated. Nobody had to get on the phone, or set up a meeting, or fly to a conference to get a bunch of fellow nerds drunk. Customers simply signed up to use the software, plugged in their credit card, and then got billed monthly. Forget sleeping in, Jason and David got paid while they slept. Their recurring revenue grew month over month, slowly snowballing into a mountain. They quickly were added to my roster of business heroes, alongside Dan

Cederholm, the author of my new design bible, and I got so obsessed with their blog, Signal vs. Noise, that I set push notifications on my phone to let me know the second a new article came out.

I wanted to make money while I slept, too.

Trying to copy their contrarian approach, I started to set MetaLab apart from other agencies by focusing exclusively on designing digital products like mobile and web apps. I started calling us an "interface design firm," which I thought sounded sophisticated.

"We're the top interface design firm in North America," I would tell a throng of startup founders in a packed bar at the SXSW conference, as I took a swig from my cheap American beer, not mentioning that I had made up this label and we were likely the *only* interface design firm in North America because there simply weren't any others.

I hadn't realized it, but this ability to sell and market is what started to really set me apart from my competition. I had reasonable taste and design sense, but my time as a barista had taught me how to make friends with just about anyone. Most of my competitors—folks who ran agencies—were nerdy programmers who looked at their shoes when talking to a potential new client. My sales technique was simple: be fun to drink with and ask a ton of questions about whomever I happened to be talking to. It worked surprisingly well.

At conferences, I quickly started to learn that the most important business connections were made in bars, gossiping with drunk executives. Buying a round of drinks often generated a huge return on investment. For instance, there was a big Facebook party in Austin, where I got a crowd of startup founders wasted on my credit card. I must have bought a hundred tequila shots that night. It was a monstrous bar bill, but it more than paid for itself a few months later, when they needed design help and one of them (whom I clearly didn't get drunk enough) remembered my name and reached out to see if my "interface design firm" was accepting new business.

Thus began the snowball and I soon started winning clients all over

the world. As the MetaLab name gained cache, people started reaching out
to me, rather than the other way around. One of these was Jerry Kennelly,
a "Tralee-born" Irish entrepreneur who had recently sold his company to
Getty Images for hundreds of millions of dollars. I flew out to Killorglin,
in the south of Ireland, the tiny town where he'd grown up and started his
company. As we walked to a local pub to get a drink, every single person
along the way said hello. "How ya' doin', Jerry?" "Top o' tha afternoon,
Jerry." "All right, then, Jerry!" He pointed out that he owned many of the
buildings in the downtown core. He was like the capitalist mayor—*the* guy
in town—and I was in awe. As we sat down with two pints of Guinness,
I asked him what it was like to be so rich and successful. To have all that
money. To own those buildings. All that respect.

"I'm drinking the same pint you are, aren't I?" he responded, looking a
bit melancholy.

His answer reverberated in my head. Not at all what I was expecting.
I wondered if perhaps I'd just caught him on a bad day? I quickly put this
out of my head as I negotiated a deal for MetaLab to design his startup's
new app.

What was strange about this time was that it all happened so quickly
that I didn't even notice I was making so much money.

For my entire life, money had been a problem. Now, finally, I had
"enough" of it. Real money. I wasn't rich, but I wasn't broke, either. For the
first time ever, checking my bank account didn't fill me with dread. While
most of the kids I went to high school with were getting wasted at fraternity
parties, I was running my own business. And a successful one at that.

Sure, I was a bit jealous about missing out on college life, but I was grateful to be where I was. I felt like I was miles ahead and the race had barely
begun.

It was around this time that we got our first really big contract from a
startup called Mogulus. The founder, Max Haot, a Belgian serial entrepreneur, had this crazy idea to create a platform where people could livestream

video 24/7. This was more than a decade and a half before Facebook Live was invented, and at the time, there was no easy way to create a livestream. It seemed like a big lift, but he had raised a substantial amount of cash after selling his last startup and hired us to help design it. We created a beautiful but hilariously glossy (all the rage at the time) interface and we hustled to try to be as unique as possible, subsequently creating many design elements that are now a standard part of the video streaming experience.

A few months into the project, Max summoned me to New York for a few days of intensive meetings. On the first day, the two of us met at the Noho Star, a bustling restaurant on Lafayette Street, where he knew the waiter and ordered a Caesar salad assembled tableside and a bevy of delectable off-menu appetizers. The entire time, I couldn't figure out why I was there. Or why he was being so nice to me. He was clearly in work mode, anxious about something, and he ordered another round of drinks. This finally clued me in—he wanted to negotiate something. I'd done the same thing countless times with new clients or would-be new hires. I was being softened up with food and spirits.

My mind immediately went to something bad. Maybe he was about to crush our monthly rate, or worse, fire us. I felt a tingle run up both hands. I had hired a team to work on this project and at the time he was our largest client, making up some 70 percent of our revenue. I cursed myself for being so fiscally irresponsible.

"We love your work; you guys are the best . . ." he started, as he tore a piece of bread and mopped up the buttery sauce on his plate. He took a sip of his gin and tonic and continued: "But . . ." Oh God, I thought, a "but." He went on: "We'd like to move you from a per-project basis, to a monthly retainer. We need to move faster."

In my head, I quickly started to panic, running the numbers, assuming it would be a lowball offer, maybe $5,000 a month at best. I'd have to lay off a designer or two, then reduce the pay for one of my engineers. But I started to think to myself: "If I can push him to $7,000 a month, I'm going to be okay."

He stopped eating. Put his drink down. And asked me, "How's $20,000 a month?"

He held the silence as I looked down at my untouched chicken. It took every ounce of self-control to not start jumping up and down and pumping my fist in the air. I could feel the excitement coursing through my veins like I'd just done some wonderful drug.

"I think I can make that work," I said, slowly, pretending to do the math in my head. "As long as you pay on the first of the month?"

"We can make that happen," he said, relieved that I'd agreed to his number.

Afterward, I told Luke, the programmer I'd hired to help on another project, hoping he'd be elated, too, but he was fully aware that this wouldn't move the needle financially for him. Instead, he was going to be doing more work, and I'd be making more money. In fact, some months, I was making as much as $10,000 in profit, and paying Luke and my freelance designers and developers the rest.

Unfortunately, I was too young and inexperienced to realize I was being greedy, or to align our incentives so we both made more money as the company grew. Instead, I quelled his concerns with a small raise and started going on spending sprees.

In one twenty-four-hour period, I went to a nearby mall, bought a PlayStation, the biggest television I could find, a surround sound system, a Canon 5D camera, and then tucked into a $500 boozy steak dinner with a friend visiting from Toronto, just because I could.

At some point, my shopping became an addiction. I didn't know what else to do with my free time, so I just started to buy all the glories I'd always wanted. Expensive clothes. Shoes. Stereo equipment. At one point I even bought a Segway, which before too long was assigned to a dark corner of my storage room.

In some weird cosmic phenomenon, the more money I made, the bigger my clients became. Dozens of Fortune 100 companies wanted to work with us and were reaching out. I bought more stuff. Got more clients. Made more money. And I quickly discovered that the human mind is naturally ungrateful, quickly habituating to what we already have, and constantly chasing after the next new thing. Psychologists refer to this as the hedonic treadmill. The idea that we have to keep running faster and faster, buying more and more, simply to maintain the same level of happiness. Before long, I was sprinting on that treadmill, but I wasn't any happier. The worst part was I was about to run into a wall.

By now it was the late summer of 2008 and I'd been so busy building a business and buying unnecessary electronics that I hadn't paid a lot of attention to the global economy. Everyone in my world seemed to be doing great. I was protected by a digital bubble, so it was all too easy to ignore the tremors coming from Wall Street as the housing market started to quake. By September of that year, however, it was becoming pretty clear that this wasn't a temporary dip; the market was crashing, and the impact was going to be catastrophic.

The problem with being a design firm is that design feels expendable. Frivolous. Aesthetic. When your stock is crashing, and your revenues are down 50 percent, the first thing you cut is the fancy design firm you're paying $20,000 a month.

Your old website will do just fine.

And that's exactly what happened. Once the big companies realized that we were entering a great recession, they immediately terminated our contracts; tens of thousands of dollars in monthly revenue vanished overnight. The small companies that could keep me afloat between big clients just stopped calling.

Warren Buffett has a saying: "You don't know who's swimming naked until the tide goes out." Unfortunately, you don't know who the jerks are either. Before the market crash, one of our largest clients was an early-stage startup that today is worth billions of dollars. We'd been working hard for them, building out their mobile app, and they'd been happy customers, giving us tons of glowing feedback on our work. But then, the day after the stock market tanked, they suddenly began complaining about our work and even demanding their money back. It felt wrong. Not only had we been hustling, but we'd done an impeccable job. Our work for them had been met with heaps of positive praise. When I asked them what had changed and made it clear that they had to pay for the work that had been done to date, they sent me a scary legal letter threatening to sue us if we didn't return their money.

That's when I started to panic. If I paid them back, I'd have a couple hundred dollars left in the bank. But what choice did I have? It's not like I could afford a lawyer. In a state of shock, I refunded their money.

Then, as quickly as it had all come, it was *all* gone.

Almost overnight I went from making seemingly endless profits to making nothing—literally nothing. A few days later, I went to the grocery store, and after I filled my cart, I had to put items back on the shelf that I couldn't afford. I left the store that night with a huge bag of potatoes. If I ate a few per day for the next few weeks, I figured those potatoes could get me through bankruptcy. An absurd thought, to be sure, but that was where my head was at. It was at this point—wandering the fluorescent aisles of a supermarket at night—that I realized how stupid I'd been.

I had gotten incredibly lucky, making more money in the past couple of years than I had ever thought possible in a lifetime. I went from mopping the floors of a coffee shop to working with Silicon Valley's most cutting-edge companies. And yet, I'd somehow spent every single cent I had earned, blowing it on things I didn't need. I had closets full of clothes I didn't wear and electronics that were already obsolete. I had shelves displaying fancy liquor I didn't even like the taste of. This was my first real slap in the face, the moment I realized that what goes up can also come down and that I had to start learning how to save and invest.

I was reminded of my father telling me about the wonders of compound interest as a kid. That if I had just invested all that money instead of buying frivolous nonsense, I could have been set for life.

There were two things that saved me from bankruptcy.

The first was a gift of Apple stock I'd gotten from my great uncle, a hobbyist stock investor, as a birthday present for his computer-obsessed nephew in the late '90s. Back then, they were worth a few hundred dollars. By 2008, those shares had increased in value to a staggering gain of around $20,000. I was desperate, so I called my uncle and said I needed to sell. My uncle thought I was crazy. "It's the worst time to sell," he told me. "Now is the time to sit on your hands." But I had no choice. I had bills coming due and an empty bank account. He eventually relented and sold the stock for me, which kept the company going. But my uncle was also right—this was the worst investment call of my life. If I'd kept those Apple shares, they'd be worth many millions today.

The second thing that kept MetaLab on life support was a laser hair removal clinic in Arizona. When times were good, I was extremely picky about what projects I'd take on. An iPhone app for a photo-sharing startup? Absolutely! A new website for a company that just raised $20 million from Sequoia? You bet! The not-so-cool brands were told, "Sorry, we're just too busy right now."

But now that I was buying potatoes in bulk, desperate to stay in business, I was saying yes to anything and everything. I was so stressed I thought I was going to lose all my own hair, and in a slight bit of irony, the one project that made the biggest difference was this hair removal clinic that reached out asking for a new site. It wasn't glamorous, and much of the work involved artfully photoshopping pictures of folliculitis and weird ingrown hairs in various areas of people's scalps. And unlike some hip startups in Palo Alto, that laser hair removal clinic was true to their word: they paid their bills on time, and I was able to make it through.

MetaLab had survived a brutal period. Our competition, the ones who held their nose when asked to photoshop infected hair follicles, were not so lucky. Most of my competitors either went out of business or fire-sold their agencies to bigger companies for pennies on the dollar, effectively selling their team for a small recruitment fee.

This was my life for almost a year. Hair follicles and potatoes.

Finally, by around 2009, tech companies cautiously started to spend again.

I'd learned so many lessons over the past couple of years: from faking it until I made it, to how to hire employees, and of course how to appropriately charge clients, but the most valuable lesson of all was that the best companies were all-weather and ready for anything.

You could fake whatever perception you wanted, but you couldn't fake the cash on your balance sheet.

After that brush with death, I vowed that, going forward, I would never spend more than 10 percent of my profits on my lifestyle. Everything else would be saved, invested, or used to start new businesses. I wasn't going to let this happen again.

Working with the least sexy clients I could find paid off. MetaLab emerged from the recession with almost zero competition and started landing some of the world's most sought-after companies as clients. In the years after, we worked on a redesign of YouTube. We helped build Walmart's e-commerce technology. We even did top-secret projects for Apple. Then one day I got a call to do a project that would catapult MetaLab into a different stratosphere of the design world and cement our reputation as a top-tier design firm.

The project was to design a then unknown app for a guy called Stewart Butterfield.

I'd always idolized Stewart as a rare Canadian tech success story: he'd founded the photo-sharing site Flickr, which he'd sold to Yahoo in 2005, before launching a massively multiplayer game called *Glitch*. The game was a dismal failure, but right around that time, as Stewart was laying most of his employees off, he sent me an email, asking if we could talk.

"Look, we're going through a really rough time," he told me over the phone, "but we have a couple of million dollars in the bank and we want to try this product idea we've incubated." That's when he described his idea: a chat platform for teams. "We're thinking of calling it Slack," he told me.

After hearing the pitch, I started to feel sorry for him. His idea had been done a million times already. A lot of people had tried to build chat products, and there was already a ton of competition, including Campfire, made by Jason and David at Basecamp. On the other hand, I really wanted to work with Stewart. He was a legend in the design world; the look and feel of Flickr had been revolutionary for its time.

"I can pay you an $80,000 flat fee, but I need a lot out of you guys," he told me, outlining that he needed a logo, website, mobile and web app design. "I really think this is going to be huge." It was a meager sum given the amount of work, but I sucked it up because I wanted to collaborate with him. He offered to pay us partially in stock, but I rebuffed him. Having learned from my hard knocks in 2008, I knew that stock was often the world's most expensive toilet paper and cash was king. (Yes, when Slack sold for $27.7 billion eleven years later in 2020, I also realized I missed out on tens, or even hundreds of millions of dollars.)

I put our best designers on the project. We worked diligently. Pulling all-nighters at the office, sleeping under our desks and barely showering, going through endless revisions because we were all so eager to impress Stewart. We started with the premise that we wanted this productivity tool to actually feel like a video game, and not just another dreary blue and gray corporate product or Facebook look-alike. We wanted to give it character and verve and pop. And we ended up designing the logo, the website, the mobile app, the web app—much of the early design DNA of Slack was designed by our team.

The end result spoke for itself: Slack became one of the fastest growing software companies of all time.

While I didn't get any of that money from Slack's sale, our work helped shine a spotlight on MetaLab, and it grew 5x over the next few years. Suddenly, everyone wanted a sprinkle of the same magical fairy dust that had propelled Slack to a multibillion-dollar company.

Of course, not all clients were as wonderful as Slack.

Some didn't pay the bills. Others abused our team and were horrible to work with. Some hired us to do work, and then ended up secretly hiring my top designers.

I realized through it all that in Silicon Valley everyone plays nice, wearing goofy hoodies and padding around in Allbirds, looking like friendly college kids. But inside, most were just as ruthless as their Wall Street counterparts. I soon came to prefer the super-direct pseudo-assholes I worked for over the fake magnanimous ones. Over time, I observed that the founders who purport their ethics in kumbaya mission and values statements are often the most dangerously full of shit.

And the more I worked with people who were selling hair follicle creams (the nice ones) and the more I worked with those trying to "change the world" (the often full of shit ones), I knew it was time to find a new strategy to procure new clients.

Going from the top down was backfiring.

I was being taken advantage of by seasoned and sometimes ruthless CEOs, and I surmised that the best way to solve this was to find new clients by going down a few levels within these organizations. I needed to befriend the project and product managers who had enough power within a company to hire my design firm (which in turn would make them look good to their bosses).

This, of course, is how I ended up blacked out in the St. Regis Hotel. Which is how I realized that there was a reason that these lower-level managers weren't in charge of these companies. They liked to party and, as my customers, it was my responsibility to make them happy.

That morning, though, felt different.

My head hurt more than usual.

My liver was rebelling.

I couldn't take it anymore.

I was desperate to escape that room that cost me $20,000 a night. I closed the door quietly, trying not to wake the engineers who were passed out in the living room. My mouth tasted of vomit, and I couldn't remember what the hell happened the night before.

All I knew, as I closed the door behind me, was that this wasn't the life I wanted to live.

Chapter 4

SCRATCH AND DESTROY

Hey everyone, it's Andrew."

"Andrew's on the call."

"Andrew here—sorry I'm a few minutes late. I was just wrapping up another call."

"I have to run to another conference call."

"Hi, it's Andrew. Sorry I'm late."

This was my day. Day in and day out.

At conferences it was the same, handing out my business card with the enthusiasm of a kid handing out flyers. "It's Andrew. Andrew Wilkinson." "Yeah, sure, my email address is at the bottom," I'd say, while secretly dreading that someone would actually email me, adding to my already inundated inbox.

My life had become a blur of endless conference calls, emails, and work trips. Most nights were spent in front of the computer working until sunrise or guzzling beer to escape the never-ending list of to-dos in my head. And yet while you couldn't have found a sliver of white space on my weekly calendar, which was filled so neatly it looked like someone who lost a game of *Tetris*, I felt constantly restless. Weekends were worse, stretched out into a dull haze of emptiness that left me feeling isolated and unfulfilled. After the anxiety of almost losing everything in the financial crash, my singular goal was to fill my bank account, and it consumed my every moment.

My biggest problem was that I had succeeded, at least in the pursuit of building my company. Where I had failed was with the rest of my life. I had no hobbies, I had underinvested in friendships, and I had a string of disastrous romantic relationships with women I was utterly incompatible with.

I had just broken up with my on-again-off-again girlfriend, Allison, this time for good. We'd been like two jigsaw pieces that just didn't fit together, with a prodigious ability to fight about anything and everything. At one point, we had a tearful screaming match over whether I should buy a Volkswagen. She already drove one and felt it would be weird if we both drove the same brand, and clearly, I disagreed. We were the perfect picture of dysfunction: constantly fighting and breaking up, only to get back together in a fit of passion, before blowing up yet again over some nonsensical argument.

In the wake of this relationship, I didn't have much of a life outside my work. My spare hours on the weekend were usually filled with expensive nights out that left me feeling vapid and empty, followed the next day by a shopping spree that made me feel vapid and empty in the sunlight as well. Everything else was business. If I wasn't *doing* business, I was *reading* about it. My bedside table was stacked with endless business books, biographies of famous business people, and magazines about . . . business. It was all I thought about. Cracking the code. Making it bigger. Making it more efficient. Figuring it out.

To help fill the white space left by my breakup, I got an adorable Siamese ragdoll kitten. And cats, I soon realized, after going through a handful of rugs and couches, need stuff to scratch and destroy. Puffy things to curl into a ball on. Places to stretch out luxuriously and sleep their lives away.

The problem was that all the cat furniture I could find was hideous. Why was every piece covered in '70s motel shag carpeting? Did they all have to come in odd, ugly shapes? Why couldn't I find a litter box that wasn't the color of dirty dish water?

At the time, I was busy reading books on entrepreneurship. If these books had a shared cliché, it was the belief that the best (and most disruptive) business ideas come from your own experience. The idea that if you solve your own pain points, odds are others share the same pain and will pay you to fix it. The classic infomercial refrain that was yelled out of a television at 2 AM: "There's got to be a better way!"

One afternoon, while sitting on another conference call, staring at some of the hideous feline furniture that now filled my home, an epiphany struck me like a thunderclap: I should start a designer cat furniture business. Surely, there must be other people who wanted cat scratching posts that aren't slathered in shag carpet and colors from the disco era. My cat deserved a nice place to play and sleep. And I deserved a place for her to play and sleep that didn't hurt my eyeballs.

Given my extensive track record of entrepreneurial success (I was one for one with the success of MetaLab, after all), I assumed it was only a matter of time before my new cat furniture designs would disrupt the legacy players and transform pet decor forever. I did the math: if I made a product (a cat scratcher or cat couch) that I sold for just $50, given that there were more than one hundred million domestic cats living in the United States and Canada, if I sold just one piece of my new furniture to just 1 percent of them a year, that could be $50 million in revenue. This could be so successful it would make MetaLab look like a failure. On top of that, given all those meetings I was constantly being dragged into, and the slog of running MetaLab, I felt like maybe this could be my way out. Another castle wall. Another revenue stream. More diversification. More freedom. Less cat destruction in my living room.

It was around this time that e-commerce was just starting to take off. It was early days for online stores, but there was a growing sense that the tools of retail were being democratized with software like Shopify, and that anyone could start selling their products online. Emboldened by my idea, I spent a weekend throwing together a Shopify store that would sell cat furniture from the few brands that already existed that were designed well (products I'd found at other cat stores) to test out the business. Then, I figured, I'd be designing my own cat furniture in no time. In my mind, I thought this would be Design Within Reach, but for cats! I decided to call the company H.J. Mews and used my design skills to make it look like a world-class furniture store. By Monday morning, I was open for business. Then, I contacted the manufacturers of the most beautiful cat products and "ordered" my first $50,000 in inventory—a container that was going to be shipped from Asia to a warehouse where I'd rented some space.

How could this not work?

The good news was that my Shopify store did get some orders; I clearly wasn't the only person fed up with traditional cat furniture.

The bad news was that I lost money on every single transaction. I'd bought the pretty litter boxes for $30, and while I had wanted to sell them for $50, I ended up having to drop the price to $44 each to compete with the large chains. That $14 of margin didn't come close to covering the cost of shipping, logistics, and the overhead of the business. I was vying for the title of "Worst Capitalist in History," managing to create a business that, unbelievably, lost more and more money with every sale.

Before long, I was losing $10,000 a month. I knew I was failing, throwing good money after bad, but I had no idea how to fix it. If I raised prices, my sales plummeted. If I spent more on Facebook and Google ads, that just cost me more money when people made purchases, compounding my losses. In fact, everything I did just seemed to make it worse. It felt like trying to nail Jell-O to a wall. My last hope was to buy a fancy model of cat litter box that wasn't yet for sale in the United States. It was beautifully designed and would have a much higher profit margin. I had one delivered to my house to test it out, and the day that it arrived, I unpacked it and set it up for my cat. That evening, I went out to meet a friend at the pub near my house.

Hours later, when I staggered back through the front door of my house, I was hit with a smell so foul it made my eyes water. The whole house reeked like a pit latrine. Gripping my nose, I walked down the hall and into my dining room. Then, I saw something I can never unsee. It appeared that my cat didn't share my fine taste in furniture and litter boxes. The sand in the box was left untouched, and in the hours since I'd left, she had defecated all over the floor around it. My robot vacuum, on its nightly schedule, had smeared a thin layer of cat feces across the room in a circular pattern, like a Franz Kline painting, and the little Roomba was now beeping shamefully in the corner.

In the end, cat furniture utterly humbled me.

After a year of crippling losses, more than $200,000 in hard-earned cash evaporating into thin air, I accepted the brutal truth: my cat furniture business was fundamentally unprofitable. It couldn't be fixed or optimized. It was time to tap out. The next day, I unceremoniously switched off the site, told the warehouse to give away my remaining inventory, and shut everything down.

But all businesses—even terrible ones—teach you something, and I realized that I had gotten extremely lucky with my first business. Partly because it was astonishingly simple, with an uncomplicated formula: Find clients. Charge them an hourly rate. Pay contractors a lower hourly rate. The difference was all profit. There was no office or physical location required, just a computer with an internet connection. My biggest overhead was an Adobe Photoshop license. If business slowed down, my contractors found other work and I could always cancel my software subscriptions. It was almost impossible to fail.

In the business Olympics, online retailing is an incredibly challenging sport. Hyper-competitive, capital intensive, logistically complex, and low margin. A million things had to go well in order for a customer to have a good experience; whereas at MetaLab, the client just had to like the designer they were working with. The cat furniture business was a painful lesson, but

I'd lived to tell about it. A flesh wound, which hopefully would build a bit of scar tissue. A lot of people aren't so lucky.

What I didn't know at the time was that this would only be the first of many business failures. What my partner Chris would later come to call "money bonfires." Poorly executed ideas where the numbers didn't work out, often run by the wrong people. And if anything, this one would look like a quaint little campfire compared to some of our future nuclear bombs.

But each one would teach me something. The key was to make sure I didn't go all in on one thing—one business—and that I not only tried to learn from each mistake, but that I did so across everything I did. That each business success or failure informed another business. We liked to joke that we "stuck forks into electrical sockets" for a living, hopefully learning something from each jolt, eventually getting better at business.

While I'd learned never to start an e-commerce business again, I was still stuck running MetaLab, which was exhausting.

When my time there wasn't spent getting wasted on the road to try to win more business, I was shaking hands and exhaustively pitching new clients. This lifestyle, where I could spend a week in five different cities, including New York, Seattle, and San Francisco, left me with the impending desire to change my life.

I was growing sick of the conference circuit, too. Having to put on a grin and give firm handshakes, even when inside I was bored stiff.

At one tech conference in Vancouver, I was seated next to a famous venture capitalist. He looked at my badge and asked me what my startup did. I told him that I didn't have a startup but instead had a profitable business that I'd bootstrapped. "Ah, a lifestyle business," he said with a chuckle. In the world of venture capital, a "lifestyle business" was pejorative. A business so small that it was only fit to pay for the founder's day-to-day lifestyle and wouldn't scale much beyond that. He promptly turned his back on me to talk to the much more interesting startup founder seated across from him. I was left, stewing and flushed, wondering why I was at yet another miserable conference sitting with such arrogant people.

I decided I needed a break. It was time to clear my head.

When a friend randomly invited me to go backpacking around Europe, I jumped at the opportunity. Then, I immediately regretted it for two reasons.

First, as much as I wanted to change my life, I also had a business to run. I didn't want to blow up MetaLab just to go on a grand tour of Europe. Second, I was still doing everything a CEO does at MetaLab. I was responding to clients, signing new business, managing designers, testing code—you name it. Every buck started and stopped with me.

"Come on, man," my friend pressed. "You'll have a great time, and if anyone could use a great time, it's you!"

I racked my brain trying to figure out who I could hire to take over while I took off, and that's when I remembered my old friend Mark. We had met at Ryerson University, where I had spent a few months before realizing journalism wasn't for me. A few days into my first (and only) semester, I had gone down to the school cafeteria. It was packed, a cacophony of chatting and clanging forks, and as I surveyed the room I spotted a corner table with a few people I recognized from my dormitory, one of whom had just started to get up right as I was about to sit down. He was pale with frosted hair and big mischievous brown eyes and he jokingly blurted out, in a thick Alabama accent, "Seat's taken!" He then thrust his hand over the seat where I was about to sit. We both started laughing at his random reference to Forrest Gump. (It's the scene where Forrest is getting on the bus, and nobody will let him sit down.)

"Hey, I'm Mark," he said as he removed his hand.

"Andrew," I replied.

We hit it off right away. It turned out that we shared a sense of humor, loved the same books and movies, and were both obsessed with the writing on *The Simpsons*. Before long we were bonding over our shared distaste for school, hanging out until four in the morning, and endlessly griping about our inability to meet girls. We embraced our status as misanthropes, Holden Caulfield twins lamenting the phoniness of everyone else around us. If you think we sounded insufferable, you'd be right.

I dropped out of college after a semester, but Mark was tougher than me and stuck it out. Although I'd moved back to Victoria, and Mark was still in Toronto, we stayed in touch, messaging daily about our existential angst and attempts at dating.

As MetaLab had grown, I started referring Mark freelance copywriting jobs from my clients. He always delivered on time, on budget, and his copy complemented our work perfectly. So, I called him and asked if he'd be interested in running MetaLab for a few weeks while I was in Europe.

"What do you mean, *run it*?" Mark asked me.

"It's more like house-sitting than anything else," I told him. "You just need to water the plants, feed the cats, and make sure the place doesn't burn down."

I could tell Mark was interested, but also a little scared—he rightfully pointed out that he didn't know anything about design, or creating websites, or how MetaLab worked.

"I have an idea," I told him. "Why don't you shadow me for a few days, and I'll teach you the ropes?"

So that's what we did. I booked my flight to London, started packing my stuff, and Mark began eavesdropping on client calls. He heard me deal with complaints, send bills, make sales calls, and work through the design process. Like so many aspects of business, these aren't discrete skills; they are instead often qualitative skills you can't teach in a class. It's all tacit knowledge, training your instincts, learning how to deal with the quirks and foibles of other human beings.

This hiring strategy is not what they teach at Harvard Business School. It was much simpler: I liked and trusted Mark. Most people I knew seemed to like and trust him, too. Therefore, I assumed my clients would like and trust him as well and he could run the business. I went with my gut. Mark agreed to give it a shot.

"What could go wrong?" I thought as I nervously headed to the airport. "A lot" was the answer, but an answer I didn't want to think about. As I sat in the airport lounge, a few minutes from boarding, I sent Mark a final email with my European cell number and the following instructions: "Only call in case of emergency."

As our plane took off, I imagined that I'd check in with Mark more than just for "emergencies" and that there would be daily calls of him asking me questions pertaining to areas of the business. I was so excited for this trip. To dine in old restaurants and eat decadent desserts. To stay in luxury hotels and talk poetically about art and the humanities with locals.

Instead, my friend Eric and I stayed in cheap hostels and got blackout drunk with random people we met on Twitter.

The only part of the trip that resembled any European culture was me and Eric asking locals, "What's the German word for *beer*?" "How do you say *beer* in Dutch?" "Is *wine* just *wine* in French?" I'm sure I ate something resembling food, though I can't really recall. As for the art, well, "The pub is just past the Louvre on the right" was the closest we got.

It was just what I needed. A form of workaholic rehab.

After a month of this, I felt rejuvenated, but on the long flight back, I started to panic. I had been having so much fun partying that I didn't even realize Mark had never called. Not once. I hadn't even checked my email after the first couple of days. As I was flying through the sky at five hundred miles per hour, I had a sickening thought: Did I still have a business? Would I return to angry clients? Any clients at all?

As soon as I landed in Vancouver, I called him in a panic.

"Mark?" I panted into the phone. "Is everything okay?"

"Why wouldn't it be?" he asked me curiously.

"Umm, I just haven't heard from you for—"

He interrupted me. "Can I call you back? I have a new client on the other line."

"Umm, yeah. Sure," I said as the anxiety dissipated. "Of course."

It turned out that not only did MetaLab still exist, but Mark had managed to sign new clients in my absence, and had even improved several of our processes. He had run the place with the precision of a general. The projects were all going out on time. Nobody seemed to even notice that I'd been gone for almost four weeks. Whole projects had happened without me being involved, or the client even uttering my name.

I guess I could have been offended. I'd built this company from scratch— how could it run so smoothly without me? But while I was walking through the Vancouver airport, I was overcome with a feeling of profound relief. I felt free for the first time in years.

I had a revelation: previously, I had thought of my business as ... *me*. It was all in my brain and it was my job to hold everything together with dental floss and duct tape. My ever-growing backpack full of stress bricks, crushing me into the trail as I trudged uphill. Every problem was mine. If I didn't show up, nothing would happen.

Now, it became clear that my business didn't have to rely on me. I could craft a machine to do everything. A machine that, if engineered just so, with the right people and processes, would convert raw material (client leads, opportunities, and introductions) into a fully formed product (an app, website, logo, whatever our clients wanted) without me lifting a finger. I adopted a mantra. I began to repeat it, over and over. I was "Teflon for tasks." Never again would I do something that could otherwise be done by someone else.

The next day, I called Mark and made him a full-time offer to become MetaLab's general manager, taking over most of my day-to-day responsibilities.

I told him I would still help sign new clients, and build the business, but I wouldn't be involved in any of the day-to-day operations. He'd hash out the concept with the client, assign designers and developers, and make sure the project was on time and budget. Basically, he was in charge of dealing with clients, making sure projects went smoothly, and that people paid their bills, all things I didn't enjoy doing anymore. Meanwhile, I would quietly handle the parts that I enjoyed: doing the marketing and strategy. In hindsight, it made all the sense in the world to do this, but at the time it was an anomalous thought that I almost felt guilty about. It's a decision that many entrepreneurs fear making. I was embracing what I came to call Lazy Leadership: the idea that a CEO's job is not to do all the work, but more importantly to design the machine and systems. Not a player on the field. Not the coach. But the owner, sitting up in a little box at the top of the arena, passively observing until the next critical fifty-thousand-foot decision had to be made.

Mark was obviously nervous about taking on such a senior role given that his only relevant business experience was a brief stint as a barista at a Starbucks in a Burlington strip mall. But, given that he was still living in the Toronto suburbs with his parents, when I offered him a steady paycheck, it was a pretty fast yes.

It didn't take long before I found myself with plenty of time on my hands.

The old days of hustling nonstop, jetting from conference to conference, working on designs while pulling all-nighters on red-eyes—that was long gone. Now Mark did most of it. And best of all, he was *excited to do it*. Unlike me, he'd spent the last few years living the life of a broke college student in Toronto, so the prospect of flying around wining and dining new clients appealed to him.

This had led me to the epiphany that there is always somebody else who loves the job you hate. You might find accounting boring, for example, but I promise you there is somebody whose idea of a great night is eight hours of pivot tables in Excel. You might find coding to be the most laborious and painstaking job on Earth; someone out there can't believe you're going to pay them to write code. And you might hate running a company, which was someone's dream job. In my case, it was Mark's.

I'd won!

I'd started a business that had become so successful I was able to walk away from it. Now, my business was running itself. The money in my bank account was growing by the day. I was sure this was it. I had made it and I'd soon want for nothing.

Now I just had to figure out what to do with all my free time.

Chapter 5

GOLD MINE

I scrambled my phone out of my pocket, dialed, and then gazed at the screen, waiting for Dad to pick up. I was grinning ear to ear. My smile spread so wide my face hurt. In my hand I peered down at the printout I'd just received from my accountant. An annual financial statement detailing how much money my company had made over the past year. I smoothed the paper with my thumb, careful not to smudge the printed text. The number at the bottom stated that I'd made over half a million dollars in annual profit, which was more than twenty times what I'd made working as a barista just a few years before.

When my father answered the phone, I shouted with sheer excitement: "Dad, can you believe it? My company made half a million this year!"

"Wow," he replied. "But did you remember to pay the taxes?"

"What do you mean?" I asked, unease rising in my stomach.

"The taxes. Did you make your tax installments?" he said, his voice rising with anxiety. "The government is going to fine you like crazy if you don't pay them on time. Just make sure you hit the deadline."

"Oh, yeah . . . right. I will," I mumbled, deflated by his reminder.

My father had always been an optimist, but after decades of never-ending financial strain, that optimism had been wrung out of him. Over the years, he had started multiple architecture firms, which seemed to career from one challenge to the next, as he, like me, tried to run an unpredictable services business with ever-shifting demands. Either too much work and not enough people, or too little work and too many people. Real estate moved in cycles, and many of his clients were high-flying real estate developers. They would swing from one extreme to another. Flush with cash to bankrupt in an instant, their bills left unpaid. Staying optimistic, he resisted making layoffs during these tough times and sunk into debt to keep his team employed, at one point putting the family house on the line. Ultimately, he recognized that running a company was not his game and he bowed out of it altogether. He sold his architecture firm to a large American company for a nominal amount, stayed for many years, then left to consult on government projects on his own. It was consistent, safe, well paid, and most importantly, in hindsight for him, didn't require the stress of having employees, whose mortgages and families depended on him. He had fought the battle in a difficult industry, and he had the scars to prove it.

Had I just gotten lucky? I stumbled into an industry where a barista with zero training could start a business and charge hundreds of dollars an hour on day one. I often wondered: If Dad were born thirty years later, would his design skills have been applied to web design instead of architecture? Had he been a victim of poor timing and chosen the wrong industry? I didn't know, but I vowed to take the baton and run with it. To make it work this time.

I remembered a line that stopped me cold during a Francis Ford Coppola interview I'd watched recently: "You can always understand the son by the story of his father. The story of the father is embedded in the son." I had watched Dad struggle in business, and this struggle was now embedded in me, too. My singular goal in life became to resolve this open thread.

While I knew Dad was proud of me, I got the feeling he feared I'd end up having a financial blowup. It felt like he was trying to scare some sense into me: Things won't be good forever. Stuff goes wrong. Murphy's Law.

And now, not only did I have a growing number of people counting on me for a paycheck, but two of them were my own brothers. Both Tim and William had joined the company. Tim, my middle brother, had joined to help with human resources, helping me build the company culture and ensure things ran smoothly. William, our younger brother, had joined as a designer while still in high school, avoiding client phone calls and carefully concealing the fact that he was only sixteen years old. I didn't take this lightly: half my family now depended on the success of the business.

To give Dad some credit, I had probably missed some tax installments. I knew I needed a counterbalance—somebody who thought in numbers to ensure I didn't accidentally drive into a wall.

I internalized this voice, realizing that, to date, I had mostly skated through on pure luck. If I was being honest with myself, I barely understood accounting or much about business. I'd recently joined the Entrepreneurs' Organization, a global network of entrepreneurs with chapters in each city, and had joined what they called a "forum," which was essentially a confidential business support group that met once a month to discuss what was going on in each of our businesses. Most entrepreneurs *definitely* need therapy, but few of us would ever go, so this was a way to lure us together and essentially trick us into doing group therapy.

At my first forum meeting, I sat across from a guy named Steve. Even though he was only ten years older than me, he made me feel like a kid. He looked like he got a haircut weekly, not a hair out of place, and was wearing a light gray business suit and a pair of impeccably shiny brown shoes. He even had two kids, something that was completely foreign to me at the time. At first, I didn't know what to make of him. He came across as serious, almost stiff, but after a few forum meetings, he revealed his warmth and an incredible sense of humor. We became fast friends, and after realizing our offices were only a block apart, we began eating lunch together often, usually at a sandwich spot that a local chef had started a few blocks away.

His office stood in stark contrast to my own. MetaLab's office was chaotic, effectively a bunch of twenty-year-olds crammed into a box. A mishmash of IKEA furniture and walls covered with quirky graphic design posters. Steve's office, on the other hand, was meticulous and five times the size. Glass offices, original paintings on the brick walls, a receptionist, and people in suits. While our offices reflected our very different personalities, I also recognized that Steve was a grown-up. He'd been in business for over a decade by this point and the library in his office was stacked wall-to-wall with business books that he'd read. He seemed to have advice on just about any topic, from accounting, to HR, to hiring. Over lunch, I'd ask him about all manner of business problems and he always seemed to have the perfect answer—he'd been there, done that, and I was reaping the benefits. In meeting Steve, I realized that I had succumbed to the Dunning-Kruger effect, the idea that people with limited knowledge or skill often overestimate their abilities. In other words: I didn't know squat about business and had a long way to go.

It was around this time that I met Chris Sparling—the same Chris from the local bank on Douglas Street who was introduced to me as "Mr. Sparling" but was so young he could have passed as the son of Mr. Sparling. The same Chris who I had somehow convinced to quit his job at the bank to come work with me as the CFO of my company.

For Chris, the initial moment of leaving the regularity and calm of the bank and joining me was clearly shocking. I ran my business on the cuff of my next gut feeling, whereas the bank had been run like, well, a bank. With rules and protocols. It even opened at a certain time and closed as the clock struck five. My company, on the other hand, was like a twenty-four-hour diner.

On his first day of work, he was waiting outside the office in a suit and tie, eager to get started. I was running late for another meeting. Rushing to get to a lunch, I screeched to a halt in front of him, threw open the trunk of my car and shoved three overflowing bankers boxes into his arms. "Here, these are all the company's financial documents. Go next door and knock on the office of the interior designers. They'll show you your office." The day before he started work, I had realized we had completely filled our current office space and didn't have room for him. I ran next door and finagled a desk in the basement of the interior designer's offices. Chris stood there in shock, likely wondering why in god's name he'd left his job at one of Canada's largest banks for this ramshackle operation. "By the way, don't wear a suit. Nobody here wears suits. Gotta go!" I told him, as I bolted back to my car and zoomed off to my meeting. I could see him in the rearview mirror, in his gray suit, arms full of overflowing boxes, not knowing what had hit him.

Regardless of this chaotic start, Chris buckled up and got things in order. Suddenly, everyone was getting paid on time. Our financials were up to date. We could get bank loans and credit cards. All things I had misunderstood or been too distracted to think about, but things that really mattered. More than these things though, Chris brought a financial eye to the business. He began analyzing our profit margins, finding opportunities to run more efficiently. He'd negotiate everything, from our office rent to the coffee beans we bought in bulk for the office. He was incredible. All the things I wasn't interested in doing, he loved and was good at. I couldn't believe my luck.

After Mark had taken over the company, I had tried to not work, but found that challenging. When I bought a turntable and started DJing for fun, I soon picked up a regular spot at a local club in Victoria, and before long had the great idea to start an online DJing school. I still can't tell if this idea was as bad as my cat furniture business, or if I was just a decade ahead of my time before online classes became a norm, but either way, my DJ school was a flop.

I was constantly coming up with business ideas. When I noticed a cluster of small pink bumps on my upper arms, I did some research and discovered that they were "chicken skin," a harmless cosmetic skin condition that was easily resolved with an over-the-counter skin cream. I immediately launched a site, ChickenSkin.org, and ordered hundreds of bottles of cream that I had a dermatologist formulate for me. I didn't sell a single bottle. As far as I know, they're still in the basement of our old office.

In a bout of extreme hubris, some friends and I even started a pizza restaurant, which worked out about as well as you would expect. We were all tech entrepreneurs and overestimated our own skills with disastrous consequences, massively overspending on the space, to the point where it was nearly impossible to get our money back. We then hired a string of chaotic managers (one of whom we promptly fired after discovering he had turned the restaurant into his personal after-hours club and apartment, partying and pilfering beer from our taps before nestling into a booth for his nightly slumber).

When any business failed, I was back to the drawing board with yet another idea. During my time away, I had watched Jason and David of Basecamp ascend from millionaires to decamillionaires, perhaps even secret billionaires. Unlike me, they seemed to work only on what they loved, generating predictable profits while they slept. While my agency built software for startups, we had none of our own, the pickaxe seller envious of the gold miners. I yearned for a calmer business, one immune to the endless scramble for clients and staff. I was sick of the roller coaster, my net worth tied to an enterprise in perpetual flux.

That anxiety that had coursed through me as a kid when I had heard my parents arguing over televisions and computers was still coursing away. I'd check my bank account and see piles of cash in it, but then the company would have a slow month and I'd spiral with images of me eating potatoes while my parents served as my landlords again.

I decided it was time to build my own gold mine. So, I went back to work.

While my cat furniture business had been a disaster, it had led me to discover a small Canadian e-commerce software company called Shopify. At a tech conference in Vancouver, I ran into Harley Finkelstein, who, at the time, was the COO of Shopify. He told me that they were looking for a partner to design templates for their platform and he liked our work. Essentially, they wanted to offer a wide range of well-designed themes for merchants to choose from when starting their online stores. For example, an electronics store might require a different look compared to a skincare brand. Shopify envisioned a one-click process for customers to choose different themes when signing up.

He told me this wouldn't be a typical paid project for MetaLab; instead, they wanted us to design and build the themes and then sell them in Shopify's newly created theme marketplace. It was similar to the App Store on an iPhone, with each theme selling for prices ranging from $49 to $249. The opportunity sounded fantastic. After hashing out the details over coffee, our conversation shifted to the challenges of managing our growing teams. At the time, both of us were hovering at around thirty employees. We both felt it was impossible to imagine ever growing beyond a team of fifty. This is particularly funny in retrospect, given that today I employ over a thousand people, and Harley manages ten times that.

I was up to my eyeballs running my various businesses, each in a different state of nuclear meltdown, so I decided I needed someone to run point on this Shopify partnership. Once again, I rolled the dice and went with my gut. I pulled aside Liam Sarsfield, who was then just an intern at MetaLab, and ushered him into my office.

"Do you know what Shopify is?"

"Yeah . . ." he replied, lips curling into a terrified smile, wondering why his manic boss, who he almost never spoke to, had suddenly ambushed him.

"Do you know how their theme language works?"

"I know basic HTML."

"Okay, good. I need to build five Shopify themes in the next two months, and I want you to manage it. Got it?"

He said yes, clearly both terrified and excited by the opportunity to go from intern to project manager, and he pulled a few designers and developers aside for the project. After some long nights, they managed to hit the deadline. Harley from Shopify was impressed. The themes were beautiful and practical, and Harley immediately asked us to make more themes and encouraged us to get into building Shopify apps, too.

Soon after, Shopify launched their theme marketplace and our business grew like wildfire. My phone started buzzing, a little paint shaker in my pocket, each buzz representing another theme sold. Another fifty bucks in the bank account. First a few times a day. Then hourly. Then every minute. All day and all night, as merchants across the globe bought one of our themes and turned it into their own online store. Before long, I had to turn off the notifications on my phone because my battery was dying before lunchtime.

The cash was pouring in by the bucketload. Five thousand, fifteen thousand, then thirty thousand dollars a month. I realized that we had stumbled into an incredible business model: we'd build a theme just *once*, which was a week or two of work, then sell it an infinite number of times. Our only ongoing cost was a trickle of bug fixes and support tickets. Before long, everyone from tiny startups to huge companies like Tesla and the LA Lakers were using our themes.

Through all of this, Liam impressed me. While he had been a lowly intern, it was obvious he was a leader and he quickly took charge as CEO. We spun out the company, gave him a dedicated team, and decided to turn it into a company we called Pixel Union, a nod to Liam's leftist leanings.

As Shopify grew, we grew alongside.

A barnacle on the whale that was Shopify, we had latched onto a wonderful business. And unlike MetaLab or the cat furniture venture or my online DJ classes, the sales were automated. The money just streamed in. We finally had our own gold mine.

This came with a very good but complicated problem. On paper, I was wealthy. But in reality, I was desperately cash poor. While MetaLab and Pixel Union were profitable, I immediately robbed Peter to pay Paul and took all of my profits and put them right back into hiring employees for my other businesses. Each of my prior business failures had been a lesson, but now it was time to learn from my business successes. I needed to figure out how to take my profits and keep them in the bank rather than reinvesting everything back into the business.

This is where Chris proved to be a genius. He completely revamped our finances and drove home the mentality that every dollar counted. He'd spend months negotiating the absolute best rates on just about everything for the business and spent hours every day hounding clients for payment. He added a level of rigor that we just didn't have until he joined.

His personality was almost exactly opposite to mine, but in the perfect way. We fit together like two expertly milled jigsaw pieces. He was the brake to my gas. The check and balance on my insane entrepreneurial ideas. Over and over, he'd build elaborate charts and graphs, trying to underscore just how much money I was blowing trying to launch these goofy side businesses.

"Don't you get it? You're already rich!" he'd bellow. "If you just stopped creating new businesses, you could retire in a few years!"

Where I was spendy, he was cheap. He drove a ten-year-old car, ate a bagged lunch, and negotiated his every purchase relentlessly, in one case spending six months haggling over a different used car (he ended up waiting out the salesman and getting it for just above cost). On a relatively modest income from managing a McDonald's in high school, then working his way up at the bank, he had squirreled away savings, which he had grown into hundreds of thousands of dollars via conservative stock market investing. I was the complete opposite. Spending on a whim, never negotiating price and stocks that frankly sounded boring. Who'd want to do that when you could start a company?

Choosing the right business partner is as important as who you marry. If your romantic partner defines your happiness at home, your business partner defines your happiness at work. But it's more intense than a romantic partner: you can't easily divorce your business partner. Unless you are able to negotiate buying them out, you're locked in forever. In speaking to other entrepreneurs, I'd learned that business partners carried a lot of risks. Some partners wrestled over control, and many partnerships ended in fuming resentment, with one contributing 110 percent while the other took too many vacations. There were a lot of ways it could go wrong.

Fortunately, Chris had none of these qualities. We didn't choose each other as business partners so much as it just became obvious that we *were* business partners. Over time, he just stopped being my CFO and became my partner, using his own cash to buy into the business over time.

Our disparate skill sets meant that we cared about different, but equally important, parts of the business, so we could divide and conquer and avoid stepping on one another's toes. We shared a few key qualities: an ability to understand people in a deep way, an obsession with reading and learning, and a shared sense of right and wrong. Outside of that foundation, he was strong where I was weak and vice versa. I was Penn, the loudmouth promoter out in front. He was Teller, quietly ensuring the tricks went off without a hitch.

Chris and I often joked that if we both owned apartment buildings, his building would be run-down and derelict, with no amenities. Just good enough for the tenants to stay. It would make a fortune, but you wouldn't want to live there or tell anyone you owned it. On the flip side, mine would be a gleaming architectural masterpiece, with endless amenities and uniformed staff to meet every need. Exceptionally beautiful and well considered, except for the fact that it wouldn't make any money.

Both approaches were flawed in their own way, but when we combined our two personalities, it created something great. A dynamic duo.

Chris became the critical eye, preventing me from pulling the pin out of too many grenades, and I pushed him to take risks he otherwise wouldn't have taken. Our partnership didn't solve every problem, but my problems were now *our* problems. We started to joke that we were two military generals overseeing a platoon. What we didn't realize was that we were about to go to war.

Chapter 6

KABUKI THEATER

I felt my phone vibrate. It was an email that would change my life. A friend had introduced me to a fellow entrepreneur named Brian. He thought we'd hit it off, and we did.

When he arrived at lunch, he plunked down a fancy bicycle messenger bag on the table, then let out a calm sigh and met me with a magnanimous gaze like a monk who was mustering beneficent vibes to send my way.

"So great to finally meet you, man. I've been checking out your businesses online and all I can say is 'wow,'" he said.

"That's really nice of you to say," I replied, still deciphering if it was a complimentary "wow."

Brian was in his fifties, with immaculately coiffed hair. He seemed fit, which I'd later learn was due to an obsession with running, and he wore a navy-blue brushed cotton oxford shirt over his lean frame. If he were a dog, he'd be a prize greyhound, lean and chiseled. I noticed he wore a dressed-down Braun wristwatch designed by Dieter Rams. At this point, most of the traditional businesspeople I'd met shuffled around in gray suits and loafers. This guy clearly had taste and seemed positively normal. I saw him as a version of what I'd want to be like in ten to fifteen years. I liked him immediately.

"I've built a lot of businesses, but by the time I was your age, I hadn't done half of what you've done," he told me, clearly impressed. "In fact, I was still working for other people at that point."

I felt my cheeks flush. I wasn't used to getting compliments.

He told me incredible war stories. About taking on a board of directors who didn't know what they were doing. About growing the revenues of another company 10x in a matter of months. He told me about some of the businesses that he had started over the last decade, everything from a music production company to a successful payroll software company that he'd recently sold.

"After selling my company last year, I spent all of last summer cycling around Spain and Italy, but even though I have millions in the bank, I realized I can't just spend the rest of my life on Mojito Island," he said. "I'm not done."

"Oh man," I responded, smiling. "If anyone gets that, it's me."

"Hi, I'm Brian, and I'm a business addict," he said, holding up his hand with a grin.

He beamed and I beamed back.

"But enough about me . . . I want to hear about *you*."

He started peppering me with questions about my story, my companies, and where I wanted to go. I went on a monologue that lasted almost an hour, as I detailed each of my businesses, by this point five—MetaLab, Pixel Union (Shopify themes), Flow (project management software), Ballpark (invoicing software), and *Clients From Hell* (a popular blog we'd spun up)—each with their own web of problems. Some were working, but most weren't growing fast enough, and a couple were even losing vast amounts of money. I was split across all five, waking up feeling like I was in a daily knife fight, just trying to stay alive, make payroll, and keep everyone happy. It felt cathartic to share. Other than Chris, I had nobody to talk to about this stuff.

I told him about how my executives were all my friends, and nobody had any experience. I told him all about my hiring strategy of "going with my gut" and he grimaced. I shared some of the metrics of my various businesses. More grimacing.

"You have a whiteboard in your office?" he asked.

"Yeah, dozens of them," I said.

"Great. Let's finish up lunch and head over there," he said. "We can talk through everything."

I paid the bill, and a few minutes later Brian was standing in front of the whiteboard as I sat in my conference room, enthralled by the lessons he was about to teach me.

"Okay, so if I understand correctly . . ." he said, as he wrote out "ANDREW'S PROBLEMS" in all caps, the pen squeaking as he scratched it onto the board. I was intensely interested, but at the same time the scene felt a bit surreal, like I was in a reality TV show about me. Where were the cameras? Who was this guy and why was he helping me? He went on: "It sounds like your key problems are that you need to hire a CEO to run MetaLab, because that's the golden goose that pays for all of this, so that you can keep starting more interesting businesses."

"Yeah. I feel a bit done," I said, explaining that even though Mark ran most of MetaLab, I was constantly getting pulled in to solve problems. "I'm technically doing the CEO job, even though I'm barely paying attention. And I don't know if I can keep starting all these businesses. It's getting exhausting."

He nodded.

"What else?" he asked. "What other problems do you have?"

"Well . . . I've been at this for almost seven years, and on paper I have two businesses that make a profit, but the money just gets lit on fire in the other ventures. On paper, I'm up, but I don't feel financially secure. I need to figure out how to build up a real nest egg," I replied, feeling uncomfortable even admitting that. While I was only twenty-seven years old at the time, I had always made every decision with confidence, something I felt my employees needed to see, and here I was with Brian, sharing every insecurity I had. It was unnerving, but also cathartic.

"Would you ever consider selling one of the businesses?" he asked as he stood back and looked at the board.

"Oh jeez," I said, rubbing my neck. "I don't know. How does that even work?"

It felt a bit like he'd proposed I sell my newborn baby for liquor money. My businesses were everything to me, and I had never even contemplated that they would be sold.

"Well, Pixel Union is the obvious choice. It's trendy; Shopify is hot right now. It's profitable and has its own team and it's easy to spin out." He turned back and looked me dead in the eyes, and waited for a beat, "I bet I know someone who'd buy it for a song. How about I run a sale process?"

As if by divine intervention, I had stumbled upon my business guardian angel, sent to save me from my own folly. Brian proposed that he'd help me sell Pixel Union for a fee, a small percentage of the deal.

Sure enough, he delivered.

He reached out to a wealthy friend, Bob, and a few short weeks later we were meeting with his entire executive team.

Bob was a video rental magnate who had made tens of millions of dollars in the '90s and early 2000s. Since video rental chains were now all but extinct, he was diversifying into other areas. Bob was interested in buying the business in what he called his "family office." (I'd later learn this is business speak for "I'm so rich I have a team of people managing my personal money.")

We spent weeks meeting with his CEO, Richard, getting grilled like we were informants for a cartel. Despite this, I liked Richard. While he was clearly an MBA type, always in khakis and a tucked-in oxford, and at least twenty years my senior, he had a warm Business Dad energy and seemed to really get what we were trying to do at Pixel Union.

Within a few weeks, he offered to buy Pixel Union for $2 million.

At first, I didn't know what to do—$2 million was a big number, so I froze, unable to make a decision. I'd been dealing in thousands for so long and now here was a number with a "million" next to it.

My hesitation led Richard to increase his offer. He doubled it to $4 million.

This made me panic even more, unsure if I was making the best or worst decision ever. If someone was willing to double their offer that quickly, was I giving away something that could grow to be worth more than that?

As I became locked in the existential crisis over selling or not selling, Richard called me and raised his offer again. Then it happened again. And at this point, to fourteen times my annual profits. "Seven million," he said to me on the phone as I sat in silence.

There's a ceiling to every negotiation. A point where you end up negotiating against yourself, and I knew if I didn't take this deal at that number, they would probably grow frustrated and walk away. Finally, at the behest of Brian, I signed on the dotted line.

Given this was my first sale of a business, I imagined I'd say "yes!" and then there would be a wire transfer in the coming days. But as it turned out, this was only the start of the negotiation. The real battle was just beginning.

As soon as I signed the "letter of intent," a document that locked me in and prevented me from negotiating with any other potential buyers while they looked through my financials, bank statements, tax filings, and operational structure, the tone immediately changed. Richard went from being my best buddy, gushing praise and complimenting the business, to having a seemingly endless number of concerns about the company.

One in particular made me laugh: There was a small discrepancy in revenue between months due to an arcane accounting rule. A few hundred dollars, an irrelevant sum, didn't add up. In reality, there was nothing wrong with our revenue and this was just a negotiation tactic, but he told me this raised "serious concerns" about the quality of our accounting and said that we would need to renegotiate.

It felt manipulative, and Chris and I decided to back out, telling Brian we wanted to walk, but he pressed us.

"I'm telling you, we're close. I can get this done. You're about to become a multimillionaire—don't blow this over a little renegotiation. I've got your back; I'll fight for you," he told us.

Reluctantly, we agreed to meet with Richard one last time.

As we walked into their office, it was clear we were going to have a problem. Our new offices were bright and modern, with lots of natural light, smiling employees, and chatter. Their offices, on the other hand, felt straight out of NBC's *The Office*. The carpet looked like it had been cut out of a vintage Greyhound bus, and the place was filled with drab cubicles and boxy Windows PCs. Richard greeted us at the elevator and walked us down the hall toward a conference room. The silence was deafening, save for the occasional murmur of a salesperson on a call or the incessant clacking of keyboards. Richard led the way, stopping periodically to introduce us to different team members. But as I glanced around, I couldn't help but notice the pervasive atmosphere of unease that seemed to permeate the place.

We met in a gray, windowless conference room and Richard's mood immediately changed. His face went slack and expressionless, like a blood-hound, and he stared at us with an opaque look. It was creepy how quickly he seemed to change, and it was clear he had soured on the deal. My gut told me this was over.

"Look, Richard, let's talk about your concerns," Brian started, grabbing a whiteboard pen.

Richard launched into a litany of grievances against the business, some of which seemed exaggerated and designed to throw us off balance. However, amidst the exaggerations, he did make some valid points. He wasn't wrong when he observed that Liam, our inexperienced intern-turned-CEO, created risk in the business, given he had never run one before. I was loyal to him and didn't want to make a change. We had become friends, and while it may have been prudent to offer to replace him, it didn't sit right given how successful he'd been at growing the business.

Richard pointed out other troubling issues, such as our complete lack of diversification and our precarious dependence on Shopify. With no executive team to speak of and a staff composed almost entirely of juniors, our company appeared to be rudderless. As Richard spoke, I could feel my anxiety mounting, and I wondered if our ship was already sinking.

As Richard shared each concern, Brian shrugged, nodded as if he agreed, then scribbled it on the whiteboard. I couldn't help feeling like this whole thing felt a bit rehearsed, that maybe he and Richard had spoken in advance and he knew where this was going.

It felt like Kabuki theater.

I became increasingly defensive. But at the same time, I now wanted that money. If before I had been on the fence about selling, now I wanted to sell more than anything. Everyone's voices drifted into the background as I imagined waking up, sun streaming into the master bedroom of the multimillion-dollar home I'd just toured with a realtor. Fourteen-foot ceilings. All glass everywhere. I imagined having coffee on the back patio, gazing into the sprawling half acre backyard. Pulling out of the driveway in a new Porsche 911.

"Look, I promise you this business will be twice as big in two years. Shopify is growing like crazy. And about the accounting issues, those won't be a problem. The revenue is all there; we're good," I blurted out, snapping out of my daydream.

I saw a glint in Brian's eye, and he glanced over to Richard.

"Hmm . . . Richard, how could we meet in the middle?" said Brian, like a teacher prompting a student to solve a math equation that he already knew the answer to. Richard looked deep in thought, eyes closed, stroking his chin, before finally responding.

"Look, the only way I can see this deal going forward is with an earn-out.

Andrew, if you're so confident it will be double the size in two years, why don't you commit to that?"

I wasn't familiar with the term.

"What if . . ." said Brian, "we did something like this . . ."

He started scrawling a potential deal structure on the whiteboard.

"You still get your $7 million, but . . . we do $3 million paid up front. Another $2.5 million once the business doubles." More writing on the whiteboard. "Then $1.5 million in stock that you continue to hold and can sell at a later date."

Seven million dollars in total, but paid out over time.

"Yeah, I like that." Richard nodded in agreement.

All eyes were on me. I didn't know what was going on. But as I started to think about the events that had unfolded, I felt as though something was amiss. Weeks before, Richard had flattered me with buttery compliments, but now I was negotiating with the bloodhound. Having seen his office, and after going through this weird experience, I knew in my gut that something was off. But then I flashed back to the Porsche. Sunroof open, ripping down the road with the wind in my hair. Rich beyond my wildest dreams.

I swallowed my concern.

"Come on, Andrew. Let's all shake hands and get this done," Brian said. "He's about to make you a millionaire."

I looked across at Chris. His hand was tapping anxiously on the boardroom table. As the company's CFO, he knew how chaotic things had been, and we both liked the idea of being flush with cash. He gave me a subtle nod.

"Let's do it," I said.

Richard lit up and we shook hands. He was suddenly my best friend again.

"All right!" he exclaimed. "This is going to be great!"

Brian marked up the letter of intent with a pen, and we all initialed and signed the new terms. I was selling my baby.

Things moved fast from there. All of their accounting concerns seemed to evaporate, and, after a few weeks of the lawyers going back and forth, I signed a pack of documents that rivaled the phone book in size. After my last signature and a handshake, the deal was done.

Up until that moment, I had a few thousand dollars in my personal bank account at any given time—and never more than ten thousand.

That evening, I got a text that the money had been wired into my account. I grabbed my jacket and walked to a local ATM machine in a nearby strip mall.

I tapped the little square buttons on the ATM—*beep, beep, beep, beep*— and selected "view your account balance." A moment went by, as I stood in the glow of a streetlight in that strip mall parking lot, until I heard the receipt contraption whirring and a slip of paper popped out. I grabbed it, held it up to my face, and just stared at it for a moment, reading the number: $3,011,640.

Three. Million. Dollars. And at twenty-eight years old.

With another two and a half on the way, if things went well. And then more after.

I felt a warm buzz crawl up my neck. Was this happiness?

I was safe, for the first time in seven years. No, for the first time in my life.

What I didn't realize, though, as I walked back to my house, still staring at those numbers in my hand, was that I had just done a deal with someone who would make every bad guy in business I'd ever heard about look like Mother Teresa. I was about to get into business with a man who was going to try to destroy my life.

But not yet. First, I had $3 million burning a hole in my pocket, and I had to spend it.

I watched him ... in rhythmic circles like Mr. Miyagi.

Chapter 7

BELGIAN TRUFFLE FARTS

I watched him wax in rhythmic circles like Mr. Miyagi.

Wax on.

Wax off.

I sat on the windowsill of my friend Ian's bedroom, two floors above his driveway, transfixed, watching his father work. As with seemingly all rich '90s Vancouver dads, he, too, was a real estate developer. But today, his job—his singular focus in life—was caring for his baby while wearing his matching PORSCHE ball cap. We watched him perform his Saturday morning ritual with the precision of an anthropologist tending to a delicate artifact. Every inch of the car gleaming in the morning sun. It was a black 1996 911 Carrera S, and it was the most beautiful car I'd ever seen.

Now, almost twenty years later, this memory came to my mind as I ran my hand along the hood of a bright red Porsche 911 at a local dealership. I slowly walked the aisles of gleaming 911s, taking in the aerodynamic silhouettes and sweeping rooflines. As I wandered, I thought about Ian's father's beautiful black Porsche, right as I happened upon the shimmering black 911

GTS, with bright red brake calipers. Those gorgeous, rounded headlights staring at me, taunting me to come closer.

"Can I take her for a test-drive?" I asked the sales rep, who was hovering behind me like a store security guard tailing a shoplifter.

He was clearly embodying the car salesman vibe, with a leather jacket and slicked-back hair. He slowly looked me up and down. I was wearing a pair of shabby Nikes, a hoodie, and some jeans. At twenty-seven, I was still boyish and invariably got ID'd whenever I bought beer, easily passing for five years younger than I was.

"Um, we save test-drives until after the paperwork is done," the sales guy responded with raised eyebrows. He had the look of a man who had to deal with annoying car nerds who just wanted to joyride and waste his time.

"How much?" I asked.

"$180,000," he responded, with a shit-eating grin.

"I'm good for it. Let's go for a test-drive," I said. He looked at me, unsure if I was actually "good for it." I looked at him, eyes wide, as if to say, *Trust me, you want to believe me.* Moments later, his whole demeanor had changed, our bodies pressed against the leather seats like astronauts in a g-force simulator as I floored it down Blanshard Street, the engine growls echoing through the street.

Ten minutes later, I screeched to a halt in front of the dealership, leaving the car to idle.

"Should I start a finance application?" he said looking sweaty and flustered, like he'd just gotten off an amusement park ride.

"That's okay. I'll wire you the money."

"This is the life," I thought, the wind throwing around my hair as I sped down the street away from the dealership toward my beautiful new house.

Sure, I'd made some money from my other businesses; when big invoices had closed in, I'd give myself a little bonus and go shopping for a new outfit or a new computer or something, but those times were nothing like this. I felt legitimately rich, especially given my age, with my other businesses still pumping out more in profits. Most of my peers had just graduated university and were, if they were lucky, slowly grinding it out on the first few rungs of the corporate ladder.

After the initial shock of seeing that gigantic number on my ATM receipt, especially considering what my childhood had been like, I had set out to do the most logical thing: convert my money into the great life I had always assumed I could buy.

I had started by filling my house with a few electronics that had previously been out of reach. A brand-new home theater, complete with a 1080P projector, Dolby surround sound, 100" screen, and McIntosh Labs amplifiers. My living room looked like a record store, with endless stacks of albums that I'd purchased brand new, cleaning out the store like a hoarder.

I wanted the best of everything. At a restaurant, I'd get the works: steak, oysters, caviar, and wine as old as me for the table, tipping 50 percent on the way out. (As I learned after losing hundreds of thousands of dollars starting my own restaurant, being a big tipper is a lot cheaper than owning the restaurant, for the same effect.)

I looked at luxury apartments and mansions of all shapes and sizes all over Victoria. There were places with floor-to-ceiling windows, others that had three times as many bedrooms as my childhood home. Some came with pools. "This property has its own hot tub," my realtor would say as we wandered through a modern condo. Then, off to the next place, where she'd say, "This one has a hot tub *and* an infinity pool."

Some places had wine cellars and built-in minibars. Little movie theaters to entertain friends. Ten-car garages. Manicured gardens and sprawling maple, chestnut, and Liriodendron trees. Even one that had a helicopter pad (which would clearly be pointless without a helicopter). I could have blown my entire net worth on any one of these properties without even blinking an eye. But while I was excited by the prospect of spending this money, I knew there were limits to how much of it I should spend.

Ultimately, I decided to buy a beautifully designed home in South Oak

Bay. The house sat on a tree-lined street very similar to my childhood home. It was just under four thousand square feet, with three bedrooms, one of which I planned to use as an office, the other for when friends came to stay. It had a marble fireplace and a sparse but well-appointed modern kitchen. There was a half-acre backyard and, most importantly, it was peaceful and tranquil. I could walk to the ocean, or nearby Windsor Park.

If I chose, this could easily be my forever house, where I could have kids, and live happily ever after.

After I moved in, I started traveling in style. I'd fill a private jet with friends and go somewhere sunny for a weekend. The cost was absurd. These short flights could put me back $10,000 or more, but it made travel feel completely frictionless. Whereas before, I would spend two to three hours going through security and waiting in dreary airport lobbies for connections, now I could drive my car right up to the plane, hop on, and be airborne minutes later. It felt like the difference between riding the city bus and being chauffeured in a Rolls-Royce.

But strangely to twenty-seven-year-old me, it didn't take long for the high of each lifestyle upgrade to wear off. Just like great food only satiates temporarily, I quickly became hungry again. I drifted into a miserable addiction, hooked on the fleeting dopamine spike that came with each notch up. I'd started swapping out my cars every few months. I then started going on increasingly expensive vacations. Nothing was quite like the first time. I found myself researching the next rung of the latter. Bigger planes. More expensive houses. Faster cars.

Another thing surprised me: instead of strengthening my relationships with my friends, it seemed to hamper them.

I had always been the kid who was broke. In high school, I'd bug my classmates to borrow a couple dollars so I could get a Coke from the vending machine, and in college I'd bum a six-pack of beer from friends. So, when I struck it rich, I decided to share my newfound wealth. When I took my friends out, I'd always be the one to grab the check, pay for the tickets to the concert, buy the drinks; later, the plane and hotel. What I soon realized, though, was that in many instances this generosity backfired and had the opposite effect.

At one dinner with an old friend and his girlfriend, I preempted the bill and paid it on my way back from the bathroom. He seemed miffed that I had paid the bill. Like I was showing off, or implying he couldn't afford it.

After that experience, I started to default to splitting the bill or letting the other person pay for it if they went for it. But oddly enough, a different annoyance cropped up. People would be equally upset with me. They felt I was being cheap and that I should just pay given my newfound wealth.

It was a catch-22. I was either implying they couldn't afford it and rubbing their nose in it, or I was rude and miserly. It triggered a cascade of weird dynamics of envy and jealousy, which caused all sorts of unspoken rifts and issues. I began hearing (soon to be former) friends make little passive-aggressive comments.

"Must be nice ..."

"Honored you made time for me ..."

"What's that, like, a penny to you?"

I could feel that they were no longer rooting for me. That I was now a competitor, rubbing their faces in it. The tallest blade of grass, which needed to be cut down to size. An envious look on their face as I told them about a recent win—something I soon learned to censor—or the almost imperceptible flash of a smile under a grave face when I shared a loss.

When I told another successful friend about this experience, he told me an anecdote about William Golding, the author of *Lord of the Flies*. At the time, he had just won the Nobel Prize in Literature, and a young writer asked Golding what it felt like to receive such a prize. His response was telling: "You find out who hates you."

Money also attracted the wrong kinds of friends. People who saw me as a ticket to the luxe life, complete with an unlimited bar tab. Suddenly, guys who had been rude and dismissive of me in high school now wanted to be my best buddies. The guy who stole my prom date now wanted to sell me a condo. To them, many of whom had become realtors or sales guys, I not only represented a fun lifestyle to tag along with, but an actual payday or career opportunity.

One guy specifically spent almost a year slowly befriending Chris, until one day he casually asked if he could meet me. When Chris made the introduction, he immediately started probing me, asking how I managed my wealth. When I told him that I managed my own money, he laughed and told me I needed to diversify and he could help. It turned out he was, of course, a wealth manager, which I soon learned was finance speak for "sales guy who knows nothing about investing and puts his clients' money in mutual funds, then charges them 2 percent a year for life." I obviously didn't say that to him, and I politely told him, "No thanks." He seemed to take it well and he backed off.

A few weeks later, he invited me to meet for a coffee. I told him I'd love to meet him socially, but I didn't need his services. He told me he just wanted to be friends. Within ten minutes of our first sips of coffee on a sunny Starbucks patio, he repeatedly redirected the conversation to the topic of investing. Then, he dropped his payload. He told me he had a funny idea: "How about this . . . you take a million dollars and invest it yourself, then you give *me* a million dollars and I'll invest it. Whoever has better results after five years wins!" (I politely passed, again.)

This began happening monthly. Bankers trying to seduce me with concert tickets. Long-lost family friends wanting to reconnect, only to spring me with a pitch for their new startup. People with dubious stories seeking loans. And I wasn't even that rich yet! This was all once word got out that I'd sold a small company.

What's bizarre is how many rich people seem to fall for these ploys. One thing I'd observed growing up in Vancouver was that, often, the same jerks and bullies who would treat me like dirt would treat the rich kids completely differently. Even the really nerdy ones. The mean bullies still wanted to visit the rich kids' pools and game rooms, and dive into their bountiful snack cupboards. To me, they'd make snide comments or bodycheck me in the hallway. To the rich kids in school, they'd give a cheery hello and invite them to a party.

Now, this same phenomenon was unfolding once again, but in my adult life. Except, this time, I was the nerdy rich kid, and everyone, for better or worse, wanted to be my friend.

Months after the excitement of the deal had worn off, the euphoria had evaporated and my fancy new life felt old again. I felt listless.

There was no "there" there.

The twentieth spoonful of ice cream never quite hits like the first. The hedonic treadmill in action.

I'm not saying that money was all bad. There were plenty of positives. It made life easier, like some sort of magical universal lubricant. When I worked at the café, a twenty-minute car drive away, I'd spend over an hour riding two crowded bus routes to get there. Now, like many people, I owned a car and hadn't ridden the bus in decades. That's what money does—it removes obstacles. But it also creates new ones.

Over time I also found myself wanting things *I didn't even know I wanted*. I'd never worn a watch, and yet I found myself obsessively researching them. I'd noticed that when I met other wealthy businesspeople, they'd often discuss their watches and show them off. I didn't get it. I had a phone, which told the time down to the millisecond—why did I need to spend thousands (or tens of thousands, even) on a hunk of metal that I had to wind every day? And yet, there I was, watching YouTube videos and reading nerdy watch blogs, learning about mechanical "movements" and why different brands were better or more prestigious than others. I started noticing the watches worn by successful people, and eventually I started collecting watches myself.

This same kind of thing happened over and over again. And it wasn't just with objects. I noticed that whatever the people around me cared about,

I began caring about, too. Business awards. Exclusive conferences like TED and Davos. Events like Burning Man and Art Basel. That was what other successful entrepreneurs seemed to care about, and I found myself wanting to fit the mold.

What caused this, I later learned, is something called mimetic desire. The idea that whatever those around you model as being valuable and important, you unconsciously find yourself caring about and wanting, too. Whether it's as simple as a fashion choice, like a wristwatch, or as complex as a meaningless professional title that you could spend decades trying to achieve.

For example, for most academics, there is nothing more important than getting published in prestigious journals. They live or die depending on where they get published, and how many times their paper is cited by others. Their refrain: "Publish or perish." To the rest of the world this means absolutely nothing. It denotes absolutely zero status to 99.9 percent of the world. But in the world of academia, it's *everything*. The same is true of writers trying to hit the bestseller list, or actors and musicians trying to win awards, or even something as simple as a corporate job title or a corner office. We all seek external gratification based on what our peers tell us we should want.

What's sad about this mimetic phenomenon is that it convinces people to sacrifice their own happiness to achieve whatever goal their peers have assigned value to, even when it's not an authentic desire of theirs. It seems to be everywhere, and it begins early, preying on the most insecure: look at any high school hallway, all kids trying to look the same, talk the same. Look at influencers on social media, implicitly dictating how the rest of us should behave.

I read a story about a chef in France who had won two Michelin stars, one of the highest honors in the restaurant industry. Michelin requires its awardees to maintain a strict standard and operate in very specific ways, and their critics frequently visit at random to ensure the standard is being upheld. Tablecloths need to be a certain way and service needs to be impeccable. Paradoxically, after winning the Michelin stars, the French chef was more miserable than ever, fixating on maintaining his restaurant to Michelin's standard and obsessing over the risk of Michelin stripping him of a star should he step out of line and spill some gravy, instead of focusing on the thing he loved: cooking incredible food.

The chef was living according to external scorecards, terrified of losing the arbitrary award that his peers had decided was valuable.

What would all the other business bigshots think of me if I rolled up wearing a Casio wristwatch? An unthinkable embarrassment.

While I now had money, my day-to-day anxieties remained. In some respects, they got worse. I was running all these companies, frantically trying to keep up with my to-do list, but now it was more intense with more at stake. I had more commitments and even more to lose. Instead of working hard for money I needed, I was now fueled by a fear of losing what I had and embarrassing myself in front of my peers.

And sure enough, there it was, that familiar voice asking me, "Now what?" The voice that no longer belonged to my father, but rather, the dust bowl farmer in my head. "Now what?"

"Now what?"

"Now..."

Every successful entrepreneur invariably gets asked, "Why keep going? Don't you have enough?" Earlier in my career, I remember my brother William ripping into me because he felt we shouldn't grow the business past ten people, a number that felt intimate and manageable. What people fail to realize is that businesses are like tapeworms—they have to grow in order to stay alive. Without growth, there's no additional revenue to increase salaries over time. If a star employee came to me asking for a promotion and I told them, "Oh, we decided to stop growing this year, so I can't," would they stay? Unlikely.

So, we grew. And grew. And grew. Most years at least 25 percent. Other years we doubled. Until one day I bumped into someone in the office kitchen and they asked me, "What do you do here?"

It was odd.

From the outside, I looked like a king in a sparkling castle. But internally, I knew my fortress's weaknesses all too well. I knew that the castle walls needed to be extended and rebuilt and the moat dug deeper. That my citizens, my employees, would become unruly without the ability to move up in society. And most importantly, that if I took my eye off the prize and spent my time collecting rubies and courting maidens at drunken feasts, my kingdom would surely be invaded by marauding hordes.

As I sat in the living room of my new, beautifully designed home, staring at my state-of-the-art television, as music blared from my McIntosh Labs stereo system, I started doing the math in my head: Even after my shopping sprees, I could invest the millions I had left. If I could earn average returns in stocks or real estate, I could make about 8 percent on my money, and would likely make enough to live a comfortable life without lifting a finger. And that's if all my other businesses went away. I still owned MetaLab and a variety of other businesses, some of which were becoming quite profitable.

But the anxiety remained.

I reasoned that if the $3 million was making me feel this way, then, surely, I'd need more money. Surely I'd need to grow my businesses and then—only then!—I'd be able to quell the voice in my head. The one asking, "Now what . . . now what . . . now what?" over and over and over.

"Now what?"

Chapter 8

THE MOST BORING AMAZING JOB ON EARTH

If someone wanted to put me to sleep, all they needed to do was to tell me about stocks. To me, they were the domain of boring wonks. Paper shufflers who added no value. I couldn't comprehend why somebody would buy stocks when they could build a business, which I'd learned was endlessly exciting and had insane upside potential. After all, I had taken my Shopify themes business, Pixel Union, which I started for all of $20,000, and turned it into a multimillion-dollar windfall in just a few years.

Building businesses was fun. I loved the act of creating something that didn't exist before.

But I noticed something. I'd have a potentially great business idea in the shower or while on a walk, as I always had, but then, after thinking about how much work it would be, I'd drop it. I no longer had the manic energy I had in the past. I was overwhelmed by the required stress that I knew came along with starting a business. And, if I was being honest, I didn't want to do what I was doing anymore.

I had been settling into a new routine, a new rhythm in my personal life. After years of nonstop work, travel, and partying, I had finally settled down, found a home, and met someone. I met Holly at a local night club. We had walked up to the bar to get a drink at the same time, and she flashed a smile at me. In an alcohol-fueled moment of confidence, I walked right over to her and we started talking. She had long black hair, striking green eyes, and something seemed familiar about her. It turned out, after a bit of mutual sleuthing, that I had gone to high school with her brother, and she had been in the same grade as my little brother, William.

I asked for her number, and a few weeks later we went on our first date.

One date turned into two and we fell in love and soon started living together and talking about starting a family. We settled into a domestic rhythm that was unlike anything I'd experienced before. It was healthy and calm. She didn't drink or party, instead preferring quiet nights at home or at the movies, so I had left my life of DJing and conference parties behind me. It was a welcome change after almost a decade of being out every night, my main companion being my corporate card. In 2015, we got married. If I wanted to maintain the calm, I realized that my work life was going to have to radically change. I couldn't keep starting companies.

All this added up to a good problem, but a problem nonetheless: I was sitting on a pile of cash and there was no way I could just keep starting more businesses. So, I reluctantly decided it was time I figured out this whole investing thing. On my way home from work one day, I stopped at Bolen Books, my favorite local bookstore, and wandered the investing section. I immediately recognized *The Warren Buffett Way*, one of the many business books I'd seen on my dad's office bookshelf all those years ago. Without thinking, I picked it up, walked up to the counter, and paid for it.

I'd always heard that Warren Buffett was the greatest investor of all time, but I truly didn't care. I couldn't imagine something more boring than investing. After all, I reasoned, Buffett had never started a business, beyond his holding company—he just bought stock certificates and traded them with other people. While he seemed like a nice guy on the outside, I couldn't see how buying stocks and bonds made the world better in any way. As I went home, sat back on the couch, and cracked open the book, I assumed I'd make it a few pages in and toss it aside like a bored child.

To my surprise, I was immediately enthralled. I inhaled the writing like an addict.

Buffett, it turned out, had cracked the code of success and figured out how to achieve the highest levels of success without doing anything he didn't want to do. It was as if he had discovered the cheat codes to business and it was all laid out in front of me, in this very book in my hands. I stayed up until well after midnight, dog-earing pages and highlighting passages like a mad professor grading an incredible essay.

I was immediately struck by Buffett's genius and realized I had completely misjudged him. Far from being some paper-shuffling stock market speculator, he was a brilliant operator who had abstracted business to the most extreme degree of delegation. While his company, Berkshire Hathaway, had over 370,000 employees across 65 businesses and 260 subsidiaries, he worked from a tiny 26-person head office in Omaha, Nebraska. Far from being stressed, he seemed like he didn't have a care in the world. As far as I could tell, he did exactly as he pleased (mostly reading newspapers, books, financial statements, and endless annual reports) and he delegated everything else to managers. Each company that he owned had its own CEO who was totally responsible for their business, and he quietly monitored the results from Omaha. Unless the leader of a company had something they wanted to ask him, he left them alone to run it. Once or twice a year, he would buy a business or make an investment, but most of the time he just sat on his hands and read.

Buffett liked to joke that his management strategy was "benign neglect, bordering on sloth." CEOs liked working for him because, unlike most captains of industry, he didn't obsess over short-term results or second-guess their strategies. In fact, he was perfectly happy if they didn't call him for years on end.

Meanwhile, people liked selling their businesses to him because he had a reputation for doing quick, fair deals, and, more importantly, not messing up their beloved companies. He would let people sell their business to him in whatever structure worked best for them. Where others would drag a transaction through the mud, taking six to twelve months of brutal negotiation to get it done, as I'd experienced with the Pixel Union deal, Buffett made the decision on a five-minute phone call, then wired a billion dollars to the founder in a few weeks with a one-page contract. Once the deal was done, he'd leave the company alone to operate as it had been.

On top of that, he wasn't living a ritzy life. He certainly wasn't trying to make himself feel better by buying silly sports cars, let alone a gargantuan yacht, as billionaires in his wealth bracket are known to do. For Buffett, it seemed the money was just a fun way to keep score, like space credits in a video game. He still lived in the same small house in Omaha that he'd bought in 1958, long before he was a billionaire.

As I rifled through the pages of the book, I came to realize a whole new way of thinking about business. I had gotten it all wrong—his approach was so much less painful. I was building businesses from scratch when it was so much easier to buy a company that already worked and leave it to grow.

A metaphor came to mind: Imagine you wanted to travel from Seattle to Hawaii by sea. My approach had been akin to hand-crafting a boat using logs I'd found on the beach, with a few buddies who had never built a boat in their lives. Sure, it was possible we'd make it to Hawaii, but it would be a miserable, white-knuckle journey, and we'd probably drown.

Buffett, meanwhile, had found a cruise ship with an expert captain who had already mapped out the ship's course and was ready to set sail. All he had to do was buy a ticket (one of many stock certificates), relax on the sun deck, and enjoy the ride.

It quickly became clear who was winning.

Buffett liked to invest in businesses with what he called "moats." If we imagine that businesses are castles, moats are the qualities that protect them and make them particularly difficult to attack. Take Coca-Cola, which is one of his largest investments. Coke has a ridiculously strong brand that makes it near impossible to compete with. Sure, you can make a cola that tastes just like Coke, but if McDonald's doesn't have *real* Coke, customers are going to be livid. Coke is the consumer's default, and this moat makes it what he would call a "no brainer" investment with an incredible brand moat.

Instead of trying to build risky startup businesses like I was, Buffett focused on finding wonderful, simple businesses with limited competition. Cruise ships, if you will.

He looked for three things: a high-quality business with a moat, an intelligent and ethical management team, and a fair price. Surprisingly, despite this hands-off approach, many of the businesses he'd invested in had thrived, with some growing fiftyfold since the time he acquired them.

While I was very different from Buffett (I'd rather eat a bowl of broken glass than spend my day reading financial statements), I wanted to board one of these cruise ships. I couldn't handle any more white-knuckle raft journeys.

The next morning, I called Chris, bursting with excitement.

"I've figured out the ultimate life hack. Do you know who Warren Buffett is?"

"Yeah," he replied, sounding slightly scared, assuming there was yet another manic startup idea coming shortly. "My dad always talks about him."

"I'm telling you, you've got to read this book. This is going to change *everything*."

While I knew the direction I wanted to go, I didn't actually know how to get there. I'd never invested in anything before. My only stock investment to date had been that gift of Apple stock, which I'd managed to sell at the worst possible time.

It wouldn't take long before Buffett and his business partner, Charlie Munger, would become my heroes in the business world. They would become the guiding light for how I would learn to invest and buy businesses and eventually put my own spin on the lessons I learned from them. But first, completely unbeknownst to me at the time, the journey I was about to embark on would be one of betrayal and backstabbing unlike anything I'd ever experienced before.

Chapter 9

PUT GRANDMA ON THE ROOF

I was so close. I had just broken his serve and we were at deuce. I served, faulted, then cursed loudly as I wiped sweat from my forehead. It was a Thursday afternoon and I was in the heat of battle. My problems had drifted out of my mind and all I could think about was the little yellow ball. And hitting it as hard as I could. Making him run.

When I stepped onto the tennis court, the world fell away. Just me, my opponent, and the fluorescent yellow ball that dictated everything. I craved the sound of the ball pounding off the racket, the screech of my sneakers sliding across the ground as I ran for dear life. The *thwack, thwack, thwack,* back and forth. Like a dance step, each shot a dialogue, a challenging question followed by a swift, certain answer. As somebody who depended on a huge group of complicated people to get things done every day, the court was my refuge. Here, I was an army of one, completely in the moment, focused solely on winning.

Then, suddenly, I felt my Apple Watch vibrate.

I ignored it and kept playing. Nailing my second serve. I was up on him. This was it.

The watch vibrated again. I silenced it.

Then again.

I looked down to see it was Mark.

These days, Mark only called me with bad news.

I walked off the court to take the call.

"You're not going to like this," he told me, "but that BookMonster account is about to blow up again and I need you to go on another charm offensive."

BookMonster was one of MetaLab's biggest clients, and it represented over 30 percent of our monthly revenue. The company's mercurial CEO was unpredictable. He would offer us millions to triple the team and meet crazy deadlines, only to explode months later over the previously agreed-upon bill. Often, these bills went unpaid for months. Bills that needed to be paid in order to make payroll and keep my many money-losing ventures afloat. In addition to MetaLab, I still had a handful of startup businesses that I was funding, each in a state of disarray, continuing to burn unholy amounts of cash. If BookMonster didn't pay their invoices, we were in deep trouble given that I had dozens of employees depending on me to pay their salary.

While Pixel Union had reliably generated cash each month, my other startups were now draining my now-finite my funds. It felt like watching an hourglass, hoping for a turnaround that would replenish my dwindling resources. Before I sold the company, I had felt like I had nothing to lose. I was taking big swings with little downside. If I failed, so what? I'd start again. Now, I had this pile, dwindling month after month. I had to figure out how to invest what I had, and where to put it that wouldn't make the hourglass drain quicker.

Around this time, on a walk with my friend Rajiv in Beacon Hill Park, I told him about my problem.

"Ahhh," he said, sagely. "You have Mole Hill Mindset. I know it well."

"What the hell do you mean? Mole Hill?"

"You have a little pile of cash, a 'mole hill,' and you want to protect it.

Now you have something to lose. The same thing happened to me when I started making serious money."

He was right. For the first time, I had something to lose and I was terrified. It seized me up. Took away my fire. Made me fearful.

Now, on the phone with Mark post-tennis match, I racked my brain about this BookMonster situation and I realized that, while Mark was a great day-to-day manager, he didn't want to be CEO. He was an incredible number two. But that still made me ... number one. The person you called when you had problems like this one.

On top of that, I was a derelict dad to my company. Barely paying attention to it. Only swooping in when something went wrong.

We needed a new number one—a new, better stepdad. But who?

During the sale of Pixel Union, the one beacon of light through the entire process was Brian, who dressed the part, talked the part, and who had said he would sell my company, and actually did, helping facilitate a deal that had exceeded my wildest expectations.

Brian was a grown-up. A seasoned business expert. We'd become fast friends during the negotiations, and we had similar ideas about how to run a business. He also exuded experience. He was fifteen years older than me and looked and sounded the part. When talking about business, he spoke in a stream of acronyms—ROI, ARR, ARPU, IRR, LTV—that I would google under the table so I could follow along. And he didn't just sound impressive to me: I watched him charm and sweet-talk countless other businesspeople, including Richard, who bought Pixel Union. Everyone I introduced him to seemed to love him. The guy could sell anything to anyone.

He constantly referred to himself as a serial entrepreneur by saying, "Once you're lucky, Andrew, twice you're good," between amazing stories about all the different businesses he'd founded, along with how much money he'd made from each. ("I sold that one to a billionaire for twelve million bucks.")

And he pointed out the problems with MetaLab that no one else, myself and Chris included, had been able to articulate. When I had explained that MetaLab was constantly struggling, always either too busy or too slow, and that I had no idea how to balance the scales, Brian knew exactly what was wrong.

"Andrew, your business lacks systems and you don't sell or market yourself," he said calmly. "You're like a great bakery that's located down a back alley with no sign, relying 100 percent on word of mouth. How are you supposed to predict demand and hire great people if you have nobody out there selling?" Brian walked me through a confusing matrix full of business terms like *synergy* and *disruption* that I didn't understand and explained how he had used this strategy at his last company to scale to tens of millions of revenue. While I didn't understand exactly what he meant, I nodded and lapped it up.

Brian seemed able to identify those undervalued opportunities that we had missed. It wasn't rocket science, but these were lessons I figured I'd have to spend fifteen years building companies, like him, to fully understand.

I called Brian and we agreed to meet for lunch, where—once again—I told him all of my worries and problems.

"I love all your companies," he told me over ramen. "I think you've got great ideas."

"Thanks," I said. "But I actually want to *stop* building companies. I want to start investing."

"And you will," he replied. "You're one of the few people I've ever met who has the potential to become a billionaire." He then leaned forward, brushed his smooth, silky hair back with his hand, and told me: "You've got a gift, Andrew. A real gift."

While I found these compliments a bit much, it felt good. Now that I was twenty-eight years old, he was the closest thing I had to a mentor, and the fact that he had seen behind the curtain—warts and all—and was still complimenting my businesses meant a lot. Here was this incredibly accomplished, seasoned serial entrepreneur, ruffling my hair and telling me I could do it.

"Why don't I help you untangle this mess? It sounds like there's a lot I could help with," Brian said as we sat back, satisfied, burping discreetly.

"That would be incredible, honestly," I said, honored by the idea that he'd come work with me.

We talked through the details of what needed to happen, and I shared some of my insights that I'd learned over the last few years. I needed to hire CEOs for all of the businesses and shut down the ones that weren't working, to free Chris and me up to focus on investing.

"Don't worry about it. I've got this," he said. It was like the president of the United States had just told me "I've got your back." Here's Brian, this Übermensch of startups, fresh off a big exit, joining my team to help. He offered to fly to Victoria and spend a few days whiteboarding with us, talking us through our crises and budgets and future plans.

A week later, Brian arrived at our office for a meeting to talk through ideas, and he was as good as I'd hoped.

Better even.

He had an unbelievable ability to cut to the core of every issue.

Chris and I took him into a conference room, and as the sun cast a warm, golden glow illuminating the ships across the bay, we laid out every problem facing us and our company. There was no bullshit, no sugarcoating, no sentimentality. Just a steady stream of hard-core problems and, in return, we got a firehose of solutions.

Hire this person.

Fire that one.

Shut down this business.

Restructure this org.

As the hours ticked by, I felt a newfound lightness: even when Brian didn't know exactly what to do, he assured me that he'd take care of it. We started doing these brainstorming meetings on a weekly basis and each one was like watching a world champion *Tetris* player solve the hardest level without breaking a sweat.

Move this piece there. That piece here. Problem solved.

I'm not going to lie. Before these brainstorm meetings, I had concerns that Brian could be just another surface sales guy, a shiny veneer. I was slightly skeptical during the final hours of the Pixel Union sale when it felt like his negotiation was rehearsed. But in the end, he ended up getting me $7 million for a company I would have sold for two.

Now, seeing him in action, solving our long-standing problems, helped me better understand his significant talents. These were issues we'd been struggling with for months, years even, and Brian helped us confront the trade-offs and see the right paths forward. We had been holding out for a Plan C, an elusive third option to avoid choosing between two imperfect paths.

Brian forced us to realize that there was no Plan C. Through all of this, in the back of my mind, I was thinking the obvious question: "Why is this guy helping me? What is he getting out of this?" Brian never mentioned pay or options or equity; I didn't even pay for his travel or hotels. But then I thought about it and realized that if I were in his situation (I assumed he was worth millions), and I found a younger version of me that I could mentor and coach, I'd do everything to help them. I assumed that maybe Brian was even bored because he had "enough" and this was his way of giving, the business equivalent of doing it all over, vicariously through someone half his age. Maybe, I reasoned, Brian was going through his own existential crisis, and I was the solution to *his* dread.

Weeks went by, and we kept reviewing our business problems. He met with key people at our companies and everybody loved him. And I mean *everybody* loved him. Even creative people who were allergic to business talk. He had an incredible knack for calibrating himself from person to person. He'd figure out what they liked to talk about and what their personality was, and dial himself up or down accordingly. It was impressive to watch.

Employees who would flinch at my erratic ideas, unsure if the company was changing direction yet again, felt a sense of calm with Brian. Finally, we had a grown-up in the building helping us out. A real businessperson. Someone who shaved every day, and wore blazers, not hoodies.

It felt like every problem he touched turned into a solution. We'd been struggling to win larger contracts at MetaLab, for example, and Brian helped us figure it out, hiring incredible salespeople who started landing massive projects. Almost immediately, business began booming. Sales numbers were up and the team seemed more motivated than ever.

It was inevitable that he would eventually want money, and I wasn't surprised when that day came. I was even a little relieved by it.

"Hey. So, Andrew," Brian said one day over what was now a regular lunch. "I'd like to start getting some compensation for all the work I've been doing."

My worry wasn't that he wanted to be paid, but that I didn't know how I could compensate someone who was worth so much. What could I add to the millions he'd made on this deal and that deal?

"Sure," I said. "That makes sense. What do you propose?"

"I'm thinking maybe we start with an hourly rate for my time?"

"Hourly?" I said, clearly taken aback. Why would someone worth so much want an hourly rate? Brian saw my demeanor change and quickly put me at ease.

"It's just simpler this way," he said. "We don't need lawyers, contracts— just good, old-fashioned wages for time."

He made a good point, and after he explained his thinking, it made sense to go with an hourly rate. After a little back-and-forth, we came to $250 an hour. It might seem like a lot, but given the amazing results he was getting, it made total sense. To borrow one of Brian's favorite acronyms—I'd still be getting an incredible ROI from his counsel, even at ten times that hourly rate.

There's an intimacy to startups, or really any small business. Boundaries are porous—everyone knows what everyone else is doing—there are few walls and even fewer hierarchies. As a result, we quickly got to know Brian very well. We spent fourteen hours a day working side by side; talking every decision over; getting his input on staffing, clients, even the best lunch orders.

There were moments where he acted in a way that was cutthroat, and when I asked if that was necessary, he said that sometimes business had to be done that way. That you have to read your opponent and figure out if they should be killed with kindness or the edge of a sharp knife.

Like with Liam.

When we sold Pixel Union, Richard had flagged then-CEO Liam's inexperience as a problem. I disagreed. Liam had grown the business tremendously during his tenure, and I trusted his taste. While he was new to it, I felt that he was learning fast.

Richard, on the other hand, was old school. He felt that the business needed what he called a "gray hair." An older, more experienced CEO. He wanted to inject one of his old executives, from the video rental company, to take over for Liam. It seemed like an odd fit. Video rental executive turned CEO of a Shopify themes business? Chris and I fought him on it, but after a few weeks we realized it was ultimately his business.

Richard told us that, because Liam was *our* hire, and we had sold him the business, we should handle letting him go. At this point, I had somehow managed to fire exactly zero people in my career. I was an inexperienced manager and hated delivering bad news, so, instead I'd put my head in the sand and ignore whatever was bothering me, hoping the person would eventually leave. We mentioned this to Brian and he told us he'd handle it.

Brian decided to use the scalpel for this one. A few days went by and he came into my office to give me and Chris an update on where the deal was going.

"You know, I think this is an opportunity to put grandma on the roof here," he said as he talked about his plan.

I interrupted him. "What do you mean, put grandma on the roof?"

Brian laughed at our innocence. "It's an old business saying: Sometimes grandma gets really old and fragile, and she's your grandma, so you obviously want to kill her kindly. You can't just unceremoniously push her off your roof," he told us. Chris and I looked at each other nervously, unsure where this was going. "First, you get grandma really comfortable and make her a lovely cup of tea inside the house," Brian continued. "Then you tell her, 'Grandma, I want to give you a tour of the house.' You walk her upstairs and say, 'Oh it's such a beautiful view out on the deck. Let's go look.' And then when grandma is on the roof, admiring the view, you push her off the roof—*THUD!*"

Chris and I looked at each other in disbelief, unsure if this was a joke or intended as an actual business parable.

"That's a bit . . ." Chris said in his soft, contemplative voice.

"Harsh," I said, finishing Chris's sentence.

"That's what you have to do when you gotta get rid of someone, boys," Brian concluded, full of bravado.

"That's a fucked-up metaphor," I said, realizing this wasn't a joke.

"Business is full of fucked-up metaphors," Brian explained. "The important thing is to make sure you're the one using these metaphors, and that someone else is not using them when talking about you." He stood up and grabbed my shoulder: "That's why I'm here. To help you and make sure you're not the grandma being pushed off the roof." As I walked out, and as I realized that Liam, whom I had nurtured and who had done a phenomenal job, was about to be pushed off a proverbial roof, I felt sick.

Brian executed his plan in a way that was astonishing and unsettling. Over the coming weeks, he built a mentorship relationship with Liam and gained his trust. He spent hours and hours with him at lunches, making him feel heard and listening to his concerns about how things could change now that we'd sold the business. After a few weeks, he told him that he really needed assistance, and that he'd help recruit an executive who could join the team. Of course, this was a Jedi mind trick. His search "found" Richard's gray-haired executive, who then became COO of the business, and ultimately usurped Liam.

Grandma got pushed off the roof. The whole time, Liam had felt like it was all his idea, until—*THUD*—it was too late.

Chris and I acted like cowards. We averted our gaze and instead focused it on our investing books, allowing the guy who had risen from intern to CEO of one of our largest businesses, and made us millions, to be unceremoniously fired from the business he had built. It was awful, but at the time, I questioned my perception. Maybe this was just the dog-eat-dog world of business?

Not everyone was as accepting of Brian's "business" tendencies. After a few months of working with Brian, my brother Tim came to me with his concerns. "I think we should keep our distance from this guy," he told me. "He's doing a lot of good things, but there's something a little unsettling about him." Despite my own nagging doubts, I got defensive. "What are you talking about?" I told him. "Look at all the amazing results he's delivered! He's making us millions!" Then, I echoed my mentor: "This is just business."

In reality, Brian was delivering more than I could have dreamed. I was making even more money. I was getting richer. When other people were experiencing similar doubts, I regurgitated whatever Brian told me, blabbing on about zero-sum games and our increasing ARR and EBITDA.

There's a famous Upton Sinclair quote: "It is difficult to get a man to understand something when his salary depends on his not understanding it."

At this moment, this quote surely applied to me.

All of this helped exacerbate the real reason I had originally reached out to Brian: to get advice about how to get out of the day-to-day operations of my businesses. He had been helping me realize this on a nominal scale, like hiring the new sales team, or helping me acquire new clients that would increase revenues, but I couldn't overlook the fact that I was still miserable at MetaLab. Ultimately, the buck stopped with me. I was still the CEO, and with all the changes going on, all eyes were now pointing directly at me.

It wasn't just the employees, but the entire agency life was taking its toll. The mercurial clients, the roller-coaster business cycle, the endless management meetings, and the trips to San Francisco to meet with people with gargantuan egos—I didn't know how much longer I could keep it up.

Then, one day sitting in my office, after a stressful conference call with my brother Tim, who was then MetaLab's COO, and a client who refused to pay our bill, I cracked.

I stood up, walked across the hall to Chris's office, a funny little all-glass fishbowl with large windows facing out onto an exterior deck, and slumped into the chair across from him. Chris and I had become so close over the last few years working together that we could immediately tell if something was wrong, and what that something was, way before we had even opened our mouths.

"Bad day, hey?" Chris said as he closed his laptop and looked at me.

"How is it that we have millions of dollars in the bank and yet here we are, dealing with the same stressful crap as before?" I said, shaking my head. "I'm done."

Chris looked at me like I was insane. "We've built an amazing business," he said. "It feels like we're making progress."

"I know it's an amazing business," I said. "But I'm *done*."

Chris knew what I meant, and that this wasn't just a random bad day. I meant it. I was done running this company and I wanted to pull the emergency ejection seat. "I want to shut this thing down, stop this madness."

"We don't need to do that. If you're burned out," Chris said, doing his best to calm me down, "let's just hire someone else to run the agency."

We talked about what that would look like, and Chris convinced me that if we found a competent CEO to take over, the business could run itself and I could focus on what we wanted to do next: investing.

"But where do we even find someone to find a CEO replacement?" I asked.

"Let's talk to Brian," Chris said.

"Great idea," I replied. "He'll know exactly what to do." I picked up the phone and called Brian right there in Chris's office. Brian said he was more than happy to help, and got on the next plane out.

That night, he sat in the conference room across from me and Chris as I paced back and forth lamenting why I wanted out of MetaLab. Brian didn't say a word—he just nodded and took it all in. Finally, I stopped talking, and Brian waited a beat, thinking through everything I had said. It felt like minutes went by in the silence of the space. All I could hear was Brian thinking. Then, he finally spoke.

"Don't worry about a thing, boys," Brian said as he sat across from us in his cashmere V-neck with his smooth smile and grown-up demeanor. "I'll take care of everything."

"You will?" I said, feeling sheer relief. "How?"

"Yeah, how?" Chris asked.

"I'm going to find you the best CEO in the business," he said. "The absolute best. Everything is going to be all right."

Chris and I looked at each other with an exhale, feeling like we'd won the lottery finding Brian, and that he was going to solve this problem, like he had the last dozen we had offloaded to him. He stood up in that conference room and began writing on the whiteboard a list of all the attributes we would want in our CEO candidate, and as he did, I began daydreaming about what my life would look like when this person joined the company. I couldn't have been more at ease or more excited. Brian laid out a vision for the agency's future that felt right. With a little space from the day-to-day, Chris and I could focus on our next chapter.

Later that night, I sat my brothers down to tell them the news. Just like Brian, they listened patiently, and then Tim spoke up.

"You're going to let Brian find your replacement?" he asked nervously.

"He'll find the best person to run MetaLab," I said. "He'll take care of the whole thing."

"He's a bit of a shark, Andrew," my other brother said.

"I know," I said confidently. "But he's our shark."

Then, perhaps convincing myself more than my brother, I reiterated: "Everything is going to be fine. He'll take care of everything..."

Chapter 10

THE FIRST $50 MILLION
IS THE EASIEST

For the first time since the last deal, at twenty-nine years old, I could taste it again—freedom.

The freedom to not feel my heart rate spike every time I checked my inbox. Hell, the freedom to not check my inbox at all. And I had one person to thank for that incoming freedom: Brian.

First, I knew we had to hire my replacement. Brian had told me not to worry about a thing, and sure enough, I didn't.

"I'm lining up a dozen folks for you boys to talk to," Brian told me and Chris. "People with vast C-suite experience; people who have run multi-hundred-million-dollar companies."

Before the interviews, I was like a kid on Christmas morning, jittery with excitement and possibility. I was eager to meet the candidates Brian had promised: the best and brightest. Leaders who could do what I couldn't. They'd have a good eye for design—taste can't be taught—but also be masters of business management. They'd care about our current employees, and be cautious when it came to hiring new ones. They'd push our profits to new heights without alienating our current customers, and they'd know how to sign new clients.

The morning we were set to start meeting the candidates that would take over for me, I was so excited about my new life of freedom that I woke up, rolled over, and literally beamed a smile from ear to ear. Later that morning, as I poured myself a coffee, I imagined standing up in front of our fifty or so employees and giving a speech about why I was moving on. This would be followed by me introducing our new CEO, who would then give an awe-inspiring oration. We'd firmly shake hands, grinning widely at the crowd, then I'd walk out the front door and into the sunlight, finally free.

Then, we met the candidates.

They were awful. Lumps of coal. Complete dinguses. All of them. They didn't know design or business; Chris and I tore them apart in the interview process with just basic questions. They had bad taste, the wrong experience, and no understanding of what made MetaLab special.

"That guy couldn't design a PowerPoint deck for someone who is legally blind," I said to Chris after meeting with one, a man in his fifties who wore a two-toned khaki and navy-blue suit and had worked at an accounting firm for most of his career.

"What's Brian doing bringing us these guys?" Chris asked. "Does he not know what we're looking for?"

When we told Brian, he said this was just part of the process. "Hiring a new CEO is the hardest job any CEO will ever do," Brian assured us. "Let me line up more candidates."

The second round of candidates was even worse. It was like he'd rounded up lobotomy patients and put them in business suits, paying them $50 for the day.

Chris and I knew that if we put any of these people in charge of Meta-Lab our business would vanish; our freedom would be short-lived, lassoed back in to save the company from a bozo.

We were sitting in my office in the middle of yet another disastrous interview and Brian (who had joined this round of interviews) was silently shaking his head; he looked despondent. Brian walked the last interviewee out as Chris and I sat unhappily checking our emails. When Brian walked back in, he slumped in his chair and shook his head again. "I'm so sorry to disappoint you both, but these are the best people I could find," he told us with a sigh. "I searched high and low and engaged top headhunters. I just couldn't find anyone else."

Although I remained committed to exiting the business, I realized that hiring my replacement would take more time. I was crushed.

As we set out to widen our search, we soon started getting some acquisition interest, and began meeting with a newly formed private equity firm run by Alexander, an old friend of Brian's. He had just raised hundreds of millions of dollars and his background seemed perfect: he had previously grown one of the largest digital agencies in Canada and sold it to a public company years earlier.

This, I thought, would be a perfect Plan B. Sell the company, and exit without having to run the place. Brian agreed, and immediately got involved in the talks to sell. He said he'd take a fee, the same deal as before. And then, almost as an afterthought, Brian also said that he'd be willing to step in as CEO in the interim, just until the deal was done. "No pressure," he assured us. "I'm just disappointed in myself that I wasn't able to find you the leader you needed and want to help make it right."

I was taken aback. While I didn't want to be CEO, I had mixed feelings about Brian taking over. Sure, he was brilliant and had delivered on his promises, but did I really want to hand over the business I built with my own blood and sweat and tears to a guy who used metaphors that involve throwing your grandmother off a roof? It was useful to have a shark in our camp, but what does that shark do to that camp if something goes wrong? How would he treat my brothers and all the employees who had stuck with us over the years?

On the other hand, though, I was miserable. Having gotten a fleeting taste of freedom, I now loathed the idea of returning to the grind. Besides, I figured that the harm was limited, since we were selling the business soon. After weighing the pros and cons, Chris and I agreed to make Brian interim CEO, structuring a deal where he could buy up to 15 percent of MetaLab if he hit certain milestones. It just so happened that, as the deal was structured, if he hit those same milestones, our equity would be worth infinitely more, so it seemed like a perfect deal.

With Brian in the CEO seat, I really was able to step away from the day-to-day stress of management. A month went by and I didn't get on a plane; my liver appreciated the break from all those drinks and dinners with clients. Holly and I were expecting our first child, a boy, and I was grateful to have this quiet time leading up to it. I started spending serene mornings reading the newspaper and playing tennis daily. I started taking guitar lessons, in awe of all this newfound free time (thankfully, I didn't try to start an online guitar school). Meanwhile, at MetaLab, Brian trumpeted the fact that we had designed Slack a few years prior, which by this time had become a multibillion-dollar company. This generated huge amounts of buzz, and he used it to sell ever larger Fortune 500 clients.

In less than a year, it appeared that Brian had doubled our revenue.

Around the same time, the private equity firm that had been circling came in with an offer to buy MetaLab for $50 million. It was a mind-boggling sum. Seven times the Pixel Union deal, and less than a year later. Chris and I could walk away completely, with a CEO in place, and $50 million in the bank to start our own mini–Berkshire Hathaway. It felt like everything was falling into place.

Unlike the last deal, where I floundered and the price went up, I knew this was the opportunity of a lifetime and I said yes instantly.

The deal went similarly to the last one. It was becoming routine at this point. They ground us on this term or that term. They played up innocuous issues. We pushed back. And, of course, the lawyers lawyered and charged us hundreds of thousands of dollars to do so. Then, a few months later, Chris and I took the elevator up to the offices of Fasken Martineau, our fancy new law firm. Their headquarters were massive, with floor-to-ceiling windows and walls covered in modernist art labeled with names I didn't recognize but probably should have.

Our lawyer, Steve, met us at the front desk and walked us into a huge boardroom with a conference table with room for twenty people. His legal assistant followed suit with a stack of documents so big she had to roll them in on a trolley. This time, it was more like four phone books. My hands shook as I signed the papers, and there, with the stroke of a pen, I signed my second business baby away.

"That's going to be a hell of a wire transfer," Steve said as he smiled and shook my hand.

I grinned a huge toothy grin. I couldn't believe it.

What I didn't realize then, was that this decision would be the starting line of two years of misery.

Chapter 11

SHARK BITES

It's hard to describe what it feels like to know that tens of millions of dollars are about to be wired into your personal bank account. The numbers ticked higher and higher like some sort of fantasy scoreboard, where I was the only player. There's a rush of adrenaline, blended with an overwhelming mix of excitement and disbelief. Suddenly, every dream and desire you've ever had seems just within arm's reach. For me, it was knowing that my bank account would go from seven digits to eight. That I could take care of my family—forever. That, unless I stupidly gambled it all away, or set it on fire, I was set for life.

It was only exhilaration that I felt when I pulled out of the parking garage of the law firm and drove to the bank, giddy at what it would feel like to see tens of millions of dollars sitting in my account.

Except, that wasn't the case. When I checked, the money wasn't there. I immediately called Alexander.

"Where's the wire?" I asked, my voice cracking.

"It's coming. We just have a minor hold-up with our investors," he said. "Just give us a couple of days."

I did just that, and again checked my account. Once again, there was nothing there.

We had the same conversation, each one growing increasingly tense. He asked for a few more days. And then, after weeks of this, he stopped responding to me. I realized they didn't actually have the money, and they had no way of securing it. When I told Brian, he was livid, and he agreed that I should tell my lawyers to pull the plug on the whole deal. "I'll never do business with that piece of shit again!" he yelled into the phone.

You'd think that in a moment like that, when you expected to be handed a bag of money full of $50 million in cash, that you'd be distraught when you opened it and it was completely empty, but after you've been in business long enough, you come to expect exactly what my father had learned over time: "Anything that can go wrong, will go wrong."

I wasn't as distraught as I thought I would be. In fact, I was almost relieved when I realized there was also an upside to the failed sale. In the process of the acquisition, I had looked at our books and we were actually doing better than ever. With so much new business, the money was flowing in.

Sure, there were certainly days when I disagreed with one of Brian's decisions and wanted to take charge again, but I also knew that my stepping aside had been the right move for MetaLab. Most founders think they need to be like Mark Zuckerberg or Bill Gates, taking their company from the garage to the Fortune 500 while staying at the helm the entire time. But I felt they were exceptions to the rule. While many founders are exceptional in the early stage—going from zero to one requires an irrational passion—it's incredibly rare to also have the skills required for the later stages of a company. I certainly didn't, which is probably why I found the idea of managing a growing agency so stressful. I realized that I was like a sprinter trying to run marathons. I should focus on what I was best at, which was starting businesses, not operating them at a huge scale.

There was another upside to the failed sale. While we waited for the money to come in (or not come in, as ended up being the case), Chris and

I had the time and space to reflect on what we wanted our lives to look like going forward. By this time, we had burrowed our way through every book on Warren Buffett and had moved onto his business partner, Charlie Munger. One of his quotes that stuck with us was the constant refrain to "invert, always invert!" Munger said that "problems are often easiest solved in reverse" and explained that it's much easier to think about what you don't want than what you do. To think about what you hate, then work backward to optimize your life to avoid the things you disliked being a part of it.

So, we decided to invert. We began by listing our complaints, writing down all the tasks that made us miserable.

Long meetings that dragged on.

Late-night emails.

People who needed constant input and feedback.

Packed calendars.

Travel that took us away from our kids.

The list went on.

We made a list of what we called our "Anti-Goals." Once Chris and I had itemized everything we hated about our jobs, we spent the next several weeks thinking about how to delegate and structure things so that we weren't responsible for any of those tasks. Most of our problems were related to issues within our individual businesses. As soon as we hired Brian, it was his job, as interim CEO, to handle all problems relating to MetaLab, and our lives got infinitely easier. So, we figured, we'd hire leaders for each business, and tell them to only call us if it was absolutely necessary. We'd set up a head office, where we'd focus our time on reading, and they could call us only when needed.

My key insight at this time was one that would become the core of how I run my businesses today: It's not enough to do what you love. You also have to stop doing what you hate. The goal isn't—as many people think—to *not work at all;* it's to only work on things that you enjoy doing. The stuff that you'd do even if you didn't get paid for it.

We soon rented our own little office. A modest room to provide a buffer from the daily demands of MetaLab and our other companies, where we could concentrate on our new investing-focused work lives. We ended up in the most generic space imaginable—a small, lackluster office with drab carpets, an old Keurig coffee machine, and a single window.

But Chris and I didn't care. It was quiet and cheap. We finally had the luxury of being able to close the door and know that no one was going to knock on it. We could have been on a deserted island with only coconuts and I wouldn't have cared.

We had transitioned: first, from players on the field, to coaches yelling plays from the sidelines, and now, finally, to the hushed wood paneling of the owner's box.

Brian was doing far better than we expected as CEO of MetaLab; Chris and I were hearing positive feedback from almost everyone and, most importantly, our clients. Even my brother Tim started to warm up to him. I was tracking the revenue numbers, and the business was growing more than I ever thought that it would. You might think part of me would be upset that I was so replaceable, that Brian could step into my job and immediately succeed, but I was thrilled to not be needed. I even let him take the lead on renovating the office, dealing with bureaucratic nonsense that I had no interest in handling. Brian was game to take all of it on.

I had my life back.

Chris and I went deep into the world of investing. Sure, we had read a few biographies, but now we wanted to drill into the details. I got copies of every Berkshire Hathaway annual report and began treating them like ancient manuscripts, poring over the numbers in search of their secret strategies. We also read up on other famous value investors like Howard Marks, Mohnish Pabrai, and Bill Ackman, each of whom we became obsessed with for their distinct investment styles, like distressed debt investing, contrarian bets, and activist shareholder initiatives.

But nobody captured our attention quite like Charlie Munger.

Munger was a college dropout–turned–Harvard Law graduate who was a career lawyer until he was in his mid-forties and then decided to become an investor. He just so happened to become one of the greatest investors of all time. For decades, he had worked alongside Buffett, generating outsized returns by buying undervalued companies. He took a contrarian approach to traditional investors in almost every way imaginable.

Where most investors sought diversification, Munger dubbed it "de-worsification," asking, "Why would you ever want to invest in your hundredth best idea?"

Where others focused on betting on short-term swings in the stock market, buying and selling depending on what was happening, Munger advocated investors should buy a great company and then "do nothing." Often for decades.

Unlike Buffett, who was generally consistent in his statements and didn't like to unduly criticize anyone, Munger was outspoken about just about everything from corporate fraud to cryptocurrencies. If Buffett was twelve-bar blues, Munger was experimental jazz—you never knew what interesting thing he was going to blurt out next.

He was a quote machine, churning out aphorisms that I wanted to tattoo into my brain. Like this one: "All I want to know is where I'm going to die, so I'll never go there." It's not a quote about death—it's about inversion and avoiding mistakes. Figure out your worst-case scenario (in business, going broke) and figure out how to avoid it. After all, the world's best investors didn't get there just by picking winners; they became truly great by avoiding dumb mistakes. They did this by understanding the pitfalls of herd psychology and steering clear of the bubbles and manias, from subprime mortgages to crypto, that captured the greedy imaginations of everyone else.

His approach was refreshing, and was particularly appealing to Chris and me for two reasons. One, it was simple and easy to understand. Make a few good decisions, then do nothing. Two, the approach of locking into businesses and holding forever came naturally to us. We'd come to realize after the failed sale of MetaLab (and more offers to buy other businesses we owned) that we distinctly *disliked* selling companies and—even when big numbers got thrown out—there was rarely a right time to sell a great business. They generally grew and grew and grew over time and nobody was going to pay up for potential future value.

Munger's approach was also marked by his deep understanding of human nature. He said that analyzing a business was about the qualitative side: human behavior and psychology. The quantitative side—the numbers—those could be sketched on a napkin. If it required any more thought, he said, it was best to pass. He advocated sitting on cash and waiting for what he called a "no-brainer." A deal so good that it was hard to lose.

"My idea of shooting fish in a barrel," said Munger, "is to drain the barrel first."

I might have been sitting in an ugly little office, drinking bitter Keurig coffee in my IKEA task chair, but I was absorbing these lessons and trying to apply them to my own life.

Now we just had to find something to invest in.

Weeks went by with Chris and I slurping up everything we could from our new heroes. We were learning to ask the right questions, and we just had to figure out how to apply the Munger framework to technology businesses like ours.

Coca-Cola was a difficult company to compete with; someone could spend $100 billion to create a new cola to compete with Coke and it would be laughable. Does anyone remember RC Cola? Virgin Cola? Jolt Cola? People love their Coke. They are loyal to the brand.

I racked my brain, trying to think of similar businesses but in the tech space. I researched different types of business moats, and one caught my eye: a network effect moat. In the 1960s, Visa had pioneered credit cards and built an extensive network across the globe. This was expensive, time-consuming work, which took decades, but now, you could walk into a store, from Toronto to Timbuktu, and use your Visa. And every time someone bought something with their credit card, Visa took a few cents for facilitating the transaction. This creates a network effect, and makes it difficult to compete with. If a store owner wants to accept credit cards, they'll accept Visa or its only major competitor, Mastercard, because that's what other stores do and they are the most widely used cards.

As I thought about this idea of network effects, I thought of Facebook. Just about everyone I knew, from my friends to my own parents, had a Facebook account, which formed a huge network. If someone is signing up for a social network, they don't want to hang out alone. They want to hang out where their friends are. And their friends were on Facebook.

Obviously, every investor on the planet had had this same thought about Facebook, but I started to wonder if there was a smaller Facebook. A smaller Coca-Cola. This brought me to Dan Cederholm, my web design idol. In 2009, Dan and his business partner, Rich Thornett, had started an online community called Dribbble, where a couple of hundred designers shared images of their work and got feedback from one another. It was cool, and for a newbie designer like me, based on a small island off the west coast of Canada, I was grateful to connect with so many other like-minded designers. I used it to find some of my first employees and even ended up getting a few clients from it. In the years since, it had grown from a hundred nerdy designers to just about every designer on the planet, becoming one of the top three thousand sites on the entire internet, with millions of visitors per month.

Years earlier, I had sent Dan a few gushy fanboy emails full of questions, which he had kindly answered, so I still had his email.

I sent him a one-liner:

"Hey Dan, Hope you're well. Not sure if you've ever considered selling Dribbble, but I'd love to talk about it if you're interested."

He sent me a nice response within a few hours: No, but thank you. He and Rich were having fun and didn't feel like they were ready to sell.

But I couldn't get it out of my head. As I looked at more and more businesses, all I could think of was the fact that none of them had a moat like Dribbble. It felt like a perfect fit. Something I understood intimately, both as a designer and a user. It was run by someone I respected tremendously, and—I suspected—had a ton of untapped potential.

I kept emailing Dan to nudge him every month or so.

"Hey Dan, just checking in. I know I'm being annoying, but please let me know if you guys change your mind."

Each time he'd pleasantly rebuff me. We'd even spoken on the phone a few times, which felt particularly exciting given how much of an influence he'd had on my early career. But a sale just didn't feel like it was going to happen. Still, being away from MetaLab and focusing solely on the potential acquisitions was the greatest experience I'd had in years. Even if he didn't want to sell to me, I was loving my new job even if I hadn't actually made a deal yet.

Around this time, I went home for Christmas dinner at my parents' house, and as we all sat around the table, devouring turkey and chatting away about what everyone was up to, I asked my brother Tim about how the office culture was with me gone and Brian in charge.

"I really like him," Tim said. "He's doing great. Everyone is really happy."

"That's so great," I said. "The financials look incredible, too."

Then my brother paused and looked at me.

"What?" I asked. "What is it?"

"It's probably nothing."

"What's probably nothing?"

Another pause from Tim. "There was something weird that happened last week," he said, then stopped himself. "Actually, it's nothing—don't worry about it. I don't want to cause any trouble."

But it was too late to walk it back. There are few things that make me worry more than someone telling me not to worry. After some pleading, my brother finally relented. "You know how we're looking at getting our new office building done?"

I put my fork down and nodded.

"Well, it's been delayed by the usual bureaucratic stuff and Brian was getting frustrated and he told me that I should pay off one of the building inspectors to get our building permits approved faster."

"Wait, a bribe? Are you serious?"

My brother nodded.

"That's insane," I said. "We could all go to jail for something like that! He literally said those words?"

"He sent it to me on Slack." Tim handed me his phone, and I couldn't believe what I was reading: a message from Brian telling Tim to "pay the inspectors graft" because "someone has to get lubed" in order to get the permits approved faster.

Obviously, I was relieved that my brother didn't follow through trying to bribe an inspector or there'd have been a chance he'd be spending Christmas in prison (and I might be in the cell next to him), but I was also unnerved. If Brian was willing to bribe a building inspector to get us moved into our new office a few weeks faster, what other shortcuts was he willing to take in business?

My brain wanted this to stop. I had reinvented myself as an investor. But I couldn't stop thinking about that building inspector, or shake the image of grandma on the roof.

Overnight, I woke up at 3 AM feeling ill. *Who had I put in charge of my company?* I wanted to throw up.

The next day, I called a friend of mine who knew Brian and told him about what was happening.

"I don't get it. Why would he put everything at risk over something so stupid?" I said, my voice straining. "He's a multimillionaire. He could go to jail over something like this!"

"Brian?" my friend asked. "I don't think he's a multimillionaire. I doubt he's even a millionaire!"

My chest tightened.

I didn't want to believe it.

But it was too late. I was already in the water with the shark.

I called Chris in a panic.

"We need to fire Brian right away," I told him. "None of this is adding up." I told Chris about the meeting and the subsequent calls. I told him about the building inspector and the Slack messages, and how nothing made sense.

As we sat on the phone, we walked through everything that had happened over the past several months, and like watching a thriller film over for a second time, we started noticing things that didn't add up. Things he'd said. Introductions he'd made. The CEO search full of moronic candidates, which, in hindsight, felt like theater. "He needs to go. Now," I said to Chris.

"Hold on. Hold on. Hold on," Chris said. Then he reminded me that we couldn't just fire Brian tomorrow—he'd almost certainly sue us for millions if we weren't careful. We had to document this meticulously and be ready with evidence. We needed ammunition.

I knew Chris was right.

It felt like we were living with a serial killer and couldn't say anything out of fear that we'd be his next victim. Was this all part of his plan from the beginning? I knew I needed to dig deeper into what was going on, and I also knew I couldn't ask him any questions. Brian would smell my fear and trepidation a mile away.

I started to delve into our accounting, looking through every single transaction in the business. There were thousands of charges each month, most obscured by bizarre credit card company transaction codes, and it took days to decipher our bills, but the more time I spent, the more glaring it became.

The charges were insane. In the last few months, Brian had spent hundreds of thousands of dollars on travel. The month before, he'd stayed at the Four Seasons and spent twenty-two thousand dollars over a few days. His palatial suite was expensive, of course, but most of the itemized bill was due to alcohol, room charges, and multi-thousand-dollar dinners.

I knew what he would say if I asked him about these bills. He'd blow them off and start blabbing about ROI, how he had wined and dined new clients at the hotel, how Chris and I didn't know how the real world operated, and so on. He was signing big clients. The business was going great. But still, this felt exorbitant and way out of line. My shark was flying first class to the world's best hotels to guzzle champagne and caviar, and I was footing the bill.

At this point, I was ready to fire Brian. Thinking of him charging us for the most expensive suites at the Four Seasons, traveling first class all over the world, then suggesting my brother bribe the building inspector, made me angrier than I knew I was capable of feeling.

Chris and I quickly hopped on the next flight to Vancouver to meet with a top employment lawyer to get the ball rolling.

Weary-eyed from the lack of sleep and nauseous from anxiety-induced inability to eat, we sat across from the lawyer in a glass office building and told him everything, putting piles of papers in front of him and pointing to this fact and that line item. The lawyer picked up the papers and reviewed them quietly as I looked out the windows, a tapestry of glass and steel framing the rugged beauty of the mountains and the inlet. All I could think of was how fucking dumb I'd been. How I'd fallen for this guy at each turn. From the serious look on the lawyer's face, I still might lose it all.

"Look," the lawyer said after a few minutes. "Situations like this are tough, but I think you have solid grounds to fire him. You can get rid of this guy and you should do it as soon as you possibly can before he takes you for everything."

Chris and I both let out a huge, pent-up sigh of relief.

Back at our hotel, we formulated a plan. I emailed Brian, asking if he could meet with us in Vancouver in a couple of days. He immediately said no problem and didn't ask any other questions. I knew we had the receipts, dozens of them, that we could use to fire him with, but I also didn't want to risk anything, so I decided I needed help. I picked up the phone and called my brother.

"Hey man, how are you?" I said.

"Good," he said. "Just got to Palm Springs, about to settle into the hotel and go for a swim." Fuck, he was on vacation this week. I paused for a moment, trying to think if there was another way, but there wasn't.

"I'm sorry, but I need you back here in Vancouver right away."

There was a long pause, then he finally spoke. "I just got to Palm Springs with my girlfriend. I cleared this vacation," he said.

He wasn't wrong. But it didn't matter. "I'm sorry, but you have to fly back today," I told him. "We need to act now. We're going to fire Brian and I need your help."

There was another long pause, followed by a resigned sigh.

"I'm on my way."

Later that afternoon, I met with my friend Tim, a serial entrepreneur who'd been in business for decades and someone I often went to with business problems. He listened calmly to my case, nodding stoically.

"Don't be too hasty," he told me. "There's no way you can fire this guy right now. He's too smart, and you're not prepared enough. Sure, his crazy spending and this bribery thing are clear to you, but he's going to argue it was just the cost of doing business, and then he'll say the building inspector stuff is just a misunderstanding. He's brought in clients, hasn't he? He's making you lots of money, right? He's going to sue you and take a percentage of the business with him, and then you'll have to buy him out at a crazy valuation or he'll ruin your life. There's a saying about people like this: 'Never wrestle a pig. You'll both get dirty, but the pig will enjoy it.' You need to catch him red-handed."

This was the last thing I wanted to hear. But I worried he was right. The lawyer might see it as a slam-dunk case because it could end up in court for a year or more, racking up legal bills for his firm. Tim had seen what people like this were capable of.

As I wrapped up the meeting, I walked out onto Burrard Street in Vancouver, and I realized two terrible things: First, my brother was now on a flight from Palm Springs back to Vancouver and didn't need to be. Second, I still had a meeting scheduled with Brian.

My brother was livid when he landed. I tried to explain what was happening, but I sounded like such a mess that it all made no sense. And even if it didn't, it wasn't his responsibility to fix it; it was mine. I was too caught up in the anxiety of the moment to think straight.

For the next two days, Chris and I couldn't figure out how to get out of the meeting. We had no choice but to go. Instead of firing Brian, Chris and I panicked and decided to present him with his quarterly bonus check in person.

Yes. A bonus check to the guy we lost all trust in and who we feared could destroy the business we'd spent a decade building. We couldn't think of what else to do that wouldn't set off his super-sensitive alarm bells.

Thankfully, it worked. Brian couldn't smell the fear on us as he was too caught up in his own accolades. He spent the entire meeting talking about how great we were, and how well the business was doing.

For Chris and me, it was an excruciating hour—we were forced to sit there knowing everything that was going on, while we smiled and praised him and pretended to be grateful for everything he was doing for us.

Our performance deserved an Oscar.

Once the meeting was over, we immediately went back to our lawyer's office and started to solidify our case. We started amassing a thick dossier of everything Brian had done. Emails, Slack messages, itemized receipts, and the attempted bribery. Our goal was to build a rock-solid case, a legal brief so strong he wouldn't even think about coming for equity.

What I thought would take a few weeks to put together took four months. Four long and very, very expensive months.

We hired more lawyers to go through every Slack conversation and text thread and company email and every line of accounting. And thankfully, while Brian was good at lying, he was also sloppy and he left us a copious paper trail.

As part of our investigation, our lawyers went through Brian's MetaLab email account. They noticed something odd, and flagged it to us. He had repeatedly forwarded client information to his personal email address, then deleted it from his work email.

That's when the alarm bells in my head started going off.

We were convinced that Brian was in the process of setting up his own secret design agency, a competitor to MetaLab, on the side. He was using his private email to forward information to clients that did not appear to be responsive to requests for information.

Brian was so brazen, and so reckless, that he had his assistant at MetaLab working to find office space for his new venture. To make matters worse, he had approached our long-standing clients, the ones we had worked with for years, and told them that he was starting a new MetaLab "spin-off" agency, which could offer them even higher-end services.

Enough was enough.

We began by setting new company policies. No first-class travel, no five-star hotels, and all financial commitments over $10,000 required my personal sign-off. We set all these new rules with a smile on our face, but the goal was to constrain him and the potential damage he, and others, could cause. His reaction was to start deleting his private emails. Thousands of incriminating messages. But we'd already backed them up and documented his attempts to get rid of them.

The last nail in the coffin came when Brian used his corporate email to set up a meeting with one of our key clients, then deleted the email thread. We figured he would pitch the client on the new agency. Our team noticed that this meeting had been left off his MetaLab calendar, and he had created a series of fake meetings in Vancouver at the same time to mask the fact that he was going to be in San Francisco with our client. Busted.

We barricaded ourselves inside a conference room at the MetaLab office. Tim and Elexa, our head of HR, stood sentry on either side of us as we paced back and forth, counting down the minutes until Brian's flight took off. When his plane finally landed, we moved with lightning speed: I left him a voicemail letting him know he was terminated and followed up in writing via email.

We had caught him red handed.

But Brian wasn't going to go gently. He assumed that many of his lieutenants at MetaLab would be loyal to him, and would back up his version of events. Unfortunately for Brian, he vastly overestimated the allegiances he commanded. Although he remained popular with many employees—he had that reality-distorting ability to make people feel deeply understood—he also left people with a feeling of cognitive dissonance. That something felt off and didn't quite make sense. That his actions didn't square with his words. People were starting to see through his mask.

Brian was in a rage when we fired him, and he frantically called an executive who he had included in his plan to start the secret agency and who Brian assumed was his co-conspirator. Instead, the colleague had realized just how unethical Brian had been, and came clean to us about his actions, filling us in on what he had been up to in San Francisco and telling us about how he was pitching the new agency and trying to steal clients. We were sitting with him in our office boardroom when Brian called him, his voice dripping with anger. "What the *fuck* happened?" he said, causing the speakerphone to crackle as we listened.

We were recording the entire conversation for our lawyers, and his colleague realized that Brian had gone too far. He was on our side now.

We all cheered and hugged, as we poured a round of scotch for everyone. I was on the verge of tears. We toasted his downfall, celebrating our victory.

A few months later, we got a scary-looking letter from Brian's law firm suing MetaLab for fifteen million dollars. As predicted, we were in for a fight. The legal battle lasted for years, but it ultimately reached a satisfying conclusion. In our examination for discovery, a meeting where both Brian and I took turns being questioned by one another's lawyers, Brian tried to refute our claims. Fortunately, in each instance, we had extensive evidence to the contrary.

When he denied telling my brother to bribe the building inspector, my lawyer read aloud from the Slack messages we'd discovered: "Pay the inspectors graft" . . . "someone needs to get lubed."

When he said he'd never started a competing agency, my lawyer pointed to a text message thread between him and another executive outlining his plan to take two of our key clients in addition to specifying which MetaLab employees he was going to convince to join the new venture.

After many hours of this, his lawyer gave Brian a look.

At that moment, I knew it was over. I drew my first unburdened breath in years, a wave of exhilarating release washing over me.

Soon after, his lawyer offered to settle for $100,000. After years of having Brian dominate my daily thoughts, I was done. As much as I wanted to fight him in court, I wanted to move on and forget about him. I had better things to do with my life.

While I didn't relish the idea of paying him anything, I assumed, based on my own legal fees, that Brian would likely be in the hole for hundreds of thousands of dollars in legal expenses. While not exactly the crowning legal victory I had hoped for, it felt like a small taste of justice.

Once Brian was gone, I had no choice but to become CEO of MetaLab again. My life as an investor was on pause; I put away my books on investing, locked up my little office, and I went back to the grind, my inbox overflowing, my calendar a back-to-back collage of colored blocks. I was miserable, again.

And I let everyone else know it. I was a pain in the ass to work with, in part because I felt like I couldn't trust anyone, not after Brian. I was like an abused dog, barking and biting if anyone made an unpredictable movement or noise. I started questioning everyone and everything, not even trusting my own gut anymore. Wondering who else was conning me.

To make matters worse, while we weren't paying attention, Brian had significantly ramped up the company's costs with an out-of-control payroll, a ridiculously expensive new office, and layers of executives doing jobs that weren't necessary. My only hope of survival relied upon becoming what can only be described as a wartime CEO—slashing costs, sending off toxic employees, and instilling a sense of anxiety across the workplace. With no clue how to rectify any of it. My brother was understandably still livid with me, not only for ruining his much-needed vacation but for putting him in a situation that could have cost him everything. I had so much to fix, and no clue how to fix it.

Then came that saying: that you can figure out what you *do* want to do in life by first figuring out what you *don't* want. Now I knew one thing for sure: I'd do anything to avoid working with someone like Brian ever again.

Chapter 12

THE ANTI-GOALS ACQUISITION STRATEGY

A biting wind hit my face as I stepped out of Logan International Airport into the gloomy Boston morning, towing a roller bag filled to the brim. Fat raindrops pelted, quickly soaking through my thin jacket. I suppressed a shiver, exhaustion sinking into my bones.

Before we ducked into the dry interior of a taxi, Chris exchanged a few words with the driver about our destination. We were both working on no sleep, and stressed about how we could pull off the deal we had come here to make. We honestly had no clue if it was possible.

As the cab snaked through early morning traffic toward downtown, I stared numbly out the window. Boston was shrouded in fog and rain. In just a few hours, Chris and I would push a multimillion-dollar offer across the table and try to buy our first business. I'd prepped endlessly, yet I still felt completely unready.

I sighed deeply, my breath fogging the glass. Chris shot me a sideways glance but didn't speak. The knot in my stomach tightened. I wished I had managed to get some real rest the previous night, or at least felt a hint of confidence in myself. But as the car pulled up to the glossy facade of the Four Seasons, I knew all I could do was walk inside, put on my best face, and try to muddle through.

Adding to the pressure of this moment was the fact that this acquisition wasn't rooted in the idea of getting richer; it was about escaping from my current predicament. I was struggling with my life as a wartime CEO, working sixteen-hour days and making hard choices as I tried to clean up Brian's mess. To relax at night, I'd lie on the couch and contemplate our first investment. How could we apply the Buffett and Munger strategy to my own industry? While I didn't know much about razor blades, freight railroads, or home insurance, I was well versed in digital agencies and the creative community. Accordingly, my thoughts always drifted back to Dribbble.

So, I kept emailing Dan. Again. And again. And again. For almost a year. Then, one day, the phone rang.

"Hey, dude," said Dan warmly. "Me and Rich have been talking and we're ready to hear you out about doing a deal. Can you fly to Boston next week?" There were no promises, just a crack of an opening.

We booked our flights immediately.

Here we were, a week later, in a rented boardroom at the Four Seasons just across from the Boston Public Garden. I had flashes of Brian ordering champagne and running up a crazy tab, but I had to look past it. Get that out of my mind and focus on the task at hand.

Dan wore thick-rimmed glasses and had a neatly groomed beard. Despite his stature in the design world, he was quiet, thoughtful, and insanely down to earth. If he was an animal, I thought, he'd be a teddy bear. Rich was the clean-cut engineer type, with a kind and contemplative demeanor. They both dressed casually in jeans and a hoodie. There was no pretentiousness to either of them. Fortunately, we immediately hit it off.

Just like us, they were two guys who had stumbled into running a big business. Accidental entrepreneurs who still didn't know what to make of it or how they felt about it. After sharing war stories back and forth and talking about all the friends we had in common, Rich started walking us through where they were at.

"Look, we love working on Dribbble. Designing the site and adding features, making it better. My happy place is coding with my headphones on. But that's not what I do anymore. We have employees to manage and we're both getting dragged into stuff we don't want to do."

I nodded along. I knew the feeling.

"Trust me, I've been there," I told Rich. "It's hard to make the transition, but we've figured out how to build teams to delegate the stuff we don't enjoy. Let's walk through it all, then work backwards to figure out the right deal."

We decided to do our Anti-Goals exercise with them, the process we'd first performed in our little office after Brian took over. We asked Dan and Rich to list all the areas of the business they didn't like. Their least favorite executive chores. It didn't take long to get them to open up. "I hate ad sale calls," Dan began. Rich nodded along. "Those calls suck. It's also really stressful managing a big team," Rich added. "It's just a layer of constant anxiety, because someone always has a problem and they expect you to fix it." Now it was Dan's turn to nod in agreement.

The conversation continued like that until the whiteboard was filled up with complaints. The big themes were the challenges of managing people, having to deal with contracts and lawyers, and juggling an overflowing inbox full of support requests and feedback. When they were done listing all their Anti-Goals, I circled each of them one by one.

"We can solve this one," I said as I circled one. "And this one." I continued until all the Anti-Goals were circled, explaining our strategy for each. I put the marker down and sat across from them. "We can solve all of these issues for you. You could wake up tomorrow and just get to work on the stuff you enjoy at Dribbble. No more ad calls, no more contracts, no more dealing with HR stress. We'd take care of what you hate, so you can focus on what you love."

Then I flipped over the whiteboard and had Dan and Rich list out the goals they would focus on if their Anti-Goals disappeared. Dan said he wanted to work less and do freelance design work for the business. He also wanted to focus on his podcast, as he loved talking with creatives and championing the Dribbble brand. Rich, meanwhile, wanted to focus on the product while also exploring extracurricular ideas he'd been mulling over for years. One of these was that he wanted to earn a master's degree part-time. At Dribbble, he wanted to work full-time on coming up with new features.

I could tell this was resonating. For Dan and Rich, selling wasn't just about the money. Sure, they wanted to de-risk and take some chips off the table. To buy houses and cars and send their kids to college and all the usual stuff. But I knew it was critical to them that Dribbble ended up in the right hands.

Given our own experience when we sold Pixel Union, we had a unique understanding of their psychological state. Essentially, we were trying to be the buyer we wish we could have sold to. Someone who wouldn't mess the business up. Who'd let them stay as involved as they wanted. Who'd treat their employees well and protect the DNA they'd worked so hard to establish, while also moving the business forward. Most of all, we weren't threatening to push any old ladies off a roof.

At the end of the meeting, we told Dan and Rich we would put together an offer that weekend.

The next day, we sent a note offering to buy a majority stake of the business for a high seven-figure valuation, which felt like a fortune given the current size of their company and the fact that it was, by far, the largest check we had ever cut. But we were confident. One of the things that Dan and Rich told us during our Anti-Goals sessions was that they didn't like talking on the phone. I asked them how they courted prospective advertisers, as they had a very small amount of advertising revenue. If they didn't make phone calls, did they meet in person?

Dan just shrugged. "People email us every day and are like, 'Hey, let's hop on a call," he said. "But we constantly put it off." It turned out they had contracted most of their ads to an outside ad network that was paying them $20,000 a month. But when I did the quick back-of-the-envelope math, it became clear that if we could build an ad sales team and sell the ads ourselves, Dribbble would net more than ten times that amount, or somewhere around $200,000 per month. At the time, Dribbble was only doing a couple million in revenue, so we were confident we could grow it to at least $10 million. This one growth lever alone would secure our investment and give us huge downside protection.

Just like Warren and Charlie had taught us, we had found a company that was highly profitable, had a competitive moat, we understood deeply, and we could buy at a fair price with a margin of safety. If the business didn't grow the way we hoped, we could make our money back eventually. If the business grew, we could do incredibly well.

After sending the email, Chris and I anxiously paced around our hotel room, barely speaking, just constantly checking our phones for a reply.

Dan and Rich called us a few hours later and told us we had a deal.

But there was just one catch.

We needed to come up with millions of dollars. And fast.

Chris and I spent the next few days walking aimlessly around Boston, trying to figure out how the hell we'd finance the deal. We had about $3 million in cash, so we needed millions more. Accordingly, we sought out bank debt, but the problem was Dribbble didn't really have tangible assets. We couldn't go to the local bank and point to Dribbble's real estate holdings or factories or inventory. Not only did they not have a factory, they didn't even have a physical office (they were fully remote way ahead of their time). The company was all bits and bites. Most bankers, who'd lend you money on a real estate deal or traditional business in a heartbeat, held their noses at the idea of lending money to a social network. They just flat out didn't understand it.

We had a lot of meetings that involved us trying to explain the potential worth of these intangibles to various financial professionals. But they didn't get it. A building with renters—they could calculate the upside of that; but a social network for creatives? That was a mystery. And banks *hate* mysteries.

The clock was ticking and we were getting desperate when Chris pulled off the impossible and managed to get us a deal with the Royal Bank of Canada. After a huge charm offensive, they came through and agreed to lend us the money we needed to close the deal. But they added one term we didn't expect: Chris and I would have to personally guarantee the deal. This meant that if Dribbble failed, they could take our houses and cars and bankrupt us.

As terrifying as that was, we felt that if we were able to execute on our growth strategy and build an ad sales team, we'd be fine. It was such a good business that we figured we'd survive and grow it even if things went poorly.

We quickly set up a new holding company that would own Dribbble. We called our new company "Tiny." We felt that all these private equity and investment firms had ridiculous, self-important (or borderline evil-sounding) names like BlackRock, Greywolf, and Maverick. We liked Tiny because it felt down to earth and friendly and, frankly, kind of ironic and funny.

Because I had more cash, Chris put up 20 percent and I put in the remaining 80, but we agreed to operate as equal partners despite the fact that I owned more. We decided that if we had a disagreement about a deal, we just wouldn't do it. We didn't write a partnership agreement or get any fancy lawyers involved. We just incorporated. After what we'd been through together over the years, Chris was like a brother. We didn't need anything but a handshake.

Then, we gulped and prepared to sign on the dotted line. It felt nice to be on the other side of a deal. After having such a negative experience selling my own business, it felt incredible to become the buyer I wish I could have sold to. Like all the best businesses, we were solving a problem we'd had ourselves. Scratching our own itch.

Then when we signed the final signature and the deal was done. We were the new owners of Dribbble.

We quickly recruited our friend Zack Onisko, a cofounder of a business called Creative Market. He was a former designer who had, like me, ended up gravitating onto the business side. He'd always led creative ventures and was adept at engaging with designers, who typically shy away from anything that even smells like business. We were confident he'd fit in with the Dribbble team and deeply understand the DNA.

And we couldn't have been more right.

In quick succession, he built out the ad sales team, just as we'd expected, and we started selling hundreds of thousands of dollars' worth of advertising per month. Then he began pulling growth lever after growth lever. All the boring stuff that Dan and Rich had been avoiding, just like me at Meta-Lab before I hired Mark.

I realized through the process that I could take the lessons I'd learned from MetaLab, often at great personal and financial expense, and apply them to a business like Dribbble. This meant that learning from failure now came with a multiplier, as I could leverage my education across companies. Every fuckup now began to pay me back in spades.

Tiny was on its way to becoming a little Berkshire Hathaway. I was hooked. Buffett and Munger had their unique strategy: they were the best in the world at finding unsexy businesses with strong brands, defensible market positions, and consistent profits.

So, what was *our* secret sauce? I realized that we appealed to founders who didn't relish the idea of selling their beloved company to some private equity firm run by people who viewed their business as a spreadsheet and would chop it up for parts then flip it to the highest bidder. Founders like us. We could come in, give the founders a huge payday, and do our best to solve all of their problems. Problems we'd learned to solve the hard way. It didn't mean they had to leave, either. We could offer deals where the founders stayed on and kept running the business, taking some chips off the table. Or, if a founder wanted, they could just advise the business and leave the day-to-day to us. Some would simply take their dump truck full of cash, hand us the keys to the house, and ride off into the sunset, never to be seen or heard from again.

My years of sticking forks in electrical sockets had paid off. As we watched Dribbble grow and grow, I knew this was it. My future was staring me right in the face, smiling at me, and I loved it.

When we announced the acquisition, I sent it to my dad. This time, he didn't mention any overdue taxes. He just told me he was proud of me. I realized, in retrospect, that he had finally let his anxiety mellow. He recognized that the fight was over. His kids were launched. We all had our own happy work lives. Nobody was counting on him anymore. I had been able to build the thing he struggled with for decades: a stable, diversified business. The baton was passed, and along with it I was able to take away the financial strain on our family.

Around that time, I asked my dad out for coffee. For as long as I could remember, Dad had been obsessed with flying. Every spare minute had been spent reading piles of flying magazines or dragging us kids to various air shows or aeronautical museums. I'd built more Spitfire models than I cared to count—a way of connecting with him when I was young—and had seen every flying movie known to man. But he had gotten sidetracked. A workaholic, he had never been able to make time for flying. It had always been a fantasy. Now that he could breathe, now that nobody was depending on him, it was time to change that.

"Dad, you're sixty," I told him. "You've got twenty to forty good years left. It's time you got your pilot's license."

I handed him a package for the flight training school I'd signed him up for. He lit up, clapping me on the back, laughing.

"Unbelievable! This is so cool!" he shouted, flipping through the brochure.

What he didn't know was that I had also bought him his own single-engine Diamond DA20, his dream plane, which was waiting in a hangar at the airport.

Now, the challenge that lay ahead was that I needed to find some more Dribbbles to buy.

Chapter 13

A $70 MILLION CUP
OF COFFEE

I took another sip of coffee as I looked at Chris, who stared at his sandwich deep in thought. We were sitting in our usual seats outside Tre Fantastico, one of our favorite cafés, lamenting the problem we now faced. We didn't speak for what felt like hours, but was probably just minutes as the world flowed by. I watched a man on a bicycle leisurely riding along, a dog sniffing the ground, birds perched on a maple tree; life going about its day.

The machine we had been working on for our entire adult lives was now constructed. Our hard-fought little investment farm, yielding a wide variety of crops. Sure, there were problems. CEOs who needed to be quelled. Difficult personalities and bad hires. And the seemingly endless compensation negotiations with hungry executives. Everyone, rightfully so, asking, "Where's my piece?"

In the years since we'd bought Dribbble, we'd built a collection of dozens of technology companies, including businesses like We Work Remotely, a popular marketplace for remote jobs; Mealime, a meal planning app; and

Creative Market, an online platform where designers could sell digital assets like fonts, graphics, and web templates.

We had even repurchased Pixel Union, the company that we had previously sold. Bringing Pixel Union back into the fold felt like an incredible win, akin to welcoming a long-lost sibling back home. Our relationship with the buyers had soured after they had—despite us telling them everything that had happened with Brian—backed him to create a new agency to compete with MetaLab. As you'd expect, the new agency fizzled, but the feelings were still raw for us. The funds to buy them out came from an unexpected partner.

Four years earlier, Chris and I went for an extremely expensive lunch with Bill Ackman, one of our investing heroes. We had followed Ackman's career from a distance for years, carefully taking notes on all his interviews and letters, and eventually investing millions into his public company. Although his investing style resembled Buffett's in many ways, he preferred a hands-on approach. Ackman loved working closely with the companies he invested in, often with incredible results. He was best known for his investment in Canadian Pacific Railway, which he transformed from the least efficient railway in Canada to one of the most effective, yielding an astounding $2.6 billion profit in the process.

In 2016, Ackman auctioned off a one-hour lunch, donating all the proceeds to charity. Even though our largest investment to date was a shrimpy hundredth of the size of his typical investment, we decided we wanted to try to learn from him in person. Plus, we figured, we were doing "due diligence." We owned a lot of stock in his company, so we figured if he was a jerk, we'd sell, and if we liked him, we'd buy more. We also reasoned that if we won the auction and had a terrible lunch, at least we would be donating some money to an important charity.

I didn't anticipate just how much money, though.

The afternoon of the online auction, my hand quivered as I punched in 5-7-0-0-0 then hit ENTER. Fifty-seven thousand dollars. It seemed insane, but we'd learned over the years that meeting interesting people always seemed to pay off in some unexpected way. Often a stray piece of advice or random introduction ended up turning into an amazing opportunity to buy a great company, hire someone great, or learn something new.

We sat watching the clock on my computer tick down by the second, until—to our surprise—it *DINGED* that we had won the lunch with Bill.

A few weeks later, we flew to New York and stepped inside Marea, an upscale Italian restaurant near Central Park. It smelled like oregano, basil, and freshly baked bread. Chris and I were ushered to a large circular table across from the bustling bar. Elegantly attired Wall Street types laughed and shouted all around us, glasses clinking loudly as mustachioed waiters danced around with steaming dishes of pasta and seafood. We felt completely out of place amid the fancy dress wear—all we had were jeans and wrinkled dress shirts that hung untucked, and our nerves were frayed from the lack of sleep, having clocked in just two hours the night before due to our red-eye flight from Victoria.

To say we were nervous was an understatement.

Suddenly, there he was. Towering over us, six foot three with a shock of white hair and sapphire blue eyes in a well-tailored suit that hugged his large frame, he exuded charm. He gave us both firm handshakes, then hunkered down in his seat, folded his hands in front of him, and fixed his eyes on us.

"Great to meet you guys. By my calculation each minute is costing you $958, so I have my work cut out for me! You guys can ask me anything you want," he said. "But first, I want to hear about you …"

Unlike many of the successful people we'd met who had a bad habit of monologuing about themselves in a one-way conversation, he spent the entire first hour peppering us with questions. He was deeply curious, wanting to understand our businesses, how we thought, and what *he* could learn from us about the world of technology, a space he had just started investing in. His enthusiasm was palpable as he listened intently, offering feedback when appropriate.

Finally, it was our turn. We asked him about everything we could think of, rattling off dozens of questions from a notepad we'd scratched questions into on the plane. Ackman surprised us with his brutal honesty about everything from investing, to business partnership, to marriage and raising children. In short, he blew us away. At one moment, when he darted off to the bathroom, Chris and I grinned at each other and laughed. We couldn't believe how incredible this was, getting to grill one of our investing heroes.

After another intense hour of rapid-fire questions, he stood up and said, "You two should come see my office." The next few hours flew by as he showed us around his office, introducing us to his team and sharing war stories from his career. Bill's conference room featured an old ejector seat from a fighter jet—a constant reminder to eject from an investment that no longer made sense. We felt like old friends by the time we reached the door, where he surprised us by saying, "I like you guys. If you ever want a partner on a deal, call me."

So, in 2019, when we wanted to buy Pixel Union back from the group we'd sold it to (for almost 4x what we'd sold it for), we decided to do something we'd never done before: take on a partner. And our first call was Ackman. It was just a few million dollars—almost too small for him to care, given his multibillion-dollar net worth—but it served as the beginning of a wonderful business partnership between the three of us. Over the years, we ended up co-investing in a variety of companies, and he became a friend and mentor—the experienced "Business Dad" we'd call whenever we were navigating a particularly challenging issue.

Sitting at Tre Fantastico, I recalled a piece of advice that Bill had given us over lunch. He told us that the best investors think not in weeks, months, or even years, but in decades. It was important to focus on the long term, not day-to-day vacillations.

At this particular moment, despite having invested in many great companies, and even partnering with one of my investing idols, we were experiencing a lot of these up and down vacillations. So many that it felt like we were on a roller coaster.

The issue with technology is that it changes. Fast. The ground was constantly shifting underneath our feet, and it was inserting huge spikes of stress and financial losses, seemingly at random. We had been disciplined about our investments, often earning our money back in fewer than three years, but we felt like some of our businesses could be vulnerable in the long term.

"It feels like we're building sandcastles and the tide keeps coming in," I told Chris between bites of a sandwich.

We had started having these scheduled lunches once a week to discuss investment ideas, a time allocated to thinking about where to put our money next. After spending the past week reading about the latest advances in cutting-edge tech, like robotics and artificial intelligence, we were at a loss for what to invest in. Chris and I were constantly debating which of our businesses would be disrupted by the latest innovations, and whatever else was around the corner, not to mention the endless stream of competitors funded by Silicon Valley venture capitalists with seemingly unlimited checkbooks.

Most venture capitalists view tech as the greatest investment on Earth because it can reap insane returns (sometimes hundreds or even thousands of times a return on an investment), but it is also one of the most competitive industries on the planet. Over 95 percent of technology startups fail. Even most of those that succeed don't turn into the next Facebook or Uber or Google. Most go to zero, while a handful of outliers become multibillion-dollar startups—hence the label "unicorns."

While tech businesses are a gamble, the beauty of the industry is that these newer tech startups are not huge bets to start with; they often cost almost nothing to grow from an idea into a prototype, and then a company. My tiny digital agency, started when I was a broke barista sitting in my boxers in my apartment, was spun up for twenty dollars, give or take a few cents—$9.99 to register the business with the government and another $9.99 to register the domain for my new website. Everything else was just code and design, both of which I produced myself. No expensive training or certification required. No factories or storefronts to build or equipment to buy. I didn't even need an office; I could work from anywhere with an internet connection.

But there was a catch to this reality. This incredible digital innovation, which had created hundreds of millions of dollars of wealth, bootstrapped from zero, was a double-edged sword: if we found ourselves on the wrong side of a technological innovation, one (or, depending on how groundbreaking the technology was, many) of the businesses we invested in could disappear in the blink of an eye.

Yes, while tech can disrupt any traditional business market, like Uber did to taxis or Airbnb did to hotels, it can also destroy its own kind, as Google, Facebook, and Twitter have done to countless brilliant startups, simply by adding a small new feature.

Our approach to investing in technology, to focus on the simple, profitable businesses in niches, worked well, for the most part. We liked to look at areas that nobody was paying attention to, or had dismissed as dead. But every once in a while, the venture capitalists would get excited about an area we were doing business in and they'd launch a barrage of competitors. In those instances, we were like an old sailboat in a race against a fleet of speedboats with engines fueled by limitless reserves of cash.

This had happened to us many times before. In 2010, we had bootstrapped Flow, a project management app, growing it to many millions of dollars in revenue. Then, Asana came out. Then Monday.com. Then Wrike. Venture capitalists poured hundreds of millions of dollars into competitors and we, being the patsies at the poker table, stubbornly refused to raise money. We kept thinking we'd beat them on merit. That our software was better designed, more thoughtful, and superior technologically. We couldn't have been more wrong. We were lambs to the slaughter, losing over ten million dollars in the course of a few years.

It was like Fiji trying to invade the United States. We didn't stand a chance.

Over the years, we had read extensively about business failures.

Historically, for example, if you owned the largest newspaper in town, it was an incredible business. Every company in a one-hundred-mile radius, large and small, wanted to advertise with you and every citizen wanted to use the classifieds because, well, why would you advertise or post a classified ad in a smaller newspaper? If somebody wanted to launch a competing newspaper, good luck—people already subscribed to yours. To start a new paper also cost serious money: you'd have to spend tens of millions on a printing press, then lose money for years while you hired teams of ad sales folks and press operators, not to mention the journalists, all while you tried to build market share to the point where you could get enough readers and advertisers to get into the black. The returns on a solid newspaper used to be astounding, pulling in the equivalent of hundreds of millions of dollars in profit each year.

But newspapers went from being one of the world's best businesses to one of the world's worst in a matter of years when the internet brought the cost of publishing to near zero. Blogs like *Gawker* and *Gizmodo* had done exactly what I had done to start my design firm: paid around $9 to register their domain and then likely sat in their pajamas in their apartment, just like me, writing news and opinions on their blog. And in a death blow, Craigslist offered classifieds in every major city for free. Almost overnight, newspapers went from being choke hold monopolies to facing endless competition.

Today, newspapers are terrible businesses and most have gone bankrupt or been sold off for pennies on the dollar.

What Chris and I were now trying to do was find investments that wouldn't turn into newspapers or taxi companies.

Investing, when you really boil it down, is just betting that the business you're buying, whether it's a corner store, a McDonald's franchise, or Microsoft, will stay *in* business, and produce more cash flow than you paid for it over the long term. And our approach to investing had become almost embarrassingly simple. We looked at a business and asked: "How do we get our money back in five years or less?" Getting paid back in five years meant we made a 20 percent return on our investment, which is exceptional.

Predicting five years out, let alone ten or twenty, was near impossible. Most of the technology in use now wasn't even invented ten years ago. When it came to our investments in tech companies, to play it safe we had to assume they could be out of business, or at least significantly impaired, within five to ten years.

As we sat eating our sandwiches and talking about what to invest in next, we also wanted to ensure that we didn't have businesses in our portfolio that were coming to the end of their lives, just waiting to be crushed by some technological groundswell.

"Everything we do is so ephemeral," I said to Chris. "Think about how good someone who builds furniture for a living must feel. You build this solid physical object and it lasts for what . . . a hundred years? I feel like most of our companies do great things, but I always wonder how many of them will exist in twenty years."

We needed more investments that could be like the former, that could last a century, and less of the latter, that could become another sandcastle built on the edge of the shore.

With this in mind, we began deep diving on brick-and-mortar businesses. Driving around town, noting successful businesses and researching each industry. Heating and ventilation. Bottle depots. Elevator repair. Gravel pits. Even porta potty rental and funeral homes. Without exception, we'd meet the owner and we were shocked by how difficult their businesses were to operate. Hundreds of employees and massive complexity, for a small profit at the end of the year, which often had to be reinvested into fixing equipment or buying a bigger facility and hiring more employees. These businesses, we quickly realized, were not only difficult to run, but they were commodities. They lacked those beloved moats. People don't say, "I want to buy my gravel from Acme Gravel Pit because they have the finest gravel!" They say, "I want gravel at the cheapest price possible." It doesn't matter where it comes from, only that it's as inexpensive as possible. Not exactly the best business to invest in.

Then we started looking farther afield. An investor we'd read about, Peter Lynch, famously recommended to "invest in what you know." For example, if you drink Starbucks every day, you might want to consider buying Starbucks stock. We took this to heart, scanning our lives for things to invest in.

I'm a coffee nerd. I've been one ever since I worked at the café after dropping out of school. One of my simple pleasures was tinkering with my coffee setup. Always trying to pair the perfect beans with the perfect grind and brew, as if there's some revolutionary cup of coffee out there that will improve my morning by 43 percent.

So, I started researching coffee businesses, zeroing in on coffee makers. I tried just about every way to make coffee. I bought a high-end La Marzocco espresso machine that cost as much as a cheap car. French presses. Pour-over and Chemex. Even a variety of Kickstarter gizmos that invariably failed to work. After tossing a series of battery acid shots of espresso down the sink at home, I almost always ended up back at my local café.

One day, I walked into our office and found a crowd encircling Ali Bosworth, one of our developers. A coffee grinder whirred and he removed a container of espresso grounds and carefully tapped it twice on the counter. He used a little dropper, the sort you'd use for eye drops, to drip a single drop of water into the ground beans.

"This removes static," he told the hushed crowd, who watched in awe.

He placed a scale on the counter, placed a mug on it, and poured the ground coffee into what looked like a translucent piece of PVC pipe that he'd picked up at the local hardware store.

"It works best with a rough grind and two filters," he told the crowd. "And my trick is to wet the filter before you use it. I saw that on YouTube."

After pouring exactly 112 grams of water into the cylinder, he stirred it delicately, then placed a slightly smaller piece of pipe on top and began pressing it down. We watched, transfixed, as the only sound in the room was a tinkling of coffee as it dripped into the mug below.

"What is this thing?" I asked.

"It's the AeroPress," Ali responded. "It's made by this really cool serial inventor."

Sure, a better mousetrap, I thought to myself, remembering my kitchen full of coffee gizmos collecting dust.

"Taste it," he told me, pushing the mug into my hands.

I made a little scene of it. I had been taught how to make a cup of coffee by my old boss, Sam Jones. I swished the cup around in a circle, like a sommelier, then brought my nose to the lip of the cup and started railing off tasting notes.

"I'm getting blackberry . . . dark chocolate . . . and waves of pretension."

Everyone rolled their eyes.

"Dude, just try it!" Ali said, slightly annoyed.

I took a sip.

"Whoa," I said, taken aback. "It tastes the way the beans smell. That's insane."

"Right?" said Ali. "And get this: it's $29. It's basically the cheapest and best coffee maker on the planet."

That afternoon, I drove over to Discovery Coffee, the local coffee shop where Ali told me he'd bought his AeroPress, and I bought one to experiment with myself. Sure enough, it was $29.

What was more unbelievable was how consistent and incredible the taste was. No more perfect tamp pressure or calibrating for humidity or voodoo dancing. It was unpretentious, dead easy, and better than any cup of coffee I'd ever had. The coffee had clarity and deep flavor, without any of the grit or bitterness of a traditional French press. I had never been able to stomach black coffee due to the bitterness, and usually opted for a latte, but this thing made coffee so smooth I could drink it black without batting an eye.

I immediately started testing it out with various beans and roasts. I was jittery with caffeine and convinced that this cheap plastic gizmo was far superior to my $5,000 espresso maker.

And that's when I remembered that I wasn't just a consumer. I was an *investor*.

I was now a buyer of companies. That's when I started to wonder about the creator of this wonderful coffee contraption.

I started googling and discovered that the inventor of the AeroPress had also invented the "Aerobie" Flying Ring, that Frisbee-like toy that flies incredibly far. (And a toy I had loved as a kid.) His name was Alan Adler, and he was a Stanford University engineering instructor and serial inventor. After having his own bitter coffee experience, he began tinkering with new methods to brew coffee and devised the ingenious design, which he released in 2005 to critical acclaim. From there, it became a cult classic sold in just about every gourmet coffee shop in the world.

Even though I was an investor, I wasn't a big-name investor like Bill Ackman or Marc Andreessen. I was just a nobody in Canada. How was I going to get this guy to even entertain a conversation with me? I thought about reaching out to a law firm or an investment bank, and paying them tens of thousands of dollars to facilitate a meeting with Adler. That, I assumed, was how the pros do it at this level.

Had I been courting La Marzocco, which sells its espresso machines for $8,000, that would have made sense. But paying a bunch of suits $900 an hour felt excessive when the product was a plastic tube that retailed for $29.

So, I did what seemed the most obvious. I found Adler's email address and sent him a three-line email. I introduced myself, praised the AeroPress as the best cup of coffee I'd ever had, and asked if he'd be open to selling the company.

The next day, Adler responded. He was understandably skeptical and he tried to brush me off. But I was persistent. I kept emailing, cajoling, and flattering. Finally, after several months of annoying his inbox, he agreed to meet me and Chris in Palo Alto—for a coffee, obviously.

Adler was in his early eighties, with a friendly, approachable demeanor. He looked like the kind of guy you'd find at NASA mission control in the 1960s, with gray hair, wiry glasses, and a medley of pens in his front pocket. He had a shy, warm smile, and was the kind of person you wish could've been your grandpa as a child because you know he would have helped you build a record-breaking go-kart or model rocket.

As Chris and I sat with him, sipping our AeroPress coffee in an unassuming office park near Stanford, we could see he was as smart as they come. I launched into my prepared spiel about my history as a barista, my obsession with coffee, and my abiding love for his simple tool. While he listened politely, the pitch clearly wasn't working. I could tell I was losing Alan. Chris could, too.

When I was done talking, Alan looked me up and down, politely, and then said he had a number for the company, but it wasn't a number I would be able to afford.

"How much?" I asked him. "If you were going to sell AeroPress, how much would you want?"

"Seventy million," he said, without blinking. He may have looked like the sweetest grandpa in the world, but he was also clearly a killer when it came to negotiations. It wasn't that he was being greedy—he just loved his inventions, especially this one. Politely, he said, "It's nothing personal, it's just that my company is worth far more to me than it is to you, and I'm already rich. The only reason I'd even consider selling it is that I'm old and my wife wants me to retire."

Chris and I looked at each other. Our businesses and investments had grown tenfold over the past few years and we now had the ability to pull off an acquisition like this.

We'd done the math before flying down. Adler, rightly so, thought two kids from Canada would never pay $70 million for a plastic tube that makes coffee. But while he was clearly a genius at engineering, invention, and negotiating, he had a blind spot that Chris and I, with our marketing and tech backgrounds, could see as clear as day.

When we had done our own research, we had found that only 3 percent of AeroPress sales were taking place on the AeroPress website—it was primarily sold in fancy coffee shops.

Three percent of sales for a company that was almost exclusively sold to hipsters, programmers, and coffee nerds, who are the kinds of people who live and breathe digital air. On top of that, there was no online marketing strategy. There wasn't even any marketing to speak of that we could find with the exception of one small line on his profit and loss statement that added up to less than $50,000 a year, just one employee coordinating reviews and press while juggling a million other things.

His business was running entirely on word of mouth, which was a testament to the incredible product. In our research, we had learned about the World AeroPress Championship with thousands of participants from 160 countries, online forums replete with people trading AeroPress recipes and techniques, and even found that dozens of people had gotten AeroPress tattoos. Now that's customer loyalty. Chris and I realized that we had found a moat unlike any we had ever seen. A business that would last for decades or more. As we did more research, we realized that AeroPress was one of only eight primary ways people make coffee. The technology was patented up the wazoo, but regardless of a patent, nobody was going to search "press coffee maker"—they were going to google what their friend told them about "aeropress." Like Kleenex, it was a category-defining brand, something that, even when it becomes a commodity where anybody can make it, people still want over the generic brand. Think Advil, Tylenol, and Coke. Not only that—it made an *addictive* product that was *actually good for you*: coffee. I felt like a mogul, reading Coca-Cola's annual report for the first time and realizing I'd like to buy the world a Coke.

Chris and I had also done the math. We knew that if we were able to increase online sales, and figure out how to reach new customers, that crazy number Adler wanted wasn't really that crazy at all.

Chris and I were clearly both thinking this as we looked at Adler in that office park, and Adler was likely looking at us thinking he'd scared us off. But instead, I turned to Adler and, with what probably looked like a confident smile, told him: "You've got a deal."

Alan was speechless. He clearly thought we were crazy, but we knew what AeroPress could become. It was a confidence born out of our Dribbble experience. We had owned Dribbble for less than five years, but we'd already scaled six times over. This charming site for creatives had, with a little marketing sweat and savvy, become a behemoth. Imagine what a coffee maker with a cult following could do in that time.

We'd learned that you didn't need to come up with a brilliant startup idea to get rich. You didn't need to buy a broken business and rack your brain for how to fix it, either. All you needed to do was find something that you believed in, and loved, and then see where you could make it just a tiny bit better.

A few months later, we signed the deal and paid Adler his $70 million. For him, it was a life-changing win. But for us, it was a game changer, too. It made us realize that we had found a new way of investing. And we were just getting started.

And sure enough, our prediction and back-of-the-envelope math proved better than we could have dreamed. In the two years after buying AeroPress, we grew online sales by 500 percent. Dribbble kept growing, too. As did all of the companies we'd been buying.

Months later, I sat across from Chris at Tre Fantastico, again in our usual spots with our usual sandwiches. I realized that, for the first time in over a decade I had a different sort of problem.

I had nothing to do.

Chapter 14

FLESH WOUNDS, NOT MORTAL WOUNDS

I sat in an Adirondack chair, my bare feet pressed into the warm sand, enjoying the breeze from the lake in front of me. I took in the serene smells—the rustic scent of aged timber, the earthy aroma of damp moss and pine needles. A perfume made by the woods around the property. I watched my two sons play in the sand in front of me, now two and four years old, slowly filling their buckets with muck from the lake, then emptying them into a deep hole I'd helped them dig. In that moment, as time seemed to slow, and almost stop, I should have been in naturistic bliss. I should have been one with the environment. As meditative as a monk.

But that's when it hit me. The random email newsletter I had seen, made by one of the designers of one of the companies I owned: it needed more white space.

The more companies we had bought, and the more I loved that particular business, the more I wanted to get involved. Sometimes, too involved.

It wasn't enough to suggest an online marketing campaign; I wanted to get my hands dirty. To get in the weeds with the copy and design. I gave detailed notes on their decks and meeting agendas, even when I wasn't attending the meeting. I'd meet frequently with a new CEO. But then I'd also Slack their designer: "Hey, have you thought about using this color on the homepage?" "I don't love that font." "The logo is a bit small . . ."

As you can probably imagine, nobody knew how to react to my feedback.

I was the "boss" of their boss, so they didn't feel like they could push back. They just did what I said, even when their idea was better, which it often was.

By this point in my career, now that I'd gotten what I hoped for (the freedom to just invest on my own time), I'd started daydreaming about the early days, back when MetaLab was just a few of us goofing around with computers.

I had coffee with a young entrepreneur, just a few years into his career. "What does it feel like to have such a big business?" he'd asked, wide eyed. I was honest.

"Okay, imagine that you love chopping wood in your backyard," I said. "You do it for fun. To relax. To enter a flow state. Then, one day, your neighbor pops his head over the fence and asks you if you could chop him some wood, too. He offers you $20. Suddenly, the thing you love doing becomes a business. Before you know it, you're chopping wood for all your neighbors. You buy a truck and start selling door-to-door. It's just you and a bunch of buddies, side by side, chopping wood and working outside. The business grows. And grows. And grows. And a decade later you wake up. You're in a little glass office, perched atop one of many sawmills. You look down at the hundreds of workers beneath you, operating the industrial equipment on the factory floor. Huge logs getting fed into machines that slice the wood. Totally automated.

"And there you are. Isolated in your little office, wearing a suit, the air-conditioning blowing a chill down your back. No axe. No fresh air. No friendly coworkers. Just you sitting in your office, doing some paperwork— alone. *That* is what it feels like to build a business this big."

He looked dejected and I wondered if I should have just shut my mouth and told him it was awesome. He could learn the truth on his own.

Every founder dreams about getting to the end—the part where they've created the billion-dollar behemoth—but ironically, once there, we all fantasize about going back to the beginning. After all, the beginning is the best part, and most of us probably wouldn't have kept going if we knew about all the speed bumps. The journey is the reward.

When I watched *Jiro Dreams of Sushi*, a documentary about Jiro Ono, an eighty-five-year-old sushi master in Tokyo, I found myself wiping away tears. Instead of scaling his business like I had, he had focused his entire life on honing his craft. For over seventy-five years, since he was just ten years old, Ono had obsessively improved every aspect of his sushi. He was so strict that an apprentice might spend years doing menial tasks, like washing rice or massaging octopus (for a full sixty minutes, ideally), before even getting to touch the fish. And *nobody* but Jiro and his son (in training for decades) was allowed to cook the rice. His restaurant was humble. Just ten seats in an unassuming corner of a Tokyo subway station. And yet, he had three Michelin stars—the culinary world's highest honor. Unlike me, Jiro was still chopping wood, just to the most extreme degree. I wondered if this approach, the polar opposite of my own, resulted in a happier life.

But I couldn't dwell on that. The reality was that at this stage in the business, I had to keep my hands off the tools and leave the CEOs who worked for me alone. While I loved the freedom, it was hard not to meddle. I wanted to get my hands dirty. I missed chopping wood.

My prying was mostly a function of habit. When you're running a company, you have to become very opinionated about almost everything. You have to make decisions, constantly. MetaLab was my baby; the company reflected my taste and preferences and goals. But now I had to learn to hold back and bite my tongue.

I also had to learn a more important lesson: that people don't like doing things that aren't their own idea. They're less motivated to execute, especially when it comes to building something special. At the end of the day, you have to accept that you've hired a jockey (hopefully the right one) and they're on the horse and you need to let them run the race. You might pay for the horse, the hay, and the vet bills, and whatever else horses need, but you're not the one riding the animal around the track.

The hardest part of managing people in this scenario is that it also means giving your jockeys the freedom to make mistakes. This was one of the most difficult things about being the "boss" of the boss. And it was a lesson I had to learn the hard way.

A year or so after we bought one of our prized businesses, the CEO came to us and said he wanted to build a new side business focused on white glove recruiting. He told us he needed to invest two million dollars to build out the concept. To Chris and me, this didn't make any sense. The CEO already had a business with revenue, and he was instead going to distract himself with recruiting, an industry where a customer only paid you once. (Once they made their hire, they didn't need you anymore.) Revenue could only linearly scale with each hire. Worse, it required hiring a huge team of expensive recruiters, given that a recruiter can only serve so many customers.

I shared my concerns with the CEO. With each worry, the CEO got increasingly defensive. My criticisms had backfired, instead causing him to double down on his idea.

"I'm not sure this is the right thing. It feels like the wrong place to invest right now, but if you want, we can disagree and commit," I said. "I'll support you, but I've lodged my concern."

"Yes, I'm 100 percent sure," he told me firmly. "I am all in on the idea."

I realized at that moment that if I blocked his idea, even though I knew it was a mistake, he would resent me. And if he didn't hit his bonus target or key milestones, there would always be this narrative that "Andrew held me back." That it was my fault. That I kept him from success.

So, I told him to go for it. I didn't want him to fail, but I had to give him the freedom to fuck up on his own terms. This wasn't going to destroy the company, just make for a bad year.

Unfortunately, as predicted, the project failed. We set over a million dollars on fire as the project floundered and eventually died. It was a lesson I had learned personally. A painful lesson. But letting this CEO learn the lesson himself was critical. He changed his behavior after that, without us even saying anything.

Chris and I were taking all of these lessons and learning how to operate dozens of businesses at once, ironically, by not operating them at all. After the meddling that I had done myself, and the million dollars flushed down the toilet, we decided on a rather simple management philosophy. We summarized it as follows: when it came to mistakes, we would allow "flesh wounds, not mortal wounds."

Our ultimate goal was to become largely unnecessary, while giving our CEOs the latitude to run their businesses as was logical. We wanted to give our CEOs the freedom to take big swings and, when required, to learn from their mistakes, even if it meant big financial losses. Our belief was that these mistakes made our CEOs better over time. If their idea worked, it would lead to business growth, a win for all of us. Failures, on the other hand, resulted in learning that would inform future decisions—flesh wounds that created valuable scar tissue.

Of course, this didn't mean we were willing to let the CEOs of the companies we owned do whatever they wanted. Brian taught us the hard way that trust should be earned, and not simply given based on your charisma, credentials, or Gucci briefcase.

If there was ever a decent chance that one of our CEOs would propose a path that could result in a mortal wound, Chris and I would take action, regardless of how it made anyone feel.

The other advantage of giving our CEOs the freedom to fail (provided they learned from their failures) was that it gave Chris and me more bandwidth to buy more companies. When you're not meddling with someone else's email templates, you have more time to find good opportunities.

Because our business idols Charlie Munger and Warren Buffett had set us off on our course to discover our own version of undervalued railroads and candy shops (in our case, social networks, coffee makers, and software companies), we decided we should pay homage to them in the office, having those bronze busts of them made and placing them on the mantelpiece.

As we sat in our office's living room, looking out at the Salish Sea, Chris and I talked through ideas for other companies that we could buy, laying out the pros and cons of each, as the bronze busts of Warren Buffett and Charlie Munger stared at us over the fireplace.

At that time, we had no idea that a thousand miles away, on a warm summer day in Los Angeles, the real Charlie Munger was sitting in his own living room, talking to a group of friends about a major problem he was facing with one of his own businesses. And that one of the advisors sitting there had suggested that two guys in Victoria, Canada, might be worth talking to.

"Oh yeah?" Munger asked him. "Who are these guys?"

"Their names are Andrew and Chris," one of his friends said. "Smart guys. They own a pretty successful company called Tiny."

Chapter 15

MONEY BONFIRES OF THE VANITIES

I looked down at my coffee, eager to gulp it down and jump-start my brain. I hadn't slept well the previous night, lying awake thinking about all the work I had to do the next day. I had woken up early, and, unable to sleep, decided to sit on my back patio and watch the sunrise over the water, a world-sized watercolor painting over the bay. I loved the beach behind my house, where the boys and I often spent summer evenings playing in the sand. It was pristine and private, accessible only by boat or a half-mile hike over jagged rocks.

As I walked out through the French doors that led onto my stone patio, I froze. There, in the center of the beach, was a large man, approximately twenty feet away from me. He was maybe thirty years old, wearing a dark-colored bandana and a simple undershirt. He was staring directly at me. I had no idea who he was, or how he had gotten there. "Hi. Hello?" I shouted. "Can I help you?"

"I have an idea I need to tell you about. I've been waiting here all morning," he replied, cupping his hands around his mouth to amplify his voice and grinning widely, his eyes boring into me.

My heart raced. This wasn't a stranded hiker who had gotten lost in the woods or a washed-up boater whose dinghy had capsized. "What kind of idea?" I asked tentatively.

"I'm going to start a business that is going to change the world," he yelled back, stepping closer with each word. "I heard you on a podcast and I knew it was important that we meet."

"Wow!" I exclaimed, stepping backward. "I really appreciate that." As I spoke, I tried to calculate how long it would take to get into my house. "You know, I'm just trying to have my morning coffee," I said, as I tried to figure out how long it would take to lock the back door. "I'd really appreciate it if you'd just send me an email." And if the pepper spray in my kitchen drawer was accessible. "Maybe don't visit me at my house—email me first!" I said, as I backed up against the patio door.

"Can I have your email?" he asked.

I yelled it to him, spelling each letter, one by one, making it inside just as I concluded with the "dot.com," then quickly locked the door. I ran from floor to floor, checking that each exterior door was locked, watching him through the window, still standing there on the beach. Finally, he climbed away on the rocks.

That evening, still a bit shaken by what had happened, I kept replaying it in my head. Could he have been mentally unstable? Violent even? What if my kids had been home? I realized that I had been completely unprepared for something like this, often forgetting to lock my doors or turn on the security system. As I anxiously lay there thinking about this, my phone dinged with an email.

It was him. I skimmed the email and was relieved to see his idea didn't seem totally unhinged. Maybe he'd just gotten too excited? Perhaps this was just a case of entrepreneurial exuberance and hustle taken to an extreme? I remembered my own endless pestering of the guys at Dribbble. I breathed a sigh of relief.

The next morning, as I drove down my driveway, a cup of coffee in the cupholder beside me, I clicked the remote for the gate to my house.

There, behind the gate, in the middle of the driveway, was that guy again. His eyes were huge, his fists clenched.

My heart started pounding as I rolled down my window, half-expecting to get stabbed.

"I'm sorry, but I told you not to come by my house. You need to get out of here, right now!"

"You didn't respond to my email," he said, glaring as he began walking toward the car.

I slammed the accelerator and sped down the street, my heart in overdrive, wondering what the fuck was going on.

The man eventually left, but this marked the beginning of a series of alarming events. Shortly thereafter, someone successfully broke into my home (fortunately, nobody was there). Then, a young man, disconnected from reality due to untreated schizophrenia, barged into our office and cornered us, demanding information on an unreleased Apple product, which he was confident we had access to (we didn't). The most unsettling news came when a wanted felon started making inquiries about me at my favorite cafés and restaurants, claiming he had an "urgent personal message" for me—one that I had no desire to receive. Unsettled by this slew of incidents, I invested in round-the-clock security, a guard dog, and various other safety measures.

Surprisingly, my experiences were almost tame compared to a high-profile billionaire friend of mine. After a kidnapping attempt, he constructed an intricate mechanical metal barrier that hermetically seals the entire top floor of his home. Each night, he engages this shield, creating a fortress-like isolation before securing himself behind a dead-bolted, reinforced steel door in his bedroom. Hardly the cozy bedtime ritual one might aspire to.

Now, it seemed, I had to think about this stuff, too.

Is this what "making it" was supposed to feel like? Nobody had told me about this aspect of getting rich. Suddenly, it seemed like everyone wanted something from me, for better or worse. Some approached me with thrilling business ventures or exclusive social invites. Others, caught in the grips of their own mental struggles, mistakenly involved me in their fantasies.

This, apparently, was my new reality, and I wasn't sure how to feel about it.

On a call, I told a wealthy friend about a few of these stories and my subsequent anxiety. He dug into me: "Look, I've been there. Money brings stress and crazy people, but come on. This is the price we pay. The tallest blade of grass is first to get cut. You're rich in your thirties—anything's possible." His words hung in the air: "Stop whining and go spend some of your money. Do something fun for once."

His words provided a much-needed push, reminding me that this new life, despite its complexities and dangers, was still a playground that afforded me incredible opportunities. Why should I let the problems that come with affluence stop me from enjoying the benefits it brings? I decided to shake it off. Sure, wealth made life more complicated, but it also opened the door to more fun. If one side of getting rich was worrying about personal security and unwanted attention, then the flip side was surely about embracing the opportunities that such wealth could offer.

I started polling my wealthiest friends about how they spent their money and soon learned that rich people don't buy normal things.

I was told by one venture capitalist about a restaurant I had to try, where chefs personally curate menus for five figures a head. (I decided to pass on this one.) A banker I'd met during one of my business deals told me that I should put down a multimillion-dollar deposit for a seat aboard a SpaceX rocket. (I didn't relish the idea of being part of an "unscheduled rapid disassembly.") A real estate mogul I'd spoken with said that I should go BASE jumping in a squirrel suit. (I decided I didn't want to win a Darwin Award.)

There was one thing that kept coming up: for some reason, rich people love boats. Huge, gleaming yachts the size of apartment buildings, each bustling with its own army of staff. The numbers were wild: while a massive mansion might cost twenty to a hundred million, a superyacht could cost many multiples of that, with some spending as much as $500 million on their boats. As best I could tell, the ultimate status symbol was having the biggest and most expensive boat, complete with the requisite number of helipads, swimming pools, and tennis courts.

It seemed like lunacy, but I figured I'd see what the fuss was about. I rounded up ten friends and chartered a yacht to Desolation Sound, one of the most stunningly serene waterways along the rugged coastline of British Columbia, filled with tranquil coves, ancient evergreens, and crystalline waters.

We began our trip full of excitement, boarding a seaplane that flew us over the gorgeous coastline, and touched down in the middle of nowhere. Jagged rock edges and seagulls and a deep blue sky as far as the eye could see. It smelled like salt and cedar.

We boarded a tender, the name given to the small boat that ferries you to the mother boat. As we pulled up, the crew waved enthusiastically at us from the yacht, all of them showing a professional excitement that said they were here to ensure we would get everything we wanted on our luxury vacation.

As we got a tour of the yacht, we were in awe. The boat was floating luxury. A hundred or so feet of sculpted metal and glass, six vast bedrooms adorned with silks and polished teak. There was a ten-person crew running around to attend to every imaginable need. The yacht boasted a bubbling hot tub, a cedar-lined sauna, a stable of eager jet skis, and a bar stocked to the gills with all the liquid distractions one could need. It made a Ritz-Carlton look quaint.

By the time we settled into our rooms, I was starting to see what the fuss was about. It was like we had our own private chalet, floating in one of the most beautiful places in the world with 360-degree views. That evening, we ate an extraordinary dinner at a table on the stern of the ship. The staff had painstakingly written "WELCOME" in seashells, something I'm sure they hated doing but had to pretend was no bother at all. We toasted with glasses of champagne as we watched the sun set over Desolation Sound. We learned from a young hostess that these gorgeous waters had been given this bleak name by explorer Captain George Vancouver, who would visit here in winter, when it was raining. Another version of the story had it that its name was an attempt by locals to keep visitors away and have this treasure to themselves. "Hear, hear!" we said, raising our glasses.

"This all makes sense to me," I thought, as a decadent dessert of molten chocolate lava cake topped with fresh berries and vanilla bean gelato was served. "Now I see why people like yachts so much."

The next day, we did it again. We ate at the same table on the stern of the ship. The staff catered to our every need. We toasted. Then, we did it again the day after that. And the day after that. And as the days wore on, the sheen began to wear off.

It wasn't just the repetition of being in the same place. It was also that we were on a boat. Everything was always swaying gently from side to side and there was a constant low hum from the engine that sounded like a phone stuck on perpetual vibrate under my bed. Everything was boat-sized: tight hallways, low ceilings, terrifyingly steep staircases. The rooms were certainly nice . . . for a boat. They were a fraction of the size of a room at a nice hotel, yet twenty times more expensive.

As lovely as it was, I felt trapped and isolated on the ocean. When I stayed at a hotel, I loved going to the bar and meeting random people, or going for a walk to take everything in. Frankly, I worried this might be a selling point for the super rich: being away from the rest of society. It's just you, your family and friends, and a team of vaguely terrified staff who are under strict nondisclosure agreements.

It all felt quite odd to me.

When we finally left at the end of the week, being transported to our seaplane on the tender, I was the one waving back at the staff with gleeful excitement. I couldn't wait to be back on dry land.

A few days later, I told a friend about my trip over lunch, trying to place the odd feeling I got from it, when I figured out what it reminded me of. "It's like a *really, really, really* nice, *extremely expensive* floating RV, that sits alone in the middle of the ocean." Don't get me wrong: It's a huge, beautiful RV on the water. It's a novel experience and has a certain beauty to it.

When I saw the bill, I went into a flop sweat.

For just seven days on a boat, I'd spent what a successful lawyer might make for a year's work. But that was the cost of total, complete isolation; for that kind of detachment, billionaires shelled out the big bucks. When I compared it to the twenty-times less expensive (and likely more enjoyable) experience of just going to a nice hotel with friends, I felt disgusted with myself.

While the yachting life wasn't for me, now that I felt I'd "made it," I started experimenting with other extravagances. Some of them I actually liked.

As did Chris.

We purchased a new office with water views. We bought new sports cars (I upgraded to a Porsche 911 Turbo; Chris replaced his ancient Volkswagen with an Alfa Romeo), and I started to build my dream home, a gorgeous structure with thousands of square feet of oak floors and handmade cabinetry. I was sure to include all the amenities I could imagine—namely, a gym, a games room, a small movie theater, and eye-wateringly expensive custom furniture. In quick succession, I purchased two more houses: a sprawling lake house and a penthouse in Vancouver. I was still technically following my rule of not spending more than 10 percent on my lifestyle—it's just that 10 percent of a very large number is, well, a lot of money.

The weird thing is, just like the purchase of a new TV or a sound system or video games when I was a budding entrepreneur and had "made it" with a few thousand dollars, these purchases—things that previously felt monumental—soon became meaningless. Buying a new car, or even a new house, without having to think about it made me feel empty and gross. Like I'd bought an Olympic gold medal on eBay instead of working for it (even though I had).

On top of that, I found that these lifestyle upgrades didn't enhance my life. In fact, they quickly did the opposite. They soon became a drag on my day-to-day happiness. I was soon overwhelmed with guilt, maintenance decisions, and logistics. My phone was constantly pinging and dinging with questions from the team of people I'd had to hire to manage my ever-complicated collection of assets: art, houses, cars, and other employees who took care of everything.

"Hey Andrew, the lake house needs a new roof."

"The gardeners want to replant the grass."

"The deck is cracking and it needs to be replaced."

"We need to install new floors."

My life was seemingly spent tending to . . . my life.

The kicker was that most of my homes were sitting empty 90 percent of the time. No one, not me or family or friends, was even enjoying these lavish abodes. I was going to all this effort to maintain these assets for no other reason than simply to have them. It became my second job. And worst of all: it made me feel like I needed to make more money to feed the beast.

There was something else that surprised me about this big lifestyle upgrade. The thing that nobody tells you is that *nobody* is impressed when you drive a flashy car or show off your crazy house on Instagram. My friend Morgan Housel put it well: "People aren't thinking: 'Wow, I'm impressed by this person!' They're thinking, 'I wish *I* had that house.'"

Or more likely: "What a prick."

Getting impressive things didn't win me more friends. At least not the kind I wanted. In fact, it made me more insular. It made me gravitate increasingly to my old friends. My world began shrinking inward to people who knew me before the money—whose intentions I knew I could trust.

Then there was the way the media started to portray me. When I started a local news publication in my hometown, I was soon painted as an evil tech-bro centimillionaire who was trying to control and pervert local journalism—the very thing I set out to support. This turned into a social media firestorm, which led to my personal address being posted online amid cries to visit my house to "eat the rich." I began to feel like the road to hell was paved with good intentions, that I was being punished for doing the very thing wealthy people are criticized for *not* doing: giving my money to good causes.

After all this, I realized that wealth came at a heavy price: risks to personal safety, envy that strained relationships, resentment within my social circles, and anger from those who misunderstood my intentions. Each taking its toll on my peace of mind.

Then, there was the weight of the money itself. As my net worth continued to grow, I set up one of those "family offices" I'd been hearing about. A team of people to manage my money. Their job: to ensure I didn't make any dumb financial decisions and lose everything. (Believe it or not, it is possible to completely blow a billion dollars, and some people have done just that, including a Brazilian billionaire who blew his entire fortune on jets and Formula 1 race cars.)

Even though I was too cautious to have a multimillion-dollar bonfire, I was spending too much, which became glaringly apparent when, one afternoon, I was sitting on my patio doing some work on my laptop when I got a call from Leanne, who ran my home office.

"Andrew, your spending is getting ridiculous ... I ran the math and you are effectively paying the equivalent of the presidential suite in a luxury hotel every day on empty houses."

"How is that possible?" I responded, flabbergasted.

"We think you should rein this in," Leanne said to me, then listed all the other expenses that came with these homes.

It's one thing to have luxuries you actually use and enjoy, but here I was, paying an astounding amount of money for empty houses that nobody was enjoying (especially me). The fact that I was doing this during a multi-decade housing crisis made it even worse.

As I surveyed where I was spending, I thought about what had actually moved the needle for me. Across the board, almost everything I had purchased had made my life worse. Sure, it was nice to have a beautiful waterfront home and drive a fancy car, but I adapted to it so quickly. It was amazing how fast something luxurious just became the ordinary fabric of life.

In reality, the things that had made me happy were simply moments of meaning. Pushing my sons on the swings at the park. Enjoying a sunset over the lake at my cabin. Laughing over dinner with old friends. A particularly challenging game of tennis. Chopping vegetables quietly while the kids laughed and played in the yard. These moments were becoming few and far between, often interrupted by stressful text messages, conference calls, and an endless stream of daily emails.

For years I'd been writing a daily gratitude journal. One evening, I lifted it from my bedside table, flipped through the pages and found page after page of notes like: "I'm grateful that I didn't have to wake up and mop the floors of the café at 5 AM," or "I'm grateful nobody can tell me what to do." I remembered what it felt like to have a boss and to be on someone else's schedule. I was still that same little kid inside who didn't want his parents to tell him he couldn't do this or that (aren't we all still that kid?). To me, the ultimate luxury was having the ability to cancel all my meetings on a whim and hang out with my kids, just because I felt like it.

After a decade of trying all these *things*—crazy shopping sprees, sports cars, mansions, and ridiculously expensive boats—I came to a fundamental realization. My ultimate goal was freedom of time and freedom from worry. And, ironically, spending and tending to my expensive toys actually ate into my time and stoked my worries. It was a pyrrhic victory: the supposed win cost me massively.

It's trite to say, but the old adage rings true: "The things you own end up owning you."

And after trying all these luxuries, I cut almost everything back.

It's not that I regretted trying this stuff. Some of it was fun and gave me experiences that made for great stories, but I started to learn the lie that we've all been told is just that, a lie. A marketing scheme dreamed up by some executives in an advertising office on Madison Avenue. The life you see on *Lifestyles of the Rich and Famous* is not any better than the lives of most other people.

The crushing financial weight of it. The crazy people and the fake friends it attracts. The million annoying details. The baffling logistics.

I'd come to the realization that I'd overshot.

On top of that, my marriage was breaking down. Every word, every action felt like we were walking on eggshells. Our relationship had become brittle, frayed at the seams. Marital stress overlapped with the chaos brought about by my business, the two combining into one inescapable mess. One particular day, during an argument that had long since passed its boiling point, the word *divorce* was yelled. It hit us both like a ton of bricks and I could feel the crack forming in our foundation, deepening with every passing moment.

Everything around me seemed to be falling apart. And the money wasn't fixing it—in fact, it was making it worse. I was caught in a painful dilemma, but I knew no one was feeling sorry for me, nor should they. No one was worrying about that young man in the gleaming fancy sports car idling by the curb, staring into space. No one was concerned that I was all alone on the fancy leather couch, the remote in my hand, thumb frozen over it, not knowing what to watch. But a dilemma it was. I certainly didn't want to blame my upbringing, my parents' constant arguments about money. Nor did I want to blame the boy who, sitting at the top of the stairs absorbing the harsh electricity of their shouts, heard again and again that money would answer any worry.

Worse, those shouts were now my own. During yet another yelling match with Holly in our kitchen, I imagined my son sitting at the top of the stairs listening to us. In no way did I want to repeat history. At that moment, I knew that our marriage needed to end.

As I resolved to close this painful chapter of my personal life, I braced myself to navigate the next: securing the biggest deal of my career.

Chapter 16

MINI MUNGERS

As the weeks turned to months and the months turned to years, our investments grew and grew as Chris and I honed our skills at not only finding the right kinds of businesses to buy but, more importantly, learning how we could nurture the CEOs of these companies with all that we'd learned over the previous decade.

Then, out of nowhere, Charlie Munger called.

Munger, our business idol, wanted to meet me and Chris, leading to what would be one of the most pivotal days of my business life.

After our dinner with Munger, Chris and I returned to Victoria and jumped into potential merger paperwork with full gusto, putting our entire team of executives to work on it.

By now, we were operating out of a creaky, waterfront 1930s mansion on Baynes Channel near a quiet little beach along the Salish Sea. The meditative sounds of waves splashing against the shoreline and the mechanical song of seagulls echoing around the bay was what I needed to be able to concentrate on this deal.

The view from my office window was an ever-changing postcard with aluminum fishing boats trolling by and the San Juan Islands hazily slicing the skyline in two. That panorama, which featured countless sailboats, also served as the constant reminder that "the two best days of a man's life are the day he buys a boat and the day he sells it." (A lesson I'd learned the hard way years earlier, after I impulsively bought my own sailboat, which promptly turned into a hole in the ocean that ate money.)

After decades of doing business, I'd learned that so much of the complexity was just pomp and bureaucracy. As I was fond of saying, "Search all the parks in all the cities, you'll find no statues of committees." As I'd experienced myself, I now knew that when buying or selling a business, too many decisions were made by committee and took months when they should take days. We had personally experienced private equity investors build committee upon committee to review the decision to buy one of our businesses, only to pull the rug out from under us and renegotiate key terms months later, which always felt like a hustle designed to grab the last dollar.

I had come to believe that buyers and sellers, or in this case merging parties, were no different from a couple that is deciding if they should date: they know almost immediately where the sticking points might be and if it's going to work. As such, I wanted to get this deal done in thirty days.

To start with, Munger wanted to see our financials, so we wrote out a meticulously detailed document about the health of our business. In addition to detailing our portfolio of over thirty companies, we also highlighted another holding company we owned called WeCommerce, a collection of software companies serving Shopify merchants. After buying back Pixel Union with Bill Ackman, we had purchased a variety of similar companies, then taken it public. We had also made over a hundred small investments in companies ranging from a St. Louis hotel, to tech startups, to Elon Musk's SpaceX.

While Munger reviewed these financials, we began sending memos outlining our negotiation and merger agreements, preparing proxy materials, and detailing what final steps would look like when we got there, including filings for a shareholder vote and exploring the SEC approvals we would need to meet to push the merger across the finish line.

As the documents went back and forth between us and Munger, our excitement grew more palpable. We were the shuttlecocks in our own badminton game—a game we were now playing with Charlie Munger.

The excitement of this moment overshadowed everything. The adrenaline of a deal with Munger created an almost fog around what I'd experienced before.

We were a private company and almost every dollar of profit had been reinvested in the business. The merger would not only make my net worth liquid—giving me some $800 million worth of stock in a now public company—but it would also diversify my business holdings outside of technology. In investing, there's something called a barbell strategy. On one side, you put high-risk investments, and on the other, you put conservative investments. Daily Journal Corporation owned hundreds of millions of dollars of stocks and real estate and would round out my barbell, giving me more security than I'd ever imagined.

I started to ready myself for the public spotlight that was about to shine on me. As the head of a public company, I'd be thrust into the center of the business world, especially given that we would be perpetually associated with Munger. I'd be filing earnings reports, talking to the media and investors, overseeing board meetings, and trying to sound smart at annual meetings, all things I'd never done before.

To prepare ourselves for what was going to come, I suggested to Chris that we should set off on a trip to meet with a handful of investors, bankers, and public company CEOs we had wanted to talk with for some time whom we would likely be working with once this deal went through. People who might want to invest in our newly public stock. Most importantly, we hoped we would be able to glean some wisdom from these business leaders about what to expect once we took the reins from Munger.

We got on the plane and set out for our trip, excited by everything we were about to learn.

Our first stop was in Seattle, where we stayed in a sprawling 12,000-foot modern mansion in the Denny-Blaine neighborhood of the city. The house had half-a-dozen bedrooms and double the number of marble-covered bathrooms. As we settled in, we were quickly made aware that Bill Clinton had once stayed at the home, as a framed presidential letterhead from the president hung on the wall with the handwritten note, "Thanks for the hospitality! —Bill."

Chris and I sat down in the gargantuan living room overlooking Lake Washington, to review the meetings we had scheduled over the next few days, meetings that would take us from Seattle to San Francisco, Palo Alto, and, finally, Bel Air and Malibu. As we looked through the names of people we were going to talk to, we realized that there had been a strange, if almost comical, fluke in the scheduling: each meeting had been set up with someone who was progressively richer than the person from the prior meeting. Our first lunch, for example, was with an investment banker who had invested early in Amazon and was worth around $50 million. The meeting after that was with a more successful entrepreneur who had a net worth of around $150 million. Then with a venture capitalist valued at a quarter of a billion. This happened all the way until our last meeting, which was with a public company CEO worth around $10 billion.

As we were shuttled to that first meeting in a long black car, I was amazed at the size of the homes in the area. These were mansions by any standard, with rolling green lawns and landscaping that I could only imagine must cost hundreds of thousands of dollars a year just to maintain.

"These houses are just insane," Chris said.

"I wonder how many acres that is," I wondered aloud.

"Six, seven maybe?"

"What's crazy," I said, "is that you could pick the largest house in all of Victoria, transport it here, and it would be smaller than most guesthouses on this street alone."

"I wish I could die and be reincarnated as any of these families' deadbeat son," Chris replied, with a chortle.

It turned out Chris and I were not alone thinking this about the homes in the area. The first investment banker we met with, the guy who was worth around $50 million, immediately greeted us in his beautiful water-front property by referring to it as his "shack." We didn't know if he was kidding or what, but it turned out that his home, which was easily a $10 million property, was sandwiched between two other mansions that were each worth around $25 million—and this bothered him, immensely.

We chatted over coffee about his career and potential investment opportunities, and while he was pleasant and cordial, he kept mentioning his "shack." Like his home was embarrassing. His mood turned downright sad when he asked who else we were meeting with, and it was clear he knew all of the people on our list and that they were all wealthier than him.

"If I'd invested in Airbnb when I had the opportunity, I'd be worth double what I am now," he quipped sadly. "I'd be the guy in the house next door."

Chris and I both noted the banker's melancholic tone. But he wasn't alone.

When we made it to Woodside in San Francisco, where the homes were even more expensive, we heard a similar sentiment. "My neighbor won't let me tear down those trees over there," a startup founder who was worth over $250 million lamented to us, while standing in the foyer of his $25 million second home. "I just need to buy the adjacent property and do it myself."

Another investor in Silicon Valley walked us through his mega mansion and said, unironically, "You know, I could've gone for a bigger house. I just opted for something more modest."

Not everyone we met with on our trip was ostentatious with their wealth, and most were actually very nice people. But each had their own uniquely surprising behavior and lamentations. We had breakfast with one investor who was worth well over a billion dollars, but who lived in the same suburban home he had been in with his family since before he had made his fortune. As we sat in his kitchen eating bagels, which he made clear he had personally picked up at the nearby bagel store, like he was just a regular Joe, he leaned in and whispered about his net worth to us, even though we were in *his* house, for fear that someone would hear him say it aloud. He wanted people to think he was poor because he didn't want to deal with a slew of problems that came with the wealth, from people he had just met asking him to invest in some far-flung idea, or a distant family member needing help with some debt, or people simply treating him differently because they knew how wealthy he was. To him, being rich seemed like the world's worst burden, and the weight of it was clearly all he could think about. And yet, he was obsessed with making more when he had many lifetimes' worth. Continuing to invest and buy businesses, obsessively counting his winnings. Having learned something of this burden myself earlier that year, I found myself nodding in sympathy.

We weren't getting advice from these people. We were hearing the envy they had of other people's lives, completely blind to what was exceptional about their own.

When we made it to Bel Air, where the homes are the same size as the hotels, the irony was truly astounding. The investors and CEOs we met there, many of whom were vacationing in their second, third, or even fourth or fifth homes, complained about the idiocy of the super-super-super rich, who lived nearby.

"Can you believe Bezos just dropped $165 million on what, his tenth house?" one CEO proclaimed. "Unreal. He's just *so fucking rich.*"

"Wait, aren't you worth like a billion dollars?" I replied, genuinely confused. "What can Bezos buy that you can't?"

He thought for a moment, then his eyes went glassy.

"I have nice yacht money. Bezos has superyacht money."

Another investor who had made a billion dollars investing in tech startups gave us a tour of his nine-bedroom, sixteen-bathroom home— yes, sixteen bathrooms, for what reason I don't know—complete with an outoor *and* indoor swimming pool, but spent the entire time complaining that a neighbor had a home with three swimming pools (yes, three). "Who needs three swimming pools?" he asked, then, without the slightest bit of irony, changed the topic to one even more garish, asking, "What kind of plane did you guys fly down here on?" We told him we chartered a Challenger—a plane twenty years older than his $44 million Gulfstream G650. "Oh . . . nice," he replied as he fiddled with his phone. We'd lost his interest.

All of them seemed to be caught up in a game of Who Has What, and yet they had *everything*. Even those who lived in normal-sized homes by most standards still managed to "leak" (a term Chris and I had come up with to describe when someone told us something they pretended they didn't want us to know) the amount of money they had spent by making their yacht less grandiose. "I kept telling the builder to make it 30 percent smaller," one billionaire told us, while showing off photos of the custom superyacht he was building. "Sherry and I don't need all this stuff; we don't need twenty staterooms and a helicopter." Ignoring the fact that he was still spending many tens of millions of dollars on a yacht he'd likely use a few weeks a year. (Chris had started referring to this kind of "leaking" as "grandiose humility.")

By the time we got to our last meeting with the richest of them all, a CEO worth several billion dollars, we were in shock at the amount of wealth we had been around in the past couple of days, and we both felt inadequate and gross all at the same time.

The last house we pulled up to told us this person was different. I've stayed in smaller hotels. It was filled with glass and marble and massive, strange sculptures. His home felt more like a sprawling office complex than a family home.

This CEO had a quality to him that I can only describe as being tiger-like, an apex predator incredible at what it did, charming, fleet-footed and regal, but still, four hundred pounds of brawn with adamantine teeth and claws as sharp as Ginsu knives. You can't get close, you can't pet it, you certainly don't want to step in the cage with it, because that tiger simply can't help himself: he's going to rip your fucking throat out.

He had a cabal of servants who waited on our every whim as he talked about his latest acquisitions and how he'd taken down this competitor or that one. He also had a way of telling us how much everything cost without seemingly realizing how crass he sounded. "Eighty-two Lafite Rothschild," he said, motioning to the wine a servant was pouring me. "Four and a half grand a bottle."

"Wow, it's ... really something," I said, unsure what else to say about the wine, which tasted like ... wine.

Later, as I looked over at a huge painting that was just a solid flat color, he interrupted my gaze to let me know that it was an "original Newman," and boasted that "we paid two for it. Two, can you believe it? It's worth about twenty now." (Chris and I looked at each other, unsure if he paid two thousand or two million.)

It wasn't until after dinner that he showed us his most recent purchase. We walked through the house, and he opened a door to reveal a vast garage filled with all kinds of vehicles that he had probably only driven once or twice. He walked us past a Bentley and a custom, completely blacked-out Tesla Model X until we came upon a Porsche 911 that was unlike anything I'd ever seen before.

"What is this?" I asked, mesmerized.

"A Singer," the tiger said, as he opened the door and invited me to sit in the driver's seat.

Nothing he had shown me had tweaked my desire, but this, this was different. It was a custom, mid-'90s Porsche that had been restored with meticulous detail and glistened like a piece of automotive jewelry. As we were told, it was as bespoke as a tailor-made suit with a molded carbon fiber body, hand-stitched leather, and a hand-crafted exposed manual shifter that looked like it might have been made from a rare, polished metal. I had purchased a Porsche 911 Turbo a few years earlier, but I had never felt the need to upgrade it. That was, until now.

"This only cost me $600,000," the CEO said.

"It's gorgeous," I said.

"Yeah," Chris echoed. "Never seen anything like it."

"Maybe," I thought to myself, "I'll buy myself one as a present once the Munger deal closes." Half a million—the cost of an entire home for most people.

The CEO knew what I was thinking. "I'll give you the guy's number who makes them," the CEO boasted. "There's a five-year wait, but I'm sure we can get you moved up on the list."

The following day, Chris and I drove to the airport in silence and boarded our jet back to Victoria. We were both lost in thought about the trip. We had set out to glean some wisdom from these business titans, which we had, but had come away feeling that they lived in a bottomless pit of envy. There was something that I couldn't get out of my head about these people. It seemed like, no matter what they owned, they were always comparing themselves to their increasingly wealthy peers. Looking up, never down. Never taking a moment to appreciate what they had, obsessively trying to add more zeros than the next billionaire.

What could be more miserable than that?

More disturbingly, I was starting to realize that maybe I was no different. Here I was, loudly criticizing yachts, while jetting around to my various homes. Grandiose humility. "I'm not like those *other* rich people—that's just silly."

If I liquidated all my assets, I'd be worth close to $900 million, and yet I still wanted to be worth more. I could already afford to fly on a bigger jet if I wanted, but for what? There were already ten empty seats on the one I was currently flying in.

And ultimately, what about my kids? Would I, should I, give them my money? On this, I was torn. At fifteen, my parents had told me that if I wanted nice clothes or other noncritical items, I had to buy them myself. There would be no handouts: money was something that had to be earned. It built a work ethic, but you know how that turned out. The difference there was that I knew my parents were broke—it's not like they were withholding anything from me. They flat out didn't have the money.

I'd recently bought my eldest son his first piggy bank and had started building little business lessons into our daily life. Explaining that when we purchased things at a café, it came from my bank account, and that money came from working; then I explained all the different ways that I made money. He nodded along sagely. I had just helped him put his first lemonade stand together, and he'd made $45.

Yes, I want my children to have a work ethic, to understand the value of money and the privileges it afforded them, but was it not insane to make them go through the same, sometimes tortuous, path I had if we already had so much?

One friend had posed an interesting question on this topic: "If you came from a long line of subsistence farmers who had been toiling in the fields for millennia just to survive, with a total inability to pursue their true intellectual passions and interests, but you, due to luck and timing, build an industrial farm and went from a subsistence farmer to a millionaire, would it be logical to teach your children how to toil the soil and grow root vegetables?"

The answer seemed deafeningly obvious.

And then there was the potential resentment. If you have a warehouse full of chocolate chip cookies and your child asks you for one, it feels a bit harsh, and maybe even borderline psychopathic, to tell them to bake their own.

All this was bubbling in my head as our plane began its descent into Victoria.

"Did we learn anything from this trip?" I asked Chris, who sat across from me in the same melancholic state.

"How not to be a whacko," Chris said.

"We're like demented squirrels, storing nuts for the winter when we already have ten trees full," I said.

As we talked, we realized it wasn't just meeting all these people that had made us feel this way. Over the past few weeks, as we'd met on the road, traveling, in back-to-back meetings, traipsing here and there to see business idols and investors and lawyers as we explored this merger and going public, we barely had time for our families. It felt like the more successful we got, the less time we had. Our inboxes were constantly full. I'd found myself doing a deal via text message the week earlier while I watched my kids on the playground.

I did some math in my head and had a shocking realization. We each had two sons aged three and five and had only thirteen summers left to spend with both of them before they went off to college and their own lives and, eventually, families.

"I mean, we've won," I said. "Why do we need more? It's all dumb stuff from here on out. Do we really want to be the 0.2 percent competing with the 0.1 percent? Comparing superyachts?"

"I read about this poll recently," Chris said, "where they asked some of the top CEOs in the world to list what was important to them in order of significance. For many of them, their families were third or fourth on the list of priorities. You know what was number one?"

I knew the answer without reading the poll. "Their business."

"Correct."

We spent the rest of the flight just sitting in silence. Mourning the week we had just had.

When I got home that evening, I saw my kids and hugged them until they had to wriggle out from under my arms like worms.

I called my friend Faisal. "How was it?" he asked, eager to hear about the trip.

"Honestly? A nightmare."

"Why?" he asked. "You were so excited to meet these people."

"I feel like I looked into a crystal ball and saw my future. These guys were all insanely rich and now they're just duking it out over accounting: the person with the most zeros wins. It was pure misery."

I told him about the banker and the investor and the CEOs and he sat silently on the phone.

"Jesus," was all he could muster when I finished telling him everything.

When I hung up, I went to play with my kids for a while, then read them a book and put them down to sleep. I sat on the edge of my son's bed, motionless.

I looked around, contemplating what to do. During my childhood, the lack of money had caused rifts in our family, and I realized that part of me (perhaps subconsciously) hoped that my own success could one day glue our family back together, finally taking away the one thing that caused all that pain. Instead, it had done the opposite. My brothers—both of whom had worked for me for a time—felt distant, like there was something left unsaid. My mother felt that I'd let the money go to my head. She was upset about the "complexities" that my success had added to our family dynamics. And here I was, working so hard now that I was barely seeing my own kids.

I was at a loss. I didn't want to become like the miserable rich people I had just met, and I feared I would if I stayed the course.

Then, of course, there was Munger, my idol. I couldn't throw the Munger deal away. But I also didn't know why I was going through with it. It was going to bring me so much unwanted attention. There would be so many more trips away from my family. The stress of integrating our businesses and building trust with our new employees. There was an irony to the fact that the more public you become, the more private you yearn to be. And, when I finally reached that vaunted net worth with nine zeros at the end of it, what would be the next goal? Would there be another zero I'd be searching for that was supposed to make me happy?

I loved so many things about my job. I loved investing and building businesses and working with smart people. I didn't want to stop doing that.

But I also didn't want to be just another broken billionaire complaining that my eight-bedroom house wasn't big enough, or feeling sorry for myself because I couldn't buy a superyacht.

I didn't want a $600,000 custom Porsche. I didn't even want the Porsche that was sitting in my driveway at that moment. I wanted to drive it into the bay at the end of our street and let it sink to the bottom of the ocean.

In that moment, I knew I couldn't walk away from the deal of a lifetime, a merger with my idol no less, but I also knew I didn't want to be someone for whom nothing was ever enough.

Chapter 17

MONOSODIUM GOBSMACKED

Stomach churning, I walked up to Bartholomew, a quiet little cocktail bar in Yaletown, and stood outside, waiting. I checked my watch, then eyed my phone for the time. I'd made multimillion-dollar deals that gave me less anxiety than this. I checked myself in the reflection of the bar window, unsure if I had worn the right outfit. Maybe I should go back and change? No. No time. Butterflies tingled in my belly as I began the ritual again: Watch. Phone. Window. I realized suddenly that I was more nervous about this date than I was about the pending Munger deal.

I felt a tap from behind and whirled around to see her. She looked gorgeous in a black top, her hair back in a ponytail, with mahogany brown eyes and a smile that made those butterflies flap frantically.

"I grabbed us a booth," she said, and gave me a hug hello. Now that I was standing beside her, I realized she was tiny. Just five feet tall, she came up to my chest. I hugged her back. If I talked during the hug, my chin would tap the top of her head.

She smelled like flowers.

As we scrunched into a plush booth across from the bar, a hip waiter approached and asked what we'd like. We ordered two Negronis, then started with the usual first date basics.

Her name was Zoe and we had met in the lobby bar of the hotel where I had been staying for the past couple of days. The first time I laid eyes on her, she walked straight toward me in a long black dress. My eyes followed her, transfixed. She was gorgeous. I'd never seen a girl like her before.

"Hi, what can I get you?"

I stuttered as I realized she was my server and nervously ordered some sushi. When she returned with it a little while later, I asked her about a small tattoo on her wrist, desperate to make some small talk.

She told me that she'd gotten it while she was at McGill University in Montreal, a school sometimes called the "Harvard of Canada." She must be smart, I thought. I started asking her about her life, we got onto a topic of films, and before I knew it twenty minutes had passed and her manager was starting to eye her. We both wrote out a list of movie recommendations for each other and she dropped the bill and whisked away, flashing me a smile as she turned back at me.

I felt like we clicked, but as much as I'd wanted to ask her for her number, I didn't want to be a creep. I was sure she got hit on all the time—I didn't want to be *that* guy. I ate my food, paid the bill, told her it was nice to meet her, and continued on my way. I reminded myself I was here to do business.

I was in Vancouver to attend the annual TED conference, the first one since the pandemic had ended. As always, it was packed with the world's top minds in science, philanthropy, art, and business. I had been attending for over ten years, and while I had been starstruck rubbing shoulders with the big names, like Al Gore, Sergey Brin, and Cameron Diaz, over time I started wandering off to make small talk with whoever was at the coffee bar. It turned out that almost everyone at TED was interesting, whether it was an up-and-coming nonprofit founder or a nerdy zoologist staring at their shoes. But while watching Elon Musk talk about sending rockets into space and Bill Gates discussing the multispecialty global epidemic response and mobilization strategies to COVID-19, I couldn't get Zoe out of my mind.

So, I came back the next day for a meeting. I scanned the room until I saw her, and then I blushed as I found her gazing over at me. We locked eyes and both grinned, then looked away, like two high school kids with crushes. I awkwardly waved at her and she waved back. Then I told myself that I'd blown it. What was I doing? "Just go talk to her, you idiot." But I didn't have the guts to follow through. I left the restaurant full of regret.

The next day, I went back for a final attempt to talk to her.

"I was hoping I'd see you," she said.

"Same," I responded, grinning.

I asked her how she was finding the conference. The lobby was packed full of TED types.

"Honestly, it's been a slow week. Lots of soda waters and three-hour meetings," she said with a wry smile. I grimaced; I had been guilty of this the day before.

I pointed out that the woman she had been serving next to me was one of the wealthiest women in the world, with a multibillion-dollar fortune.

"No way! She ordered the cheapest wine on the menu and tipped 15 percent!"

We both laughed.

"How much longer are you here?" she asked.

"I leave tomorrow afternoon," I told her.

"Aw, that's too bad..." she said.

Without thinking, I blurted: "I'm going to a party tonight. Wanna come?"

She thought for a second, grinned, then scratched her number on the back of a receipt and told me to text her.

I left, gripping the receipt like Indiana Jones clutching a long-lost artifact. When I texted her, we decided to meet for a drink at Bartholomew first.

At the bar, we shared our life resumes. She told me her dad was Icelandic and her mom was Taiwanese, and aside from going to school in eastern Canada, she'd lived in Vancouver her whole life. When she asked me what I did, I demurred, saying I was a web designer and had invested in a couple of businesses. She told me that, while she was working as a server to make ends meet, her real passion was nonprofit work. For years she had worked with an organization focused on helping women transition out of abusive homes, but it barely paid her enough to make rent, let alone live a normal life in Vancouver, so she was working double-time at the restaurant.

"I'm working as a waitress to pay for my nonprofit job," she joked.

"Oh, wow," I replied. "Good for you." Not only was I impressed, but I was also now extra nervous.

She went on to tell me about how tough it was at the nonprofit she was working at. Her coworkers were working 24/7, but getting paid half of what they could make in the private sector. As a result, it was a revolving door. People were constantly leaving, reaping chaos and operational meltdowns as employees were forced to step into interim positions on top of their existing ones, or replacements took months to find while roles stood vacant. I was shocked. There was no way I could run a successful business if I lost half my team every year.

"Wait, how can they pay people so little?" I asked. "That seems insane."

"There's a lot of reasons. Part of it is cultural. It's a bit of a taboo to ask for more money as a nonprofit employee. Plus, a lot of donors stipulate that their money only goes to fund the services, not overhead. They want to know their money is helping people directly, not being spent on salaries," she responded. "Of course, the nonprofits wouldn't run without the staff."

I had made a few donations to local charities and done exactly that, thinking I was doing the right thing. Helping more people, but forgetting the employees. I shifted uncomfortably in my seat.

As if I weren't nervous enough, she told me story after story about all the wacky rich people she encountered, and what it was like to go between working in a lavish hotel serving caviar to the uber rich, to a chaotic non-profit to help people who sometimes didn't even know where they would sleep that night. She inhabited two starkly different worlds.

"Yesterday someone asked me to pick the hibiscus leaves out of the mountain berry tea because they wanted hibiscus tea."

"Oh my God," I said, holding my hand to my mouth. "What did you do?"

"I told him no way! There's like fifteen ingredients in that tea," she said, as we both broke into laughter at the absurdity of the request.

"That's only scratching the surface," she continued. "There's this one regular, some rich guy, who bought all our Louis XIII because he wanted to reserve it for his future consumption." She widened her eyes to emphasize the crazy. She caught my blank look and explained: "It's this ridiculously expensive cognac. Basically, he paid like $10,000 to make sure all the other rich people would be jealous and only *he* could drink it."

How could I come clean that I was, technically, in the lavish camp?

I was, on paper, almost a billionaire, depending on how you calculated it. And yet, Chris and I were still playing endless whack-a-mole. We woke up every day to hundreds of messages, and hundreds of problems. All day we'd put out fires, and the next day be greeted by hundreds more messages. Somebody wanted a huge raise. One executive was feuding with another. A company was underperforming and needed help understanding why. A CEO was leaving. AI was pulling the rug on a business. It never stopped. I'd come to accept this, after twenty years of it, but I'd been wondering lately what I was doing it for.

It had been different in the early days. If we solved one problem, there was a reward at the end of it: a new car, a better night's sleep, more money saved for a bigger goal.

But at this new scale, it felt pointless. More money was just a number in the bank. It didn't change my day-to-day. During a lunch the week before, a similarly overworked friend had shared a quote by John D. Rockefeller: "I know of nothing more despicable and pathetic than a man who devotes all the hours of the waking day to the making of money for money's sake."

In that bar, looking across the table at Zoe, listening to her talk about how she was so dedicated to helping others that she worked a second job to do so, I was not only in awe of her and the choices she made in life, but feeling like this Rockefeller quote applied to me. In this way we were so different. I had dedicated my life to enriching myself. I worked for money's sake. It felt weird to think that out loud. But there, enjoying drinks with this wonderful person, I realized it was true.

Sure, I had employed a lot of people who were now able to buy homes and put food on their tables and save for their own retirements. I had provided valuable services for countless customers. Turned the wheels of capitalism to increase GDP. All that Ayn Rand stuff. But ultimately my life was selfish. I wasn't doing a whole lot for my community, and certainly not for the world at large.

I quickly had the sense that Zoe was deeply critical of people like me.

Indeed. She began describing a podcast she loved called *Behind the Bastards*, which profiled terrible people. Each episode was a multi-hour deep dive into the ethical failings of a new dictator, cult leader, or billionaire who had abused their workers or bribed and cheated their way to the top.

"Do you think all billionaires are evil?" I asked, worried I already knew the answer.

"Well, I think that a system that allows a select few to accrue amounts of money that could literally end world hunger is *maybe* flawed and in need of some restructuring," she said with a wry smile. "And, I mean, is it evil to have enough money to feed billions of people and ... not?"

I knew that it was a common misconception that wealthy people were just sitting on billions of dollars of cash. In reality, I knew that most billionaires' wealth was on paper in their company ownership, in stock in their company, not hoarded gold bars in some Swiss bank.

But saying that seemed like a bit of a mood killer.

"Not great!" I said, laughing nervously.

From that point on, I gingerly changed the topic whenever anything work-related came up. Fortunately, we hit it off in just about every other way and serendipity seemed to strike over and over. We were both voracious readers, a result, we agreed, of neither of our families having cable TV growing up. We shared some similar family dynamics and a mutual anxiety around money, stemming from our parents' financial stresses.

At one point, she was telling me a random fact she'd recently read, that monosodium glutamate, or MSG, a food additive often used in Asian cuisine, had been unfairly maligned when a rogue scientist shared in a 1960s edition of the *New England Journal of Medicine* the (false) idea that it was toxic. Gobsmacked, I opened the Kindle app on my phone and tapped on Bill Bryson's latest book, *The Body*—I had read that exact fact, in the exact same book, the day before.

As the Negronis kicked in, she asked me a question: "Have you ever heard of 36 Questions to Fall in Love?"

I was shocked again. Not only had I heard of it, but in my nerdy, nervous prep before the date, I had actually written a note of things to talk to Zoe about in case the conversation faltered. Number five on my list: "36 Questions to Fall in Love," a series of questions that a team of psychologists had created, designed to create intimacy between two strangers.

Once again, I pulled out my phone and showed her my list.

We both laughed. This was weird. Like some universal force was bringing us together.

I knew eventually I would have to tell her my terrible secret, that I was in the tax bracket she despised. That I was, on paper, one of the bastards from her podcast. But that could wait until the second date.

It shouldn't have surprised me. Zoe's views were not unique. On a daily basis, in threads and jokes on Twitter and videos on TikTok, in all the major news outlets around the world, on Netflix, *SNL* skits, innumerable books, and now at the bar on a date with Zoe, I heard how rich people got rich by doing bad deeds. I needed to change the subject, quickly.

"Another, um, Negroni?" I asked, gazing into her mahogany brown eyes, feeling the butterflies again. I hadn't felt this way in a long time.

As I walked up to the bar to get another round, I thought about it. I hadn't expected this date to swerve into my lane of traffic around capitalism and wealth. But it had, and she wasn't wrong. Some billionaires are horrible people. Some of them are selfish, narcissistic assholes—though you don't have to have money to be any and all of those. But in my experience, *most* people who got rich were there because they provided society with some kind of service. Whether they created a new prescription drug, started a popular restaurant chain, or invented the iPhone. Society chose to use the company's product, ergo the owner of the company got rich.

I agreed that a lot of billionaires suck. There are psychopaths who run scammy multilevel marketing schemes. There are people who abuse and underpay their workforce. Some engage in corruption and bribe politicians. But, having met many of the world's wealthiest people, I'd found that most of them are just very complicated. They grew up without money. A teacher told them they wouldn't amount to anything. A parent was too hard on them or hadn't been there at all. Sure, they might have obsessive personalities. After all, what kind of person dedicates their entire life to delivering packages as fast as possible? A lunatic. And yet, most people who hate Jeff Bezos probably use Amazon Prime.

I remembered a saying by investor Josh Wolfe: "Chips on shoulders put chips in pockets." When I looked at the *Forbes* Rich List, I mostly saw well-intentioned but messed-up people with chips on their shoulders.

"Here you go!" said the bartender, sliding two crimson cocktails toward me on the bar.

I plunked back down in the booth with the drinks and took a deep breath.

"So, what's your family like?" I asked, putting the pin back in the grenade.

One hour turned into five (and two Negronis into six), and we ended up chatting, holding hands, and eye gazing, until the bar finally closed and I got her an Uber.

"I'd love to see you again," I told her as I kissed her goodbye.

"I'd like that," she said with a smile. And I closed the door behind her.

As I watched Zoe's car drive off, I started walking back to my hotel. I was smitten, but I wondered: How could two people with so much in common have such polar opposite viewpoints? My thoughts returned to our (almost) debate. There was so much I had wanted to say to her, before I thought better of it. Could capitalism be improved? Of course! It had to be, if we didn't all want to fry from global warming. But it had done so many incredible things for the world. I was convinced that, to date, it was the best system we'd come up with. As Churchill said of democracy, "It's the worst form of government, except for all the others that have been tried."

In my eyes, capitalism was just a system that rewarded people for solving problems. Do something people like, and they'll pay you for it. If a lot of people like it, you make a lot more. Yes, not all people solve society's problems for financial reward—there are plenty of people who make things and innovate because of the creative pursuit—but when people solve them at scale, it's usually as a result of capitalism's giant turning gears at work.

I felt that people viewed this billionaire problem in a strange way. If a local woman starts a beloved restaurant and she makes $250,000 in profit, nobody thinks she's evil. But if she takes that same concept and turns it into a chain, she might become a billionaire. Is she suddenly evil? Just because her restaurant is . . . larger? If her customers were satisfied and she charged a reasonable price, and her employees were paid fairly and treated well, I didn't see the harm.

Like everyone, I was addicted to my iPhone, where I caught up with my friends' lives on Instagram, texted them *Simpsons* quotes, and ordered granola bars on Amazon. I'd bet Zoe was no different. Did she know that none of these things would exist if it weren't for a deeply complicated billionaire? Steve Jobs. Mark Zuckerberg. Bezos. Rupert Murdoch. Well, maybe not Rupert Murdoch.

These were people I didn't necessarily like or agree with. Complicated people. And I didn't think it was a coincidence. I felt that complicated people produced incredible work. After all, some of the world's best art had been created by people with mental illness (think Amy Winehouse, Ernest Hemingway, and Vincent van Gogh). The same thing was true in business, sometimes with a dash of megalomania or narcissism or psychopathy. As I read more and more biographies of famous businesspeople, I found deeply sad and complex stories: Steve Jobs was put up for adoption by his mother at birth. Oprah Winfrey was badly abused in childhood and left home at just thirteen years old. Elon Musk was subjected to physical and emotional mistreatment by his father and is on the autism spectrum. Their complex lives formed these extreme personalities, which resulted in an obsessive drive to move the world forward.

As I walked into my hotel room that night, plopping down on the bed and processing everything I'd talked to Zoe about, I wondered what she would make of my current situation and all these ideas. Would there even *be* a second date?

I was still debating it all with myself, and I didn't know the answers. All I knew at that moment was that I really liked Zoe, and with the Munger deal mere weeks away from moving forward, I'd have to come clean with her eventually.

Chapter 18

WHO WANTS TO BE
A BILLIONAIRE?

W e'll be landing in about forty-five minutes," our pilot said over the intercom as I looked up at Chris, then over to Steve. All three of us smiled with excitement. We were on our way to Los Angeles to meet with Munger again, and this time we had invited Steve. I looked out the window and saw that we were somewhere over Marin County, California, the golden coastline shimmering below, divided into neatly organized grids.

Steve held out a cardboard box packed with freshly baked croissants and strudels that his wife, Heidi, had baked for us the night before. She had been a professional pastry chef in a past life and had a wonderful habit of sending him off on trips like these bearing goodies.

"Do it . . . Your paleo diet can wait a few days. Cavemen loved croissants," he said, like a drug dealer making a first sale.

I stuffed a strudel into my mouth and let out a moan that was far too loud for a grown man eating a pastry. I took a picture of what was left of the pastry and sent it to Zoe, hoping to make her jealous of the perfectly crunchy treat.

The morning after our date in Vancouver, she texted me: "Ok, confession: I Googled you. Sorry for saying all billionaires are by nature disassociated from their humanity and evil?"

I responded immediately: "I hope that you will come to realize that billionaires are wonderful, humble folk with one simple desire: to build penis rockets to Mars."

We had a good laugh about it on our second date. Then we went on a third date and a fourth. Before long, we were inseparable, either together or constantly texting. Despite viewing the world's problems through two different lenses, we just clicked. I appreciated the way she looked at the world and what she taught me about it. While she wasn't thrilled that I was a pawn of capitalism (her words), she had warmed to a few of my ideas and we had spent many evenings debating the merits (and demerits) of our current economic system and what I should do with my wealth.

Now on the flight to LA, Steve began asking more questions about Munger. In many ways, Steve was my opposite. Where I hated details, he thrived on them. Where I would do anything to avoid hosting a meeting, Steve built custom software to make his meetings more efficient. Where I preferred shorts and a T-shirt, he was most comfortable in a charcoal business suit. He was a business operator, through and through. He liked being a coach, whereas I wanted to be up in the owner's box, away from the action, where nobody could bug me. In spite of this, we had grown extremely close over the years. We'd been in a business support group for over a decade and had seen each other go through just about every business and personal problem imaginable. We'd seen each other cry more times than I'd like to admit, which isn't something I could say about many of my male business friends. I trusted him more than almost anyone other than Chris, and today, even if he didn't realize it, his life was about to change in a profound way.

Steve had sold the software company he built to a private equity firm a few years ago. After ticking off a bucket list item and moving his family to the south of France for a year, he was getting restless again. But what was interesting about Steve was that he had *enough*. Even before he sold his company, he'd paid for his house in cash and had calculated that he needed less than $250,000 per year in income to live his dream life. He put the proceeds from his exit sale into a hyper-conservative stock and bond portfolio, and never looked back.

On the day he sold his company for tens of millions of dollars, I called him to congratulate him.

"Did you do anything stupid to reward yourself? A convertible? A fancy watch?"

He told me he had treated himself to a nicer pair of garden shears that he'd had his eye on for a while. That was Steve. So disciplined that he wouldn't allow himself to spend money on such frivolous things when he already had a perfectly good pair of garden clippers, even if they were a bit rusty.

I thought back to that moment as I glanced over at him, wondering how we could swap brains.

Steve also idolized Munger, and jumped at the chance to meet him. He might have even traded me his garden shears for the opportunity.

For Chris and me, though, there was a slight problem.

This dream—this incredible opportunity to partner with Munger, that was right there in front of us—was giving us doubts.

We realized that, in merging with Daily Journal Corporation, we would potentially lose what I'd come to realize was our primary goal: freedom. After all, this would no longer be *our* business, a collection of two decades of careful decision-making to build Tiny in our image. Brick by brick, following our passions and working with people we loved. This was *his* business, a 130-year-old conglomerate with shareholders going back decades and businesses in areas we didn't necessarily understand or choose. A wonderful company with all sorts of potential for the future given their investments in software, and no doubt great people on the other side, but it felt like we'd be two divorcées integrating families, with results that would be both complex and unpredictable.

On top of that, all of these conversations with envious billionaires and meeting Zoe, not to mention my bouts of stress and emptiness over the past few years, had made me question everything. Why was I doing this? For money? For a label next to my name that started with a *b*? To check off a box of doing a business deal with my idol?

I'd flipped back and forth over the past few weeks, egging myself on when I was ready to walk away and convincing myself to stay the course. Then, the next day, reality would flood in. I'd think about how I'd have to spend years trying to learn how to run a newspaper business. Wrestling with shareholders, board members, and executives that I didn't pick. It felt like turning a cruise ship. I'd tell myself I was done; I didn't want to go through with the deal. Then, twenty-four hours later, I'd be back to yelling at myself: "But this is *Charlie Munger*!"

We all struggle with this type of conundrum in one form or another. A CEO friend once said to me: "Some mornings I wake up and I want to work my ass off day in and day out to be the next Steve Jobs. Other mornings I wake up and daydream about buying a tiny house, an old beat-up car, having no overhead, and leaving the stress of the business world behind." A by-product of capitalism is wanting everything, or believing you can only have that—everything—or nothing. Too often, we press forward and double down into new stress when we would have been happy—in fact, happier—where we were.

I just couldn't figure out yet if this was one of those moments.

We also dug into what was happening at the company that we were going to take over, Daily Journal Corporation.

They had a steady newspaper and publishing business, hundreds of millions of dollars' worth of stocks (purchased with profits Munger reinvested), and a shining light: a successful legal technology software company called Journal Technologies that had contracts all over the world. That said, they had their work cut out for them. Their largest competitor was Tyler Technologies, a multibillion-dollar publicly traded company that was extremely aggressive. Munger wanted to execute on a David vs. Goliath strategy and do well by doing good—structuring contracts in deeply fair ways and not charging their clients until the work was done, whereas competitors were known for endlessly nickel-and-diming their government customers.

It was solvable, but we realized that it would be a heavy lift. We needed to hire a CEO who knew how to sell complex software to government agencies. Somebody who could think long term and understood the unique way that Charlie operated.

"Steve. One hundred percent, it's Steve!" gasped Chris.

I couldn't have agreed more. Steve's last business had remarkable parallels to Journal Technologies. He idolized Munger.

But the question remained: Did this make sense? Were we doing it because of mimetic desire or authentic desire? For the approval of our peers or for ourselves?

The next morning, Chris and I sat in the garden of our office overlooking the calm sea and listening to the seagulls. It was quiet and contemplative.

"I know this sounds crazy," I said. "But I..."

Chris bluntly finished my sentence. "...don't want to do the deal."

I talked him through all of my worries. There were the practical logistics, that we'd adopt Munger's board, his shareholders, and a legacy newspaper business that we'd have to figure out how to grow. Years ago, I would have thrown caution to the wind and dove headfirst into that chaos. But I was trying to be rational. In my mind, over the past few weeks, I had thought about the approach to merge with Munger in the same way I had convinced other CEOs to sell their business to me.

I had used the Anti-Goals strategy on myself.

The idea of being a billionaire had seemed like it would be the perfect antidote to my childhood money anxiety. And yet, here I was, wealthy beyond my wildest expectations, and I still had problems. I still worried about my kids and was consumed with anxiety about all manner of problems: in business, relationships, friendships, and day-to-day life. And of course, there was the ego of it all. Perhaps the worst thing Chris and I had seen when we'd visited all of these billionaires on our West Coast trip. In reality, that had been the hardest part of saying no. My ego. Mimetic desire. Wanting to be a "Mini Munger."

"Am I crazy?" I asked Chris.

"No. For the first time since I've known you, you're actually being the opposite of crazy," Chris said.

And finally, after weeks of turmoil, we made a decision. At that moment, I felt like the weight of the world had been lifted off my shoulders.

Next, we told Munger, who understood and completely respected our decision. We told him that while we didn't want to merge companies, we had the perfect CEO candidate for him. Fortunately, Steve and Charlie immediately clicked, and before our lunch in Los Angeles was over, Munger had decided that Steve would be the next chairman and CEO of the Daily Journal Corporation.

"So, what next?" Chris asked. "Should we retire? In our thirties? Drink margaritas on a beach somewhere?" We both laughed, knowing full well that neither of us could handle lying on a beach with nothing to do for more than a few days, let alone years.

"I have no idea," I said.

A few days later, as I lay in bed with my kids, reading them *The Adventures of Captain Underpants*, my phone dinged with a text. We'd received an unsolicited offer for many hundreds of millions of dollars for one of our businesses. I quickly did the math in my head and realized that—at least on paper—I was now a billionaire. I chuckled to myself, then turned my attention back to the book, eager to read more of Captain Underpants's latest escapades.

Chapter 19

BURN THE BOATS

I was awakened by the song of a korimako bird, a more soothing alarm than I was used to. I slipped out of bed and gently closed the door behind me, the floorboards creaking as I tiptoed through the dimly lit room. It was six in the morning, and I didn't want to wake Zoe, who was still asleep in bed.

We were celebrating our one-year anniversary at Anderson's Cove, staying in a small cabin on a sprawling farm built by a New Zealand family. Our cabin was a converted four-hundred-square-foot potting shed, surrounded by the pristine beauty of the Northland. A tiny two-room cabin, it contrasted starkly with the yacht I'd chartered the previous summer.

I sat on the deck, mesmerized by the garden and trees, watching the dawn break, casting shades of rose and tangerine across the sky. Towering trees swayed in the wind, their branches providing shelter for the chattering birds. The garden, rich with native ferns and vibrant pohutukawa blossoms, came alive as the sun's rays touched dew-kissed leaves, each droplet reflecting the new day like a tiny prism.

Suddenly, like a pack-a-day smoker reaching for a cigarette, I jolted from my reverie and patted my pocket, grabbing my phone, only to see "No

Service" staring back at me. I tapped into the settings menu. No Wi-Fi either. Then to my calendar: completely empty. I oscillated quickly between anxiety and happiness. What if I missed something? What if someone was trying to reach me? What if there was a disaster at one of my companies? And then . . . pure bliss. I felt my blood pressure drop. I had no emails to contend with. No texts. No one could reach me. I slid my phone away and picked up the dog-eared book sitting at my side and took in a deep breath of the warm, fragrant air.

I was on day ten of this. Completely checked out of my day-to-day life in a country on the other side of the world. I smiled, imagining my vacation autoresponder working overtime, shielding me from a deluge of messages twenty-four hours a day. And it couldn't have come at a better time. This shield from the outside world. Because I was contemplating something I needed time to digest.

For the past year, I'd been wrestling with meaning. I'd done the thing I always wanted to do. Then there came a resounding question: Now what? Everyone rolls their eyes and thinks, "Oh, not me. If I had that much, I'd be just fine." But trust me, you wouldn't.

For me, the money had become a burden, and quickly. Something overwhelming, which didn't seem to bring me joy. I'd tried spending it, which only left me feeling hollow. I'd tried focusing on growing it—building the castle walls—but that, too, felt kind of meaningless. I already had enough to live the life I wanted forever—why keep going? Fear? Insecurity? My motto for decades—a quote from Andy Grove, that "only the paranoid survive"—was beginning to feel unproductive. I worried I'd just keep going forever. Get addicted to more. A workaholic scratching at my pocket to jolt off emails, to take action for action's sake.

I'd once met a man who had been nicknamed "The Homeless Billionaire" because he didn't own a home, but essentially lived out of his private jet. He'd fly from country to country around the world, having his team book multiple hotels in the same city, and then decide at the last minute which one he'd sleep in that night. The rest of the time he slept on his Gulf-stream G650.

I was starting to feel like "The Aimless Billionaire." I'd read a hundred books on how to get rich, but none explained what would happen if you actually pulled it off. Now I was searching for a model. Somebody who had cracked this. And what I'd found, as I met more and more successful people, is that most were like sharks: automatons unable to stop swimming forward, eating whatever was unlucky enough to cross their path. Never once taking a moment to hold a mirror to their lives. For some, their fuel seemed to be insecurity or childhood trauma. For others, it seemed like a personality disorder. Many suffered from both.

As I sat in the dawn, thinking about this, I was searching for something, and as I always did when I had this feeling, I read. And at this very moment, I had found a book that was lighting my brain on fire and causing me to question everything.

An hour or so later, Zoe came out in a robe, two coffees in hand. As she passed me a mug, I set my book down and turned to her.

"Okay, imagine this: you're dressed in a beautiful outfit and designer shoes, when you see a child drowning in a nearby pond. What do you do?"

"Wow. Good morning to you, too," she replied. "Obviously, you jump in and save the kid."

"Right. Obviously. Even though you'd ruin your expensive designer shoes." I said. "The child's life is more important than designer shoes."

"Wow, you really know how to start the day off right. I've been greeted with a question about drowning children this morning because?" said Zoe.

I told her about the book, an essay called *Famine, Affluence, and Morality*, by Peter Singer, an Australian philosopher who argued that anyone with the means to do so has a moral obligation to give to those in need. He suggested that when faced with the choice of spending money on anything in excess of what we need versus donating the equivalent amount to help someone in need, the morally correct choice should be clear. However, this decision becomes complicated when the suffering is often out of sight, happening far away in the developing world, making it easier to ignore. When the kid is drowning in front of you, it's obvious. When you read a story in the newspaper, your brain abstracts it away and ignores it.

I read Zoe a quote:

"If it is in our power to prevent something bad from happening, without thereby sacrificing anything of comparable importance, we ought, morally, to do it."

We began to run through an inventory of our excess and realized that we too were guilty of this. Not only did we own lots of nice shoes, but we had well in excess of what we needed to be comfortable. Multiple homes. Multiple cars. Designer furniture. Not to mention jet fuel.

Were we watching people drown to save our fancy shoes? Many kids? Hundreds? Or even tens of thousands?

Should we give it all up, move into a small apartment, and give the rest to charity?

I thought about all the super rich people I'd met over the past year. Their palatial houses. Their helicopters and private jets. The yachts.

I told Zoe that Jeff Bezos was building a $500 million superyacht. I had read that GiveWell, an organization that conducts research to identify highly effective charities for donors to support, estimates the cost of saving a human life in the developing world is around $4,500.

I punched the math into my iPhone's calculator, then wondered aloud: "Is it ethical to build a $500 million yacht for twelve people to vacation on a few times a year when that same amount of money could be used to save 111,000 lives in the developing world?

That's roughly the population of Boulder, Colorado.

What if you can afford to do both?

What if you gave away all your money but kept $500 million for a superyacht—does that make you a bad person?

According to Singer, it might.

This contrast made me feel slightly queasy. Was Bezos just a modern-day Marie Antoinette, shouting "Then let them eat cake!" from the bow of his superyacht, or was that his silly billionaire reward for building Amazon?

Was this just the Richest Man on Earth equivalent of a successful lawyer buying a bright green Lamborghini to celebrate becoming a partner at his law firm?

We all know the guy. Ripping by, top down, revving the engine too loud, his bald head and aviator sunglasses shining in the sun.

Nobody *likes* him or his car, but I don't think anyone wants it to be illegal for him to buy that silly car. We roll our eyes and move on. We tolerate it because we live in a society where we let people do what they want with their money, however insane the rest of us might think it is.

"How much reward is okay?" I asked Zoe. "I think people need *something* to work for. You get a big raise at work, you want to buy a new car or a nicer couch. Is it okay for rich people to enjoy luxuries if they otherwise give the rest away?"

Zoe and I went back and forth on this for over an hour and didn't reach a satisfying conclusion. Obviously, when we used Singer's heuristic, imagining a pool of drowning children for almost any luxury, it left us with a lump in our throats.

This was a typical morning for us. Our debate about billionaires and capitalism and philanthropy had become just that, a daily debate, though mostly a playful one. Zoe had made me realize that I had missed a few things, and vice versa. And reading this book had reinvigorated my urgency in regard to philanthropy. This image of the drowning child was a proverbial slap across the face.

In the coming days, I kept thinking back to a conversation that I'd had a week earlier. When Zoe and I had first arrived in New Zealand, we'd landed in Wellington, the country's windswept, hilly capital, and I had looked up who I knew in the area. I came across an old friend, Derek Sivers, who had moved to New Zealand a few years earlier, and whom I had emailed and asked to meet.

I hadn't seen Derek in person for over a decade and I was looking forward to catching up.

We met at August, a hip little café on Taranaki Street. I showed up early to check my emails and get some work done, and when Derek walked in, his blue eyes sparkled with intensity. He was wearing a beautiful tailored gray suit with a turtleneck. He had this way about him that seemed to constantly exude a level of calm, and no matter who he spoke to, he made them feel like they were the only person in the world worth talking to.

While a decade had passed, he was just how I remembered, with perhaps an extra line or two of aging now showing across his forehead.

I had mostly kept up with Derek via the occasional email conversation, and by reading his books and newsletters. He was a fascinating contrarian who seemed to live his life how he pleased, and he'd spent the past several years focused on writing and philosophizing to his hundreds of thousands of readers. He had written a book called *How to Live*, a treatise on living the best possible life by avoiding things like dependence on others, owning too many things, and, counterintuitively, pushing yourself to experience painful things.

Despite all his success and fame, I had always appreciated how down to earth he was.

Derek and I had met at the TED conference in 2009, and while you could count all the employees at my company on one hand at the time, and he had already sold a business for tens of millions, he still treated me as an equal and took an interest. Back then, he had taken me out for lunch and introduced me to his friends, even though I was a twenty-something dork who had just started his company and he was a well-known entrepreneur. The way he had treated me, despite our disparate success and status, all those years ago, had always inspired me to pay it forward. Now, nearly a decade and a half later, he treated me the same way as a successful entrepreneur as he had when I wasn't one: talking to me with respect and kindness. He didn't need anything. He just wanted to catch up.

"So, tell me about your life," he said, with a warm smile as we sat with our coffees.

I launched into a monologue that would exhaust even the most seasoned Shakespearean actor. I verbally vomited every thought, worry, stress, and existential debate I had been having with myself over the past few years, telling him everything I'd been through since we last caught up. Through sips of coffee, and him listening intently and patiently as I told him about starting all the companies, about nearly losing it all to Brian, about my strained relationships with my brothers, and about where I was now, the anxious billionaire, he just listened. When he thought I was done, I rattled on about all the money I had made, and how unsatisfying it was to be at the top of the business mountaintop. "I feel like I have no idea what to do," I concluded.

"Wow. That's a lot . . ." he told me, calmly nodding along, like a horse tamer trying to quell a spooked mustang. After a beat, he then said: "But I've been there. I went through a lot of this after I sold my company."

"You did?" I replied, leaning forward.

I realized that despite having followed Derek for years, I actually didn't really know much about his backstory. Sure, I knew that he had founded a company called CD Baby, an independent music company that was often referred to as the "anti-music label." I also remembered a mutual friend whispering to me once that he'd sold it for "a shitload," but I mostly just knew him from his writing and enjoyed spending time with him.

Derek told me he had never intended to become an entrepreneur. He had a difficult childhood and grew up in a dysfunctional family. He had dropped out of high school at sixteen years old. He later joined the circus as a clown (yes, a clown), which led him to become a professional musician, playing in bands and touring the world. It wasn't until 1998 that he stumbled upon an idea that would change the music industry forever. While trying to sell his own CDs online, he realized that there was no easy way for other independent musicians to sell their music on the internet. Thus, CD Baby was born. He clearly found an audience, because his site quickly became the biggest seller of independent music online, with $100 million in sales and over 150,000 musicians using the service. This got the attention of everyone in the industry, including Disc Makers, a CD and DVD manufacturer, who offered to buy the company in 2008.

"I was about to sell the business for $22 million and yet I was more miserable than ever," he told me as I listened intently. "It felt like a huge burden. And I felt this weird itch to do it all over again."

"Never enough," I thought.

He went on: "I started thinking, 'Now I need to prove that this wasn't just luck—I need to build a new company, just bigger and better.' I started dreaming up all these business ideas before realizing that this was just insecurity. I was scratching the same itch, trying to do the same thing I'd just done. And it wasn't about me. It was about proving myself to other people."

"So, what did you do?" I asked him.

"I decided to let go of business and try something new," he said. "To focus on music and writing."

"Right, but what about the money? Now you have all this money to manage and grow. Did you invest it or what?" I asked.

"I burned the boats," he responded, sounding like a Viking.

"What do you mean?"

"In war, when you burn the boats, you're giving yourself no option for retreat. You *have* to follow through on your mission," he explained. "I knew that, left to my own devices, I would stay trapped in the business world, solving the same problem over and over. I was an addict, so, like an addict who wanted to quit, I had to remove all the drugs from my house."

"So how did you quit?" I asked, ready to hear that he literally burned $22 million—thankfully, he had not.

"When I really thought about it, I didn't need or even want the money from the sale of the company. I just wanted to make sure I had enough for a comfortable life. It was never the money that did it for me; it was the freedom and the fun of building something."

"So did you give it away?" I asked.

"Kind of," he said. "A few months before the sale, I transferred the ownership of my company into a trust. My entire net worth was irreversibly and irrevocably gone. It was no longer mine. It all belonged to the charitable trust. When I die, all of its assets will go to music education, but while I'm alive, it pays out 5 percent of its value per year to me. On paper, my net worth is next to nothing. It was my way of opting out of the burden of the big pile of money and accepting that I had enough. That I was done with the game."

I took this and thought about it. I'd been where he was a hundred times by now, and I couldn't do it. I wanted to know he had pulled off the impossible. "Isn't that a huge hit to your ego? How do you feel when you're hanging out with other wealthy people?" I asked him.

"I feel like I went to rehab and got clean, and I'm hanging out with a bunch of addicts. Their lives revolve around drugs, but, for me, having space from it now, it seems insane."

I felt my cheeks flush. I was one of those addicts he was talking about.

"I have a conversation with someone like you about this about once a month now. A lot of people talk about doing what I did, opting out, but not many people end up doing it. It's like the whole tiny house thing. Everyone loves the idea of a tiny house in theory—the simplicity of the humble life—but very few people actually go do it. I did the business equivalent. Except I burned down my mansion," he said with a chuckle.

"Okay, so now what? It's been, what, thirteen years since you sold the company?"

He told me how he started writing books and blogs, and how he focuses his time on making music and writing an email newsletter, which has hundreds of thousands of subscribers around the world. "I think. I write. I travel. I hang out with my son. I play music. I just got back from India, where I spent three days just meeting interesting strangers who read my newsletter and just learning about their lives. I go on a lot of hikes. I don't know—I'm busy."

He told me about a heuristic he uses to decide whether to do something: "Either it's 'hell yeah!' or it's 'no.' Life is too short for 'nos.' This is the ulti- mate freedom."

I laughed. I often groaned when looking at my calendar and badly needed to implement the same strategy.

"Okay, so now everything is perfect?" I asked.

"Of course not!" he said as he laughed at the seeming absurdity of my question. "I get stressed out. I got divorced. My family is complicated. I have the occasional existential crisis. It's not like I cracked life. It's hard and com- plicated, but the one thing I did that's different from so many of my friends in business is that I started solving different problems and opted out of the money game."

I sat there somewhat stunned. I kept turning around the idea of burning the boats over and over in my head. I felt like I had grown up in some sort of cult, and now, in this cute Wellington café, I was being deprogrammed by a former cult member. My brain instantly hated this idea. Akin to someone suggesting Gollum from *Lord of the Rings* throw away his precious ring. Inconceivable.

"Don't you miss it?" I asked.

"Miss what?"

"Business. Having a yardstick to measure yourself by. Money. Status," I replied.

"I have enough money, and I've proven myself to the world once. I don't know why I need to do it again. Does anyone roll their eyes at the guy who won Olympic gold once, wondering, 'Why didn't they do it twice?' No. The yardstick is no longer useful. Think about it: Why do you love business so much?" he asked.

"Well, I like making stuff better. I've always had ideas for how things should work or problems in the world I'd like solved or ideas I'd like to make happen. For me, that's the fun part," I responded.

"I *still do that*; I just don't do it for money," he said, talking about some of the recent digital projects he'd been working on, but with no financial upside. "Instead of money, I got the joy of manifesting an idea and then interacting with all these interesting people in the process," he said.

"How do you feel around businesspeople? Do you feel judged?"

"Well, two things. One, they are mostly jealous of the fact that I quit and they dream about doing the same thing. And if they get weird about that, then, well, I don't think I want to be friends with them. Two, I bought a few *very* nice, *very* expensive suits last time I was in London. I wear them every day, like a uniform," he said, gesturing to his beautifully tailored gray suit. "It's amazing how wearing nice clothing changes people's perception of you," he went on with a shrug.

I laughed and sat in silence for a moment. As we looked out the window of the café, contemplating what Derek had told me, I realized he had hacked life.

He had enough, and I wanted the same.

Chapter 20

ASSHOLE

A few weeks after I returned from New Zealand, I lay in bed, doom-scrolling through my inbox, when I stopped at one of the emails, excited to see a name of someone that I hadn't heard from in years. I clicked into the thread, and began to read.

"Hey Andrew," it began. "It's been a while . . . any chance you're free for coffee or dinner one evening? Best, Brent."

Brent was an old colleague from the early MetaLab days. He was a talented designer who had worked with me almost a decade ago when we only had twenty employees across the entire company. We'd been friends at the time. Grinding away on design projects and then celebrating wins together afterward at bars. But over the years, we'd fallen out of touch. I was excited to tell war stories with an old colleague, so I happily arranged a time to meet for dinner.

Brent was 5' 8" with wavy brown hair, and even though I hadn't seen him in a few years, he looked like he hadn't aged a day. I had chosen a fancy steak house in Vancouver for the occasion. The restaurant had mahogany walls, black leather banquets, and a meat locker in back enclosed in glass that was filled with beef. I ordered an expensive bottle of wine to celebrate and looked forward to a nice evening talking shop. Not stocks, but design. UI and UX. Color schemes. Typefaces. The stuff I loved.

As we opened the menus to consider which steak we should order, I could sense that Brent was a bit flustered. He seemed off.

"Wow, this place is great," he said, unemphatically. "Come here much?"

His eyes gazed over at the cold slabs of meat hanging in the glass box across the room.

"Well, sometimes I do like a good steak," I said, for some reason sounding a little apologetic.

When the waiter poured our wine, Brent grabbed his glass and guzzled it down as if it were a glass of ice water, not a nice cabernet sauvignon. As I watched him drink, I realized that this might not be the friendly catch-up I had hoped for. And as he put the glass down, I could see him steeling himself to say something he'd been meaning to say for a very long time.

I braced myself.

"I've been thinking about it and I wanted to let you know that I don't think I was treated fairly at MetaLab," he began.

"What do you mean?" I asked, quickly trying to remember anything I might have done a decade ago that would have offended him.

"You exploited me," he said. "You didn't pay me what I was worth. You always said we couldn't afford more, that we needed to stay lean, but now look at you. You have a goddamn movie theater in your house."

How did he know that?

"I know how much you were charging for our work. *Our work*, not yours. And you were just pocketing the difference."

I wanted to interject, to point out that it wasn't that simple. That when he worked at the company, it was chronically a month away from going out of business and held together with duct tape and shoestring. But I kept my mouth shut.

"It's not fair," he went on, as he poured himself another glass of wine. "You and Chris made hundreds of millions of dollars and I got a salary."

I waited a long minute, trying to decide what to say. It was clear he had been following what we'd been doing at Tiny, and had seen the rumors about how much the company was now worth.

"Aw man, I'm sorry you feel this way," I said. "And I get the feeling. You were there early and you worked hard. We obviously couldn't have grown MetaLab without you—"

"Okay, so if I was so important, why didn't you give me equity? Why didn't you give us *all* equity?" His eyes were bugging out. He looked more pissed off than before.

So, this was what this was about. "We did offer you equity, twice. Do you remember when I came to you with that big stock options package? You turned it down." Then I reminded him why: "You said you wanted a bigger salary, even though we couldn't afford it at the time. Which was why we were offering you equity."

"Because I needed the money," he responded.

"That's why I found the money to give you that raise. And I understood your choice—at the time the business wasn't doing well. I was pretty worried we weren't going to make it, too."

He was still glaring at me but I kept going.

"And then I came to you again. In 2012. I offered you another options package. But you turned most of it down for another big raise. Again, I get it—cash is valuable and the business could've easily failed and that equity would've been worth nothing. You had bills; you wanted to buy a house—it's hard to take a risk. So, you got another raise," I said. "But now you're pissed at me because it turned out my bet was a good bet and you didn't make more than you were paid?" I waited a moment while he pondered this. Then continued: "I know those options you didn't want are worth a lot now. But I can't go back in time and make you take them. That's not my fault."

I braced myself for his response. But I saw I'd made a mistake: he didn't need a reminder of his regrets.

"You're such an asshole, Andrew. Don't you get it? You made me choose between paying my bills or getting equity in the company I helped build. So, I did what I had to do. And then you kept the entire company for yourself, while it was growing thanks to our work." He took a breath, and then continued: "So you felt like a nice guy giving us little raises while you just kept charging more and more for our designs."

"Dude, the company had been going for years by the time you joined," I responded, my voice rising. "And we paid you $150,000 a year! That was a huge salary for a designer back then. We paid you well, and you turned down the stock options! What would have happened if the company had failed? If it had blown up and gone to zero and you took the stock options and they were now worth nothing, would you be coming back to me demanding lost salary? You can't have it both ways."

He just stared at the table, furious.

I thought back to those early days and the dozens of draconian contracts I'd signed with Fortune 500 companies who could sue me into the Stone Age. Office leases and lines of credit I'd personally guaranteed. Screaming matches I'd had with clients who refused to pay on time. The time Chris had to loan the company money at the last minute, to pay Brent and his coworkers' salaries and save us from the brink. All things that had been invisible to him—as they should have been.

In my eyes, I had put everything on the line. I had bootstrapped every cent and poured my own money back into the business, constantly doubling down and hiring more people. This was the bargain every employee and employer enter into.

Yes, in the long term, we had made the profits, but we had also taken massive losses. I'd paid everyone's salaries, even when we (not infrequently) lost money. And when we lost $10 million building the company Flow, that came directly out of my bank account.

So often, when we offered employees stock, they balked at the idea—and I get why. It was like being handed a pile of chips at a casino. You could cash them in or put them on the roulette table. In their eyes, it was the logical thing to do—most people value a steady paycheck versus a risky bet that could take decades to pay out. Over and over again, Brent had chosen the immediate, consistent paycheck. Like clockwork, every two weeks. Stability and safety.

Chris and I had had hundreds of conversations like this. Occasionally, people would take stock options, and some of those who held on, who took the risk, made a fortune.

I wanted to tell Brent all that, but I knew I was wasting my breath. There was no point. His narrative was cemented in his mind.

I was an asshole.

So, I stopped talking. I let him vent. I couldn't go back in time and change his choice. My job now was to let him hate me.

We never ordered steaks. I'd lost my appetite anyway.

Before too long, the owner of the restaurant delicately slid our bill onto the table. A not-so-subtle cue to stop yelling in his restaurant. I looked around. The place had gone silent and the other tables were eyeing us. I wondered if they thought I was an asshole, too.

As I walked to my car in the rain, I replayed the conversation over and over in my head. While I was sure Brent had it wrong and was holding onto an inaccurate version of things, I also wondered who I truly might have overlooked. And how much did they deserve?

———

The next morning, I began the wild dash to get the kids to school. I shoved their tiny limbs into their school uniforms, quickly slathered toasted bagels with cream cheese, and jammed a variety of crackers, fruits, and vegetables into two lunch kits, knowing one thing for certain: the fruits and veggies were aspirational. As we pulled up into a parking spot in front of the school, I saw another boy get dropped off in an older station wagon. The paint was scuffed and his mother looked frazzled as she ushered him out of the car, kissed him on the cheek, and then quickly pulled away. He had dirty blond hair and a jacket one size too small, with a distressed look on his face. I looked up in the mirror, to my boys sitting in our plush black BMW SUV, both wearing brand-new Patagonia jackets. Then I looked down at my own outfit. Khaki pants. Nice shoes. As I watched the boy walk inside, I felt a tug in my chest.

I could spot the feeling that boy felt a mile away. That used to be me.

It was a feeling my own boys would never know. Now, I was the wealthy dad in the nice car. I had gotten the thing I wanted, but it felt wrong. Like I'd sold out.

"Daddy!" yelled my eldest son, piercing my existential trance. "What are you doing? Let's go!"

I got out of the car, unbuckled them from their car seats, and gave them a quick kiss. As I watched them run off to their friends on the playground without a care in the world, I shouted: "I love you! Have a good day!"

I got back in the car but didn't go anywhere. I just sat in the silence of that moment. I thought about what Brent had said. I thought about that little boy. I thought back to my earliest employees. I remembered people I couldn't have built the business without. People who made true sacrifices and got paid poorly in those early days.

Then I thought of Liam, the intern-turned-CEO who had grown Pixel Union from a harebrained side project into a business that I had sold for $7 million in a matter of years. Liam, too, had turned down a 10 percent equity stake in the company in exchange for a higher salary and so got nothing when the business sold. As a thank-you, Brian had shoved Liam out the door, and we had let it happen, thinking that's "just business."

I thought of Ali, who joined as a web developer (employee number three), then stayed with the company for over fifteen years. He was insanely talented, a joy to work with, and his sense of humor became the cultural DNA of the company. Over time, he bounced between various startups we'd launched and unfortunately, through bad luck, only received stock in the ones that didn't work out. Yes, he'd been paid more and more each year, but his salary did not reflect his contributions. He was never the sort of person to say anything, but he had recently left the company and I wondered how he felt reading the headlines about me and Tiny.

I thought of Luke, my very first employee, who used to be one of my closest friends. He had gone on to have a successful career at other places, but I had recently texted him to catch up and it immediately became clear he had grown bitter toward me.

I needed to fix this. I wanted to share my success, not because I owed them, but because I wanted to say thanks. Because it felt like the right thing to do.

This wasn't "just business." These were my friends.

Fuck. Maybe I was a bit of an asshole.

Sitting in my car, now the only one left parked in front of the school, I opened a notes app on my phone and started typing a list of names.

Chapter 21

THE ORACLE
OF OMAHA

The gravel road stretched into the distance as I drove through fields of wildflowers—vibrant colors punctuated by the occasional cluster of Garry oak and Douglas fir. I rolled the window down so I could smell it—life. My hands rested lightly on the steering wheel, the car humming smoothly beneath me, the playful tickling of gravel underneath. Everything I was worrying about—the meetings, the money, what I was going to do next—seemed to just dissolve like a dream. And then, Matt Damon popped back into my head.

I'd just that morning heard a podcast about the time Damon, along with his best friend, Ben Affleck, won the Academy Award for writing *Good Will Hunting*. Damon was twenty-seven at the time, and Affleck twenty-five.

In the euphoria and glitz of that starry night, Damon remembered feeling an odd, overwhelming sense of relief that he had won so young. Not so he could be listed as one of the youngest to win the award, which he was, but for a different reason. The Oscar, Damon noted, was an accolade almost every actor and screenwriter aspired to, yet only 0.002 percent in Hollywood ever win. At twenty-seven, Damon held it in his hands—a gold-plated figure symbolizing a weighty achievement—at a time when many spent lifetimes chasing such honors.

But as the night wore on, the allure of the statue began to fade. Returning home, his girlfriend went to bed, leaving Damon alone, pondering the weight of the 13.5-inch-tall Oscar in his hand.

He realized the fortune of winning it at a relatively young age. He imagined the hollowness of winning it at ninety, after a lifetime of yearning, only to realize that it was just that: something to yearn for, nothing more. Damon concluded his story by noting how grateful he was that he now had the rest of his life ahead of him to focus on what truly mattered: honing his craft and telling stories, instead of fixating on little gold trophies.

I understood Damon's perspective.

I was thirty-seven and I'd won my own version of an Oscar, and, like Damon, I was relieved I'd done it long before I was ninety. There was one stark difference between me and Matt Damon (other than the significant disparity in our facial symmetry and muscle mass), and that was that, once you've won an Oscar, it's yours forever. It usually sits on your mantel or bookshelf. A fortune, on the other hand, is a different story.

I had been struggling with this conundrum for months, trying to figure out what to do with the money I had earned. As I made a soft U-turn into a dead-end parking lot and pointed the car back south toward Victoria, I mulled over all the options.

I could spend it ceremoniously:

Richard Branson once hired Robert De Niro to jump out of a cake at a birthday party he threw for himself. (Just writing this made me cringe.) Steven Cohen spent $12 million on a fourteen-foot preserved shark submerged in formaldehyde for his office. (This seems straight out of the Bond Villain Handbook.) Mark Zuckerberg almost fought Elon Musk in a cage match because they have competing businesses, and they're two of the richest people on Earth. (It may come as a surprise, but I didn't earn the nickname Palm Pilot for my physical prowess.)

No. I'd already learned the lesson of how it felt to spend it on frivolous and largely pointless things. It's fun for a moment, and then a hollowness arrives.

As I pulled into town and drove past the old coffee shop where I'd worked as a barista, I wondered what nineteen-year-old me would think of thirty-seven-year-old me, and if he would have agreed with these thoughts on business and capitalism. Or, if he would have given me the middle finger as I drove past the bus he took to work.

I pulled up to my house, and parked in my garage. I walked into the kitchen and was engulfed with hugs from my two sons, now four and six.

At our kitchen counter I sat drawing with them as we looked out the window, watching the boats stream by in the bay, the seagulls squawking. And I wondered what they'd think when they were old enough to understand what I did with the money I had made over my lifetime. I thought about how important it was that money didn't pull apart our own little family for the opposite reason it had in my own childhood: too much instead of too little. I wondered how their friends would treat them at school when they found out they were rich. Whether they'd be motivated to get jobs and forge their own path. If they'd feel pressure to get into business, like me, or follow their own passions. Would they resent me for giving them too much? Too little? These thoughts weighed on me as I left them to draw. I marveled at how industrious they looked, how steady and eager they were, hunched over, committing their fantastic ideas to paper.

A few months earlier, I had sat in this same kitchen, looking out at a similar view, only with more clouds in the sky and fewer boats on the bay, as I chatted on the phone with Bill Ackman, our now business partner, whom Chris and I had had the expensive lunch with all those years ago. Bill had been at it for decades, was worth many billions of dollars, and seemed to work harder and harder each year.

"What keeps you going?" I asked him. "It can't be money. What's the point? Why are you still working?"

"The point is I'm giving it all away," he told me. "I used to work for myself. Now I think of myself as the world's greatest fundraiser for charity. I work my ass off to make as much money as possible to give back to society."

He went on to explain that a decade ago he had signed The Giving Pledge, an agreement that Bill Gates, Melinda French Gates, and Warren Buffett had convinced hundreds of billionaires to sign. It was simple: signatories pledged to give away the majority of their wealth, either in their lifetimes or in their wills. In fact, Buffett, Gates, French Gates, and many other billionaires had taken it a step further and committed to giving away the vast majority of their net worth before they died.

"You should sign it. Today."

"What do you mean *today*?"

I was, by no means, an accomplished philanthropist. Sure, I'd given away some money, but it added up to a tiny percent of my net worth. A string of donations to scientists whose work I thought was interesting, and a few local charities. Bill had to run to a meeting, and as he wrapped up our call, he blurted out, "Check your email." Then he hung up the phone.

I glanced over at my laptop, opened it on the table in front of me, and sure enough, there was a one-line email my brain couldn't quite parse. The email read: "Warren, Meet Andrew. He should sign The Giving Pledge."

Within minutes, I had an email from Buffett's assistant: "Call Warren anytime this morning, here's his personal number."

I couldn't believe it. The Oracle of Omaha, in my inbox.

I punched in the number and hit the call button. After a few rings, a familiar voice answered. "Great to meet you, Andrew. Bill speaks very highly of you. Tell me about your business . . ."

It was Warren Buffett. Kind and grandfatherly. Just sitting in his little office in Nebraska, looking out the window while overseeing his empire of over 375,000 employees and over sixty businesses and a net worth over

$100 billion, and he was asking me about my life. What the actual hell was going on?

People say not to meet your heroes, but Buffett was everything I'd hoped he'd be. He listened intently and spoke in folksy aphorisms, just like on TV, except now he was a real human, in my ear.

After an hour of Buffett asking me questions about my business and my various problems, he stopped me and laid it out: "Look, if you just hand it all to your kids, you're going to spoil them. They should have enough to do something, but not so much that they end up doing nothing. In my life, the money I've spent is much, much less than 1 percent of what I've earned. The rest, more than 99 percent, is going to others. It's no use to me, so why not share it with the world? As long as I'm around, I'll keep running my business. But when I'm gone, it all goes back to society. All of it."

This approach resonated with me. I had loathed entitled rich kids growing up, and while I knew my kids would be raised around wealth, I wanted to do whatever I could to ensure they didn't become like some of the children I'd grown up around.

"But didn't your kids resent you?" I asked.

"I don't think so. I always made it clear that we had a duty to give it back to society. They always knew they'd be taken care of. And I included them in giving it away."

Buffett went on to tell me how he had given each of his children huge sums of money in foundations to give back to society, but they otherwise lived normal lives. He said they were a non-dynastic family. If everything went as planned, there wouldn't be any billionaire sixth-generation Buffetts living it up with fifteen houses a hundred years from now. The money would go back to helping those in need.

I liked this approach. It felt fair. It felt good. The 1 percent that Buffett spent on his home and lifestyle and a private jet was a bit of cream skimmed off the top. The prize for his eight decades of maniacal work. Everything else would go toward saving lives and improving society via his foundation.

But he warned me: "Giving away billions of dollars is no small task. It took me until I was in my eighties to figure it out," he said with a chuckle, "and it's still hard."

Later that day, sitting on the couch with Zoe, I told her about the phone call. I told her about the push and pull of giving it away, of giving it to people who I felt deserved it, of how my kids would feel, and how weird it was to reach this pinnacle I'd worked so hard to achieve, only to consider pushing all the money right off the top.

"What else are you going to do with it?" Zoe said. "We've got more than enough."

Enough. There was that word.

But did we?

I got out my phone and started tapping numbers into the calculator.

If my business kept growing for a few decades, an already large number would become an almost unfathomable number. Billions of dollars. If I did better, maybe tens.

And if I spent just a few percent of that in my lifetime, it would be more than enough to live almost any lifestyle imaginable.

I thought about what Derek had told me.

"Okay," I said to Zoe. "Let's *burn the boats*."

It felt weird. The letting go of money. My obsession since I was a little kid. Decades of blood, sweat, and tears.

I didn't want to hesitate. I was afraid I'd lose my nerve. I picked up the phone and called Chris.

"We need to take Tiny public," I told him. "Over the next fifty years, I'm going to give all my stock away."

He didn't think I was acting crazy or that I had come up with some bizarre (and terrible) new idea, like starting a cat furniture business or opening a pizza parlor. This time, he needed no convincing.

"Let's do it," Chris said. I could hear his smile on the other end of the phone.

The emptiness of making money taught me something I had been so slowly learning: that the payoff wasn't the point—it was the process. The act of building something. Of designing the life you wanted. Scratching itches and solving problems. The struggle of creativity. Helping people reach their potential. The flow state. The journey itself. It's all so obvious in retrospect. If a million dollars didn't give me joy, why would a thousand more millions?

We all know this. We've heard it a million times. And yet, everybody—myself included—seems to need to learn the lesson the hard way.

As G. K. Chesterton put it: "To be clever enough to get all that money, one must be stupid enough to want it."

Over the next few weeks, I set my inbox to say I was away on vacation. I sat down with Zoe and Chris and started working on a list and a letter. Both of which would prove to be incredibly challenging.

When you decide to join The Giving Pledge you have to write a letter to state why, and what you hope will come from your philanthropy. Some of the most successful CEOs alive today have written and signed these letters. I read them all with intent curiosity to see where these business leaders wanted to leave their mark.

Bill and Melinda French Gates were the first pledgers, and hence the first letter. They pledged to give the majority of their wealth to improving healthcare and reducing extreme poverty around the world. Warren Buffett talked about the importance of humanitarian causes. Azim Premji, the Indian billionaire, committed to improving education in rural India. Others were working on wilder stuff, like protecting the world from bioweapons and artificial intelligence. Each had found a niche they were passionate about and they were pouring billions into it.

I jotted down notes about the lessons I'd learned along the way. My favorite passages in books I'd read by philosophers and novelists. The areas and people of the world that I wanted to try to help fix. The more I worked on the letter, the more I knew I was doing the right thing. Not only because it's morally right, but because we need to show the rest of society that we aren't all little Marie Antoinettes. That we can share our cake with others.

Sitting at my laptop one night with Zoe, we wrote our letter for The Giving Pledge:

> This quote by John Rawls succinctly captures what drives our giving: "Those who have been favored by nature, whoever they are, may gain from their good fortune only on terms that improve the situation of those who have lost out."
>
> We have been incredibly fortunate in life, and much of our luck has been due to circumstances outside of our control. The opportunity we now have, to support those who have not been so fortunate, is one we find impossible to ignore.
>
> We look forward to working in partnership with those we aim to serve, listening to their stories, heeding their advice, and practicing humility in our philanthropic approach. We pledge to give the majority of our wealth back to society before we die.

After we published the letter, I had another, more private giving pledge to write. A few days later Chris and I reached out to some of the earliest employees who had worked with us as the company grew, and we told them we were giving tens of millions of dollars to them. Back when we had started the company, we didn't have the foresight to see what it would end up being, and now, in hindsight, we felt that they deserved the financial upside of their hard work. Of sticking with us.

Their responses were filled with shock, elation, and gratitude. These were life-changing sums for most of them.

There were four other people I wanted to give money to whom I didn't call that day, but rather, drove to them to tell them in person: my mother, father, and two brothers, all important to my success in different ways.

I told them each over coffee and tea. I paid off the mortgages for my parent's home, the one I had grown up in, where as a child I'd sit on the stairs hearing my mother and father argue over overdue bills. "I want to give you enough money to retire, stress free," I told them. Then I went to see my brothers to do the same. I knew this wouldn't fix the problems with my family. It was only money, and families are more complex than that. But I hoped it would do a little to resolve some of our past wounds.

And with that, I closed the loop.

The one that had been eating away at me since I was eight, when my dad jokingly told me that instead of having a 401(k), he had me.

Not everyone would be happy. Chris and I accepted that. But we did our best to ensure that those who had made the largest contributions in the early days were taken care of in a way that felt right.

In the end, I expect to give away the majority of my wealth by the time I die. The rest, well, I'm not Mother Teresa. Like Buffett, I'll treat myself to a few luxuries for all the hard work. No superyacht or phallic rockets for me, I hope, but a couple of nice homes. Furniture and comfortable clothes. Jet fuel for the odd vacation or business trip.

But in the coming decades, everything else will be transferred to my foundation, earmarked for a philanthropic impact on society at large. The most ethical solution I could come to.

Now, I'm reframing things as much as I can. No longer striving to be a billionaire, but rather, an anti-billionaire, intentionally working to shrink my wealth over time as I give it away.

In reality, I'm not even a billionaire anymore. A few months after Tiny went public, the stock market crashed, and my net worth was cut in half.

And the strangest thing happened as a result: absolutely nothing.

I still woke up in the same bed. Did the same routine. Rushed the kids to school. A pint of beer tasted the same. Life went on. I just saw a smaller number every month on the report from my accountants. A number I'm hoping I can shrink over the long term as I give it away.

It turns out it was just a number.

A big number, don't get me wrong, but just a number.

Of course, life isn't perfect, and it won't be, no matter what that number is. The pit in my stomach is still there. The voice asking, "What's next?" Maybe a little less now than a decade ago. Like anyone else, I wake up irritable some mornings. Have moments of existential dread. Get in disagreements with the people in my life. Feel overwhelmed. Worry about how I'm messing up my kids. Money is just a small piece of the puzzle, and one that, paradoxically, adds many additional ill-fitting pieces.

Of course, I'm still going. Growing the pile, but reframing a bit. Fundraising for society.

Continuing to yoke my childhood anxiety to do some good.

Still obsessively running my businesses.

Still compounding.

Still shouting ideas into Siri.

Still harnessing anxiety for productivity.

Almost enough.

ACKNOWLEDGMENTS

In crafting this book, I've been fortunate enough to be supported by an amazing circle of people whose contributions, encouragement, and critiques have made this a far better book than I ever could have produced on my own.

First and foremost, a huge thank you to my editors, Katie Dickman and Matt Holt at Matt Holt Books. Your edits, insights, and exceptional editorial skills leveled things up in innumerable ways. A huge thanks to Liz Parker, my agent at Verve, whose expertise and guidance helped bring this book to fruition.

To Chris, who tolerated many multi-week absences from our day-to-day work to write the book, and who was crazy enough to leave the comfort of the bank to build what we've built today.

A special thanks to my family, for supporting this project and allowing yourselves to be part of the book. To my two boys, your endless energy and curiosity are my daily reminders that none of this really matters. And a special thanks to Holly, who was with me through many of the most challenging parts of the story and without whom I wouldn't have two wonderful sons.

I am deeply grateful to my friends who read early versions of the book and sent me feedback and tweaks (and told me when I sounded like a jerk): Steven, Bill, Liam, Troy, Rajiv, Mohnish, Faisal, Nick, and many others. I appreciate your candor and thoughtfulness.

To Charlie Munger and Warren Buffett, who gave Chris and me the blueprint for everything we do today and set an incredible example for all of us in the business world.

To my girlfriend, Zoe, who spent endless afternoons reading and re-reading this book, helping me shape it into something wonderful. I'm so grateful we got to navigate this together and I love you.

Finally, to you, the reader. I can't express deeper appreciation to everyone who has taken the time to read this book. I appreciate you allowing me to live in your head for 5–10 hours and hope it was reasonably enjoyable.